THE
PRISON
EXPERIENCE

ALSO EDITED BY
KAREL WEISS

UNDER THE MASK—
An Anthology About Prejudice in America

THE
PRISON
EXPERIENCE

AN ANTHOLOGY

EDITED AND WITH
INTRODUCTIONS BY
KAREL WEISS

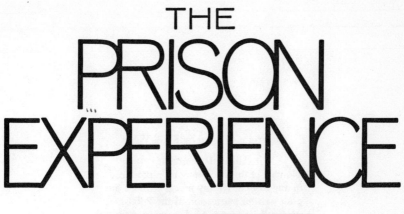

DELACORTE PRESS / NEW YORK

Library of Congress
Cataloging in Publication Data

Main entry under title:

The Prison experience.

Includes index.
SUMMARY: The writings of prisoners, their
families, friends, and other outsiders discuss various aspects, attitudes, philosophies, and implications of imprisonment and criminality.
    1. Prisoners—Addresses, essays, lectures. 2.
Prisons—Addresses, essays, lectures. 3. Crime
and criminals—Addresses, essays, lectures. [1.
Prisoners and prisons—Addresses, essays, lectures.
2. Crime and criminals—Addresses, essays, lectures.]
I. Weiss, Karel.

    HV8665.P73   365'.6'08   75-32920
    ISBN 0-440-06017-6

Grateful acknowledgment is made to the following for permission to use copyrighted material.

Bantam Books, Inc.: From ATTICA: THE OFFICIAL REPORT OF THE NEW YORK STATE SPECIAL COMMISSION ON ATTICA. Published by Bantam Books, Inc. and Praeger Publishers, Inc.

From SOLEDAD BROTHER: THE PRISON LETTERS OF GEORGE JACKSON, copyright © 1970 by World Entertainers, Limited, published by Coward, McCann & Geohegan, Inc., and Bantam Books, Inc.

Basic Books, Inc.: From THE FRYING PAN: PRISON AND ITS PRISONERS by Tony Parker. © Hutchinson Publishing Group Limited 1970, Basic Books, Inc., Publishers, New York.

Boston Phoenix: From "Peaches and Me" by Joseph La Bonte (May 22, 1973). Reprinted with permission.

Broadside Press: "The Freckle Faced Gerald" and "Hard Rock Returns" by Etheridge Knight. From POEMS FROM PRISON, Copyright © 1968 by Etheridge Knight. Reprinted by permission.

Curtis Brown Ltd., London: From THE CRIME OF PUNISHMENT by Margaret Wilson Turner.

Collins Publishers, London: From THE JOURNEY INTO THE WHIRLWIND by Eugenia Ginzburg.

Thomas Y. Crowell Company, Inc.: From THE DESPERATE AND THE DAMNED by Beatrice Freeman Davis.

Doubleday & Company, Inc.: From WOMEN IN PRISON, copyright © 1973 by Kathryn Watterson Burkhart. Reprinted by permission.

From THE JOINT, copyright © 1970, 1971 by James Blake. Reprinted by permission.

From THEY SHALL BE FREE, copyright 1951 by Allan K. Chalmers. Reprinted by permission.

From SCOTTSBORO BOY by Haywood Patterson and Earl Conrad. Reprinted by permission.

for Warren

CONTENTS

ACKNOWLEDGMENTS

For their cooperation in making much excellent material available, I should like to thank David Rothenberg, Executive Director, Fortune Society; Jim Peck of the War Resisters League; Spencer Coxe, Executive Director, American Civil Liberties Union of Pennsylvania; Bella Green, National Headquarters, American Civil Liberties Union; and Tom Cornell of the Fellowship of Reconciliation.

I am greatly indebted to the New York Public Library for the many courtesies extended to me during the compilation of this collection: to George Louis Mayer and Mary Kay Carlson of the General Library of the Performing Arts, The New York Public Library at Lincoln Center; the reference librarians of the General Research and Humanities Division (in particular, Robert Allen); and the staff of the Mid-Manhattan Library. Without their assistance much of the research for this book might never have been accomplished.

For their special knowledge and encouragement, I should also like to express my appreciation to Anne Katherine Markowitz, David Willis, Una Corbett, Arthur H. Friedman, and Beatrice Weiss.

To Ron Buehl, who commissioned a book on the prison experience, and to Marilynn Meeker, for help in editing the book, my gratitude.

I am indebted, most of all, to the prisoners. Living lives beyond endurance, they show us man's capacity to survive, and thereby set an example. Whatever strength pervades this book is a gift from them.

INTRODUCTION

This is a book about people in prison.

The authors are the prisoners themselves and the men and women who know them—families, friends and various outsiders. Although writings by correctional officers, lawyers, journalists, and sociologists have also been included, *The Prison Experience* is not a sociological study, but primarily an account of the prisoner's own journey through the world inside. Instead of charts and statistics, these are narratives of madness and despair. Instead of case histories, these are statements of political awakening and hope which have grown out of imprisonment, expressing not only optimism but the durability of man.

Although the history of punishment is old, prison as punishment is new. In primitive societies (and in nonliterate societies today), when religious belief and taboos were the regulating forces, the violation of tribal taboos, the profanation of sacred truths, were judged as the gravest public offenses and punished by death or banishment. Murder and theft, posing no threat to the religious institutions of the tribe, were considered private matters— and accordingly ignored by society at large; these acts were settled by blood feud, fought by the families or persons directly involved. Such feuds (often lasting through generations) could prove costly in terms of lives and property, and were gradually replaced by the more practical punishment of restitution—compensation paid by the offender to the victim.

With the coming of the Bronze Age, almost six thousand years ago, and as the institution of kingship emerged and society began to codify its taboos, authority of the family gave way to that of the state. Murder and theft, once considered private wrongs, were now judged as public offenses; compensation formerly paid to the kindred became the newest source of revenue for the king: punishment, then as now, was profitable.

Earliest records show that legal codes originated in Egypt in 2900 B.C. But it was not until the period between 1700 B.C., when King Hammurabi gave his Babylonian subjects the *lex talionis* (the law of retribution), and 1350 B.C., when Moses received the law on Mount Sinai, modeled after Hammurabi's, that they were widely acknowledged. Although "an eye for an eye, a tooth for a tooth" and the Mosaic Law were severe in their emphasis on corporal and capital punishment, they nevertheless give evidence of remarkable legal sophistication—for the first time punishment was made to fit the crime. That the punishments prescribed were less civilized than present-day imprisonment is questionable, for if vengeance maimed or destroyed the body, imprisonment, at its worst, destroys the mind.

Although prisons have existed for thousands of years, they served for lowliest offenders only, as places of detainment until trial and sentencing. Prison as punishment was restricted to religious heretics, kings and queens, and nobles fallen from power. It was not until the mid-thirteenth century in England, when imprisonment was first used as a penalty for perjury, theft, breach of forest laws, and as a means of securing fines, that prisons opened their gates to the general population.

As the Enlightenment spread throughout Europe, eighteenth-century philosophers, reassessing man's place in the universe, called for a new approach to criminal law. Believing that deterrence rather than retribution should be the chief justification for punishment, champions of freedom—such as Voltaire, Montesquieu, and Beccaria—wrote impassioned discourses on the subject. In the name of humanity they condemned still-existing corporal punishments as unworthy of man, advocating a more extensive use of imprisonment as the civilized alternative. What they wrote helped form the theoretical basis of our own prison system.

In 1790, Dr. Benjamin Rush and a group of Quakers, influenced by reformist talk from abroad, formed the Philadelphia Society for the Alleviation of the Miseries of Public Prisons; this society was instrumental in establishing the Walnut Street Jail. Motivated by the highest Christian principles—seeing the convict as an errant child of God, but a child nonetheless capable of ultimate redemption—the Quakers imposed on their prisoners *total* solitary confinement: in the proper atmosphere of isolation, through constant prayer and reflection, the sinner was to find his way back to God. Since, however, the Walnut Street Jail bred more madness than salvation, work periods—silent, solitary, and also good for the soul —were subsequently provided, allowing the prisoner a necessary respite from the tensions of prayer. With this and other modifications, the Philadelphia Prison System was born.

As a reaction against the failure of Newgate Prison built in New York City in 1797, which was, at best, but an inadequate reflection of the philosophy of the Philadelphia system, the New York legislature provided for the building of a new state prison in Auburn in 1815. Though completed in 1816, it was not until six years later that Auburn had perfected its prison system. Stressing solitary confinement by night, but congregate, silent work during the day, the Auburn System became the prototype not only for the American prison of the future but European prisons as well. With its emphasis on prison labor (again the prisoner as a source of revenue), even today the Auburn concept dominates much of correctional thinking.

There is also the rehabilitative approach. Having made increasing headway among the "enlightened" during the last fifty years, it now threatens to displace the Auburn System as the prevailing mode of punishment. In the attempt to modify the so-called deviant personality, counselors and therapists too often play at being gods, making the prisoner over, if not in their own image, then in an image sometimes grotesquely stereotyped, acceptable to the parole board. Inability to see the prisoner as a person with differing cultural values, plus too great a concentration on the prisoner's criminality at the expense of the total personality—in short, taking the partial view—are but some of the shortcomings of our rehabilitative approach. The growing rate of recidivism, estimated by some to be as high as 70 percent, indicates that rehabilitation is as ineffective in creating a crime-free society as the theories that preceded it.

For over four thousand years, from ancient Egypt to Auburn, New York, the history of punishment is reflected in social mores and in the history of criminal law; punishment is society's response to the instinctive nonconformity and aggression in man. Since, according to Freud, there exists "primary mutual hostility of human beings," a world without law is as terrifying a prospect as a world without freedom. Yet law restricts our liberties even as it secures them, for law does nothing so much as ensure continuing power of the class that maintains it. Our freedom is relative: once we threaten the security of the dominant class, either through action or words, we are liable to criminal sanctions.

Throughout history, behavior and beliefs at variance with the interest of the dominant class have often been brutally suppressed by law. Jesus, called "King of the Jews," was feared as a threat to the established order, was condemned by the Great Sanhedrin for reformist activities, and crucified; early Christians in Rome were persecuted for withholding allegiance to Caesar and the state religion; Quakers in seventeenth-century England were condemned as political dissidents for refusing to bear arms and support the Crown. In each case, their crimes were in having acted according to religious beliefs.

In the United States during the late nineteenth and early part of the twentieth centuries, Socialists, trade unionists, and anarchists, like Eugene Debs, Mother Jones, Big Bill Haywood, Emma Goldman, and Alexander Berkman, were denied their most basic civil liberties. They were often imprisoned, and, in the case of Berkman and Goldman, finally deported because they fought against social and economic injustices. In our own time, we have only to look at the imprisonment of civil rights leaders Dr. Martin Luther King, Jr., and Bayard Rustin, and the arrests of Vietnam war protesters A. J. Muste and Dorothy Day, to realize the repressive use of law.

As many laws suppress nonconformist belief, so they may also attempt to regulate morality, thereby creating unnecessary crime. That over six and a half million people (one out of every thirty persons) were apprehended in 1970 for the commission of some crime indicates not so much that the United States is the most crime-ridden nation in the world, but that it is the most over-legislated one. Laws against victimless crime—vagrancy, gambling, drunkenness, crimes against nature—account for over one-half of all arrests. Though Prohibition was repealed in 1933, over two million arrests were made for drunkenness in 1970—more than all the serious crimes of violence and crimes against property combined. Prohibition, adopted in

1919, was government's response to the fears of rural America, who saw in the increased urbanization of America and the new wave of immigration a threat to their Protestant values of temperance and self-control; the revulsion was not against alcohol but what it represented. Although the accomplishments of Prohibition were extensive—the creation of the bootlegger, the bloody gang wars, and the highest per capita consumption of alcohol in our history—they were not what the Women's Christian Temperance Union had envisioned.

Similarly, laws against possession of marijuana were enacted not out of fear of the marijuana itself, but of those who smoke it. Long associated with underground cultures —the world of jazz, the beat generation, the hippies, the Yippies, with all that is "un-American"—marijuana has become a symbol of freedom, a rebellion against American middle-class constraints; as such, penalties against its use have been severe, ranging now from $100 fine in Oregon to a fifteen-year prison sentence in New York State. But the imposition of criminal sanctions has had no deterrent effect. In 1973, over 420,000 arrests were made for violations of marijuana laws, as opposed to 188,682 in 1970, proving that marijuana, like alcohol, refuses to be legislated away.

Through law, the dominant class legislates morality, regulates nonconformist belief and behavior, and also uses its power to create a convicted class that can be blamed for all the failures of society. Today in the United States, it is, if not a crime, at least a dangerous disadvantage to be poor, black, or both—especially when confronted by the law. FBI crime statistics for 1970 report that over 53.3 percent of those arrested for murder, rape, robbery, and assault were black. This reveals not so much that blacks are the perpetrators of crime as that they are the most likely to be apprehended. Of the 53.3 percent arrested, each had averaged no more than six years of schooling, 85 percent were school dropouts, and almost all were poor. Our courts are selective in whom they confine. That the average prison sentence for whites is 42.9 months as compared to 57.5 months for nonwhites is explanation enough of how our prisons have become, in the words of New York City Criminal Court Judge Bruce Wright, "nigger and Hispanic zoos with mostly white keepers."

Prisons reflect the caste and class prejudices of society; they serve to perpetuate the economic and social injustices inherent in our social order. As cited by Frank Browning, The President's Commission on Law Enforcement and the Administration of Justice reported that, in 1965, white-collar crimes (embezzlement, tax fraud, forgery, et al.) amounted to $1.7 billion, while crimes of the poor (robbery, auto theft, burglary, et al.) totaled $608 million. Yet only 14 percent of the prison population is of the white-collar class, other white-collar offenders having been diverted from prison either by payment of fines, through probation, or simply by nonprosecution for crimes.

Diversion from the criminal justice system as an alternative to imprisonment should be, if not for all, then at least for more than just the few. According to Ronald L. Goldfarb and Linda R. Singer, correctional authorities estimate that between 85 and 90 percent of all prison inmates could be safely released from confinement without detriment to themselves and society. A more extensive use of fines, by which the offender could make restitution to the victim, would allow the offender to assume responsibility for his crime. Community service (working for the handicapped, participation in environmental projects, and similar activities) would serve not only as an alternative to imprisonment but would help reconcile the criminal to society. Programs such as the Manhattan Court Employment Project, begun by the Vera Institute for Justice, have recognized the need for counseling prisoners *away* from the prison setting, and have been successful in integrating the offender into society. That there will always be that small number of persons who, because of psychopathic or sociopathic behavior, can never be released into society, is hardly reason to perpetuate a correctional system that on any given day incarcerates 214,000 prisoners in federal and state prisons.

Until we realize that imprisonment serves neither as a deterrent against crime nor as rehabilitation for the prisoner, that punishment is always a vengeance—a form of counteraggression—our prisons will continue to stand as monuments of futility. They have always been—for all but the prisoner—the easy way out, reassuring us that life can become the Utopia **we** have always wanted it to be, since all of society's evils are finally contained behind prison walls. We have not yet come to realize that by separating the criminal from society and condemning the already condemned, we are ourselves guilty of a crime— the crime of imprisonment.

Karel Weiss

New York, 1975

1.

ASPECTS OF CRIMINALITY

Criminality proceeds from the very nature of humanity itself.

—Adolph Prins

We think of crime as acts committed by others, yet rarely reflect upon what it is that separates the accuser from the accused. Anger and envy are considered common to all, but when anger is intensified by emotional instability and envy by economic deprivation, the result may be murder or theft, or both.

"Crime is normal," wrote Émile Durkheim, the nineteenth-century French sociologist, "because a society exempt from it is utterly impossible . . ." Excessive crime is not normal, and must be seen for what it is: a symptom of social and economic ills. Increasing alienation among the young and widespread poverty within minority groups are important causes of crime; improvement of these conditions, as recommended by The President's Commission on Law Enforcement and Administration of Justice, is but the beginning in the fight against rising crime.

As we examine the socioeconomic implications of crime, we should confront, also, our own attitudes toward criminality: our need to condemn, to project inner fears upon the outsider; our belief in privilege; our indifference to the causes of crime; our self-righteousness in viewing criminals as a people apart, as others.

THE EVER-PRESENT CONDITION

Crime is eternal—as eternal as society. So far as we know, human fallibility has manifested itself in all types and forms of human organization. Everywhere some human beings have fallen outside the pattern of permitted conduct. It is best to face the fact that crime cannot be abolished except in a non-existent utopia. Weakness, anger, greed, jealousy—some form of human aberration— has come to the surface everywhere, and human sanctions have vainly beaten against the irrational, the misguided, impulsive, and ill-conditioned. For reasons too subtle and too complex to understand, the ordinary pressures and expectancies that pattern the individual's conduct into conformity break down in given instances. They have always done so: they always will. No way of drawing the scheme of the good life has yet been discovered which will fulfill the needs of all human beings at all times.

Crime is therefore an ever-present condition, even as sickness, disease, and death. It is as perennial as spring and as recurrent as winter. The more complex society becomes, the more difficult it is for the individual and the more frequent the human failures. Multiplication of laws and of sanctions for their observance merely increases the evil. Habituation becomes more difficult in a complex society, and the inner strains grow more obvious.

—Frank Tannenbaum, from Foreword to *New Horizons in Criminology*

CAUGHT

Only three percent of all crimes known to police are serious; ninety-seven percent are minor offenses.

There are only a small number of serious crimes in the human catalogue. The rest result from the growing complexity of civilized life. Cultural and social changes alone create criminals. Men were still serving sentences for violation of the Volstead Act five years after the repeal of Prohibition.

Over 375,000 new state laws have been passed in the United States in the last thirty years, and these are in addition to the more than one million then existing state, municipal and Federal laws and ordinances.

Surveys have been made concerning the effect on the ordinary law-abiding citizen of such a mass of unknown statutes. One study estimates that the average citizen in one American city, considering himself entirely law-abiding, would unwittingly break sufficient laws to spend over 1,825 years in prison, and to accumulate fines in excess of $2,085,919.55, within one year of orderly living. While such a citizen does not constitute a crime problem, the fact remains that legally he should be serving time under our existing laws. He is a criminal, if a criminal is anybody who commits a criminal act. Is this a supportable definition?

You work in a garage. Have you never stolen a tool? You're a beautician. Have you always paid for the shampoo or the hair nets you took home?

Have you never been overdrawn at the bank? Never postdated a check? Never fudged on your income tax returns? Made personal use of the company car?

Have you never had illicit relations with anyone? Or indulged a fleeting homosexual contact in college? . . .

Have you ever been a party to collusion on divorce? Finished a cocktail after hours in a bar?

. . . Entertained a "convention girl?" Visited a prostitute? Somebody visits them.

If you have done any of these things, you have committed a criminal act. You are a criminal, according to the above definition.

. . . Perhaps you have always been absolutely honest about your income tax, but you know someone who hasn't. You have never stolen, but you have witnessed a theft. You should have reported these criminal acts. Not reporting a criminal act is a criminal act.

This definition of a criminal does not imply repeated offenses. One theft, one blackmail, one abortion, one incident of withholding knowledge of a crime, and you are a criminal, according to our definition. It is easy to see that if this definition were adopted as a working concept in our Commonwealth, our business houses, underworlds, universities, homes, farms and churches would be largely without constituents.

Do *you* think a criminal is anyone who commits a criminal act?

Perhaps a criminal is anyone who is convicted of a criminal act by a duly constituted court of law. This is the legal concept of crime. But let us examine its philosophy. You are a criminal only if you get caught. The trick is not to get caught.

This is a convict's concept of society's concept of a criminal. You hear it on every side. "You know the difference between me and the guy on the outside? I got caught!" A man is punished, not for his crime, but for getting himself caught. It implies that crime is not an absolute moral offense, but a legal caprice.

—Donald Powell Wilson, *My Six Convicts*

THE WAR AGAINST CRIME

Warring on poverty, inadequate housing and unemployment, is warring on crime. A civil rights law is a law against crime. Money for schools is money against crime. Medical, psychiatric, and family counseling services are services against crime. More broadly and most importantly every effort to improve life in America's inner cities is an effort against crime.

—From *Report of The President's Commission on Law Enforcement and Administration of Justice, 1967*

THE POWER TO CHOOSE

I remember that when I was first losing in the prison atmosphere my rather determined prejudice against criminals, after I had been forced to acknowledge that burglars at nearer sight are not such terrible fiends, I still was determined to hate men guilty of what I called the unpardonable crime of indecent offenses against children. I questioned the rightness of letting men guilty of rape have the privileges of interesting evening classes in prison.

There was one such man at the time guilty of "carnal knowledge" of a little girl, who at an age when any woman would have said it was impossible, gave birth to a child. Every detail of it was repellent and disgusting to a degree. And then I learned that that "brute" had said casually, as if there was nothing strange in the remark, that never in his life until he got into prison had he slept in a bed in which there were not men *and* women. Investigation showed that his statement was probably literally true. Life . . . had given that creature practically nothing but carnal knowledge. What the effect of such an environment had had on an adolescent lad one hesitates even to imagine. He had lived, as it seems probable his forefathers had lived, one large family in one room. Within a few yards of that "home" stood a cathedral which people come from the ends of the earth to see. He had never been inside it. An exquisite choir sings there, week after week, "Glory be to the Father, and to the Son" and one wonders what the words would have meant to him if he had heard them. For it was commonly said by the neighbors, and likely in his hearing, that his mother had had children by both her half-witted father and her half-witted son. Until that time I had not known—I say it to my shame, for the lack of such realization is disgraceful—that a child under ten can no more protect itself from moral corruption than it can from smallpox or from diphtheria, and having suffered from moral infection, can no more of its own efforts recover from it than it can of its efforts recover from the markings of the smallpox. Until that time I had ignorantly shared the conventional but unpardonable belief that even criminals had the same power and the same duty to choose between right and wrong as I had, that they had had the same "chance." To the best of us, to the most clear-sighted of us, virtue is not always shining white, nor vice as black as night, that we distinguish at once and easily between them. The antithesis of promiscuity, violence, and casualness in the sexual relations, that is, . . . privacy, and tenderness, had possibly never even once been put before this man's consciousness. And he was sentenced to prison—not because he had committed a disgusting crime, but so that we may not commit the disgusting crime—by a judge who probably had learned before he was five years old that men don't enter women's bedrooms without knocking. And the criminal's family, rather surprised, every member of whom may well have been guilty of a similar crime, with the terribly begotten child and its little mother, went on living in the one room and sleeping in the general bed. And in the cathedral the choir went on singing beautifully, "Glory be to the Father, and to the Son." But I began wondering if there were many criminals, . . . whom one would not pity more than one hated—if one knew all about them.

—Margaret Wilson, *The Crime of Punishment*

SPECIAL PRIVILEGES

I will guarantee to take from this jail, or any jail in the world, five hundred men who have been the worst criminals and lawbreakers who ever got into jail, and I will go down to our lowest streets and take five hundred of the most abandoned prostitutes, and go out somewhere where there is plenty of land, and will give them a chance to make a living, and they will be as good people as the average in the community.

. . . It's easy to see how to do away with what we call

crime. It is not so easy to do it. I will tell you how to do it. It can be done by giving the people a chance to live —by destroying special privileges. So long as big criminals can get the coal fields, so long as the big criminals have control of the city council and get the public streets for streetcars and gas rights—this is bound to send thousands of poor people to jail. So long as men are allowed to monopolize all the earth, and compel others to live on such terms as these men see fit to make, then you are bound to get into jail.

The only way in the world to abolish crime and criminals is to abolish the big ones and the little ones together. Make fair conditions of life. Give men a chance to live.

—Clarence Darrow, "Address to Prisoners in Cook County Jail, 1902"

THE CRIMINAL AS SCAPEGOAT

The criminal . . . becomes the handy scapegoat upon which he [the ordinary citizen] can transfer his feeling of his own tendency to sinfulness and thus by punishing the criminal he deludes himself into a feeling of righteous indignation, thus bolstering up his own self-respect and serving in this roundabout way, both to restrain himself from like indulgences and to keep himself upon the path of cultural progress. The legal punishment of the criminal today is, in its psychology, a dramatic tragic action by which society pushes off its criminal impulses upon a substitute. The principle is the same as that by which an emotion such as anger is discharged upon an inoffensive lifeless object.

—William Alanson White, *Insanity and Criminal Law*

BEING-FOR-OTHERS

. . . when children are subjected, from their earliest days, to great social pressure, when their Being-for-Others is the subject of a collective image accompanied by value judgments and social prohibitions, the alienation is sometimes total and definitive. This is the case of most pariahs in caste societies. They internalize the objective and external judgments which the collectivity passes on them, and they view themselves in their subjective individuality on the basis of an "ethnic character," a "nature," an "essence" which merely express the contempt in which *others* hold them. The Indian untouchable thinks that he *is actually* untouchable. He internalizes the prohibition of which he is the object, and makes of it an inner principle which justifies and explains the conduct of the other Hindus toward him.

The situation is exactly the same for the small caste of untouchables whom our societies have charged with personifying Evil and whom they overwhelm with prohibitions under the name of criminals. Yes, they are criminals. This means, in all good logic, that they *have committed* one or more crimes and that they are liable to punishments set down in the statute book. But by virtue of the ambiguity of the term, society convinces them—and they let themselves be convinced—that this objective definition actually applies to their hidden, subjective being. The criminal that they were to others is now ensconced deep within them, like a monster. They thus allow themselves to be governed by *another,* that is, by a being who has reality only in the eyes of others. Their failings and errors are transformed into a permanent predisposition, that is, into a destiny.

—Jean-Paul Sartre, *Saint Genet*

THE BADGE OF DEVIANCE

When the people of a community decide that it is time to "do something" about the conduct of one of their number, they are involved in a highly intricate process. After all, even the worst miscreant in society conforms most of the time, if only in the sense that he uses the correct silver at dinner, stops obediently at traffic lights, or in a hundred other ways respects the ordinary conventions of his group. And if his fellows elect to bring sanctions against him for the occasions when he does misbehave, they are responding to a few deviant details scattered among a vast array of entirely acceptable conduct. The person who appears in a criminal court and is stamped a "thief" may have spent no more than a passing moment engaged in that activity, and the same can be said for many of the people who pass in review before some agency of control and return from the experience with a deviant label of one sort or another. When the community nominates someone to the deviant class, then, it is sifting a few important details out of the stream of behavior he has emitted and is in effect declaring that these details reflect the kind of person he "really" is. In law as well as in public opinion, the fact that someone has committed a felony or has been known to use narcotics can become the major identifying badge of his person: the very expression "he is a thief" or "he is an addict" seems to provide at once a description of his position in society and a profile of his character.

—Kai Erikson, *The Wayward Puritans*

Biographical Notes

DONALD POWELL WILSON. Served for three years as a psychologist in a drug-addiction research program conducted at Fort Leavenworth during the 1930s.

MARGARET WILSON. Wife of a governor of an English prison. Her book, *The Crime of Punishment,* was published in 1931.

CLARENCE DARROW (1857–1938). Noted criminal lawyer and champion of unpopular causes. Defender of Socialist Eugene Debs, defense attorney in the famous Scopes trial of 1925 as well as in the Leopold-Loeb murder trial in 1924.

2.

THE LAW

**Prisons are built with
stones of Law.**

—William Blake,
Proverbs of Hell

Frequently it has been pointed out that once the upper or middle classes engage in an act ordinarily considered a crime, law will be changed to accommodate them. Nevertheless, people are still doing time for a "crime" that is now an accepted form of behavior. However, the double edge of this truth should not be overlooked. Organizations such as the American Civil Liberties Union, Community Action for Legal Service, and the Human Rights Commission were begun and supported by the upper and middle classes to benefit the whole of society—not simply to protect the special privileges of the few.

In 1974, Vice-President Nelson Rockefeller was able to applaud as a courageous and compassionate act President Gerald Ford's pardoning of Richard Nixon; yet three years earlier, as governor of New York State, he ordered state troopers to fire on Attica inmates, in response to their demands for amnesty; clearly there is a breakdown of law and order. With the Watergate break-in and the Agnew scandal, we see, as never before, the problem of inequality before the law.

"The law in its majesty," said Anatole France ironically, "draws no distinction, but forbids rich and poor alike from begging in the streets or sleeping in the public parks."

. . . The gentleman really believes that he is a creator of national prestige, a defender of the faith, a pillar of society; and with this conviction to strengthen him he is utterly unscrupulous in his misplaced pride and honor, and plays the wholesaler in evil to the criminal's petty retail enterprises.

—George Bernard Shaw, *Doctors Delusions, Crude Criminology*

AGNEW COPS A PLEA

Spiro T. Agnew has copped a plea and bargained himself out of going to jail. Conceding income-tax evasion and the acceptance of money gifts outside his official salary, while the Justice Department dropped numerous other criminal charges against him, Mr. Agnew is getting off with a $10,000 fine, a suspended sentence and a "Dear Ted" letter from the President. That, apparently, is what the public trust is worth to the Nixon Administration that made this deal.

The charges, massively detailed, were that Mr. Agnew as a county, state and Federal official, in the latter case as the second highest in the nation, consecutively betrayed each trust. The "pattern" of payoffs to him, said Attorney General Richardson, had been established—and although Mr. Agnew does not concede that, the circumstances of his plea bargaining and the willingness of Mr. Richardson to make such a statement in court, even while pleading that Mr. Agnew not be sent to jail, speak louder than any denials.

Even for such crimes as those not contested by Mr. Agnew, men who had no public trust are ordinarily and frequently sent to prison. For stealing $75 from a service station or grocery store, people—especially poor people

—are imprisoned for years. What were once minor drug offenses in New York now carry mandatory sentences of 15 years or more. In most cities, accused persons routinely spend months or years in jail even before coming up for trial; and some political dissenters of recent years spend more time in jail, without being convicted of anything, than Spiro Agnew will for evasion of taxes and betrayal of public trust.

The appalling prisons of this country are full of people who committed crimes no more serious than those not contested by Mr. Agnew and who held no high office of trust. The cities of this nation are full of people who know they would go to prison for almost any crime, who know friends and relatives who are rotting in prison now for lesser crimes than the second highest official in the nation has conceded. But he is getting off lightly, and for millions of Americans the lesson of the Agnew case is merely the confirmation of their bitter belief that prison is for the poor and the powerless, while mercy is for those who can swing it.

—Tom Wicker, *The New York Times,* October 12, 1973

BRINGING THE CRIMINAL TO JUSTICE

Throughout [the President's] speech, the sixth in a series on his domestic programs, Mr. Nixon took a stiffly uncompromising attitude on the need for heavier penalties and stronger public weapons against crime and on the deterent [*sic*] effect of threatening criminals with harsher laws.

"Americans in the last decade," he said, "were often told that the criminal was not responsible for his crimes against society, but that society was responsible. I totally disagree with this permissive philosophy.

"Society is guilty of crime only when we fail to bring the criminal to justice. When we fail to make the criminal pay for his crime, we encourage him to think that crime will pay. Such an attitude will never be reflected in the laws supported by this Administration, nor in the manner in which we enforce those laws."

—*The New York Times*, March 11, 1973

THE TIME FOR TRUTH

From disclosures in recent days, the public is finally getting a picture of what was going on at the highest levels of the American Government in 1972. To wit:

• His own campaign organization was apparently deluging the President of the United States with thousands of telegrams to create the false impression that his war policy had much more enthusiastic and active support than it actually enjoyed.

• The then Attorney General of the United States was participating in meetings that discussed illegal wiretappings and burglaries and took no action against the persons who made those criminal proposals in his presence.

• The counsel to the President and the head of the President's domestic policy staff were discussing whether incriminating documents should be thrown into the Potomac River or destroyed in some other fashion.

• The acting head (now resigned) of the Federal Bureau of Investigation obliged his White House friends by having those same documents burned.

• The former Secretary of Commerce and chief fundraiser for the President's campaign organization was, with the active assistance of the President's brother and the President's personal attorney, pressuring shady businessmen and organized pressure groups for large sums of money, preferably in cash.

• Experienced intelligence agents in the employ of the White House and the President's re-election committee were burglarizing the files of a psychiatrist in an effort to find something damaging to one of his patients who is a defendant in a criminal case—a case based on Administration charges of breach of privacy.

• The White House press spokesman who repeatedly issued false statements about the Watergate affairs in 1972 asserts that those lies and slanders are now to be regarded as "inoperative."

The instances of infamous behavior accumulate day by day, each more appalling than the one before. Their still incomplete sum is a picture of men in the highest offices of the Government engaged in lawless and ruthless actions and utterly contemptuous of the restraints which apply to ordinary citizens.

—*The New York Times,* April 29, 1973

"VAGRANT"

Every prostitute . . . has a repertoire of true stories about having been solicited and arrested by young men they believed to be grocery clerks, farmers, factory workers, doctors, lawyers, or college professors—but not police officers. The officers arrest the women for offending against the Vagrancy Statute, Section 887 (4) (a) and (c) of the New York State Code of Criminal Procedure.

Clause (a) defines a vagrant as "a person who offers to commit prostitution." Since this is the law invoked when a girl solicits or approaches a plainclothes police officer, it is obvious that, in order to effect a valid arrest, the officer must be the person solicited and that if the officer is the one to solicit the girl, "the sense of the statute," according to New York City's Chief Criminal Court Judge John M. Murtagh, "must be deemed inapplicable. . . . But," Judge Murtagh adds, "in point of fact, women are entrapped every day by police officers and although, as judges, most of us are aware of the sordid entrapment procedures plainclothes officers sometimes use, we cannot often throw their cases out of court as we might like to do. It's asking rather a good deal of a judge who is called upon to decide between the conflicting testimonies of a law-enforcement officer and an accused prostitute to take the prostitute's word and, in effect, to call the officer a liar."

Admittedly, however, despite the entrapment tactics many plainclothes officers use for arresting prostitutes, there are not many women sentenced for prostitution who are not actually prostitutes. The fact is that, although the prostitutes did not, as the officers claimed, solicit them, they still went to strange rooms with strange men they believed to be customers. But what good does it do, either for them or society, to jail them? Certainly, if a policeman must solicit prostitutes in order to make arrests, they are not, at least at the time of the arrest, hurting anyone. We are legislating against them, therefore, not because we know them to be our enemies but rather because we are disapproving and even repelled by their morals. And our criminal law, based, in part as it is, on the moral law, holds prostitution to be a crime. But the question must present itself to thoughtful people who know the situation: should prostitution continue to be considered a crime?

—Sara Harris, *Hellhole*

DRUGS AND THE LAW.

(Excerpts from the message by former Governor Nelson Rockefeller to the New York State Legislature, January 3, 1973)

I will now turn to other major program recommendations.

Virtually every poll of public concerns documents that the number one growing concern of the American people is crime and drugs—coupled with an all-pervasive fear for the safety of their person and property.

This reign of fear cannot be tolerated. . . .

I therefore am proposing the following program for dealing with the illegal pushers of drugs including heroin, amphetamines, LSD, hashish and other dangerous drugs.

(1) **Life Prison Sentences for All Pushers**—The hard drug pusher destroys lives just as surely and far more cruelly than a cold-blooded killer. He threatens our so-

ciety as a whole, whether he engages in large scale trafficking or small-time operations.

I therefore will ask for legislation making the penalty for all illegal trafficking in hard drugs a life sentence in prison.

To close all avenues for escaping the full force of this sentence, the law would forbid acceptance of a plea to a lesser charge, forbid probation, forbid parole and forbid suspension of sentence.

(2) **Life Sentence for Violent Crimes by Addicts**—In order to deter effectively the violent crimes committed by the addicted, I will in addition: propose that crimes of violence committed by persons under the influence of hard drugs be punished by life imprisonment. The avenues of escape would similarly be closed.

(3) **Removal of Youthful Offender Protection**—It is just as important to have maximum deterrents effective against pushers in their late 'teens as against adult pushers, since both destroy youth and corrupt society.

(4) **Payment for Information on Hard Drug Pushers**—If these deterrents are to be effective, there is need to create incentives to support the law, in order to counteract the incentives which already exist to subvert the law—particularly in the field of drugs. Therefore, I will propose the payment of a $1,000 state cash reward for the person or persons providing information leading to the apprehension and conviction of each hard drug pusher.

—*The New York Times*, January 4, 1973

MY SON–PERHAPS YOURS

. . . Once I was prepared to go Governor Rockefeller one better than his proposal to imprison all drug sellers for life without chance of parole. Once I seriously considered taking my rifle and killing a drug peddler. I didn't know his name or what he looked like. All I knew was that he —someone—was selling heroin to my son and killing a family in the process. . . .

My son did the same thing at times, buying bags cheap in Harlem and the South Bronx, and selling them at a profit in our Connecticut suburb, the profit going back into his arm. To be consistent, I would have had to shoot him too, and his middle-class white addict friends who were also doing it. . . .

A friend of my son was arrested a few years ago for a so-called accommodation sale worth $15 to an acquaintance. He was sentenced to from three to five years, a terrible sentence in itself to a first offender who—the judicial process laggard as it is—had been straight for almost a year by the time he entered jail. Through great effort, possible because he was white and middle-class, the boy was released early, returned to his program, entered college and found a job. If Mr. Rockefeller had his way, that young man would be in a cell today, at 23, unable ever to leave it.

My son—his once-bright promise returning now after two-and-one-half years off heroin—might be serving the same sentence beside him—never to taste full manhood, know fatherhood, be part of a family of love.

I watched my son's best friend die of drugs. I saw my own son come so close to going down forever that I don't like to think about it. I hate drugs and the cold-blooded merchandisers of them and all of their protectors. But adequate penalties exist to put them out of business. I believe that some criminals, drug peddlers among them, are seemingly incorrigible and releasing them into society is a criminal act against the citizenry. But even men once thought to be depraved beyond hope of salvage have reformed.

At the least, let's not descend to the level of Governor Rockefeller who would have put my boy—or perhaps yours—in a cell forever.

—Paul Good, *The New York Times,* January 29, 1973

"DEFECTIVE DELINQUENTS"

Dallas is a small town ten miles from Wilkes-Barre, and a hundred from Philadelphia. The State Correctional Institution is a prison for "defective delinquents." Through the high fences and barred windows, the inmates can look out on the beautiful mountains and woods, but until recently many of them had no hope of ever seeing beyond the closest range of hills, because they were committed to stay at Dallas until the institution thought they were "ready" for release. Recently the American Civil Liberties Union has attacked the whole idea of imprisoning "defectives" indefinitely and has found an ally in Judge Adrian Bonnelly of the Philadelphia County Court. Judge Bonnelly agrees with the ACLU that prison is certainly no place to send children who have never been convicted of a crime, and he has served notice that he intends to release every person now at Dallas who was committed by the Philadelphia Juvenile Court. Some of these "boys" are now well over 21, like Walter, who was 39 when Judge Bonnelly released him a month ago. Walter, abandoned by his mother at the age of 4, has spent his life in institutions since then, and finally wound up at the prison at Dallas in 1950, though he has never committed a crime.

When Judge Bonnelly has fulfilled his purpose, he will have released approximately 150 inmates. There are another 650 who Judge Bonnelly cannot release because they were committed as adults, or because they do not come from Philadelphia.

So far as the ACLU can determine, each of the 800 inmates was sent to Dallas under the Defective Delinquent Act of 1937 (as amended). This act is worth careful study. Under its terms, any male of 15 or over who is convicted of a crime *or* is adjudicated delinquent by a juvenile court may be sent to Dallas *indefinitely* if the court is satisfied—after an examination by a psychiatrist and a psychologist or by two qualified physicians "that the person thought to be mentally defective is not insane, nor can be classified as an idiot or imbecile . . . nor a psychopath or an infirmary case, *though in fact mentally defective with criminal tendencies*" (emphasis added). The Act nowhere defines "mentally defective" nor "criminal tendencies." The commitment is indefinite; the inmate will be released only if the committing court orders it, or when, in the opinion of the institution, "his mental condition has so improved as to warrant his discharge." . . .

Dallas is a prison, not a school. Run by the Bureau of Correction, an agency of the Department of Justice, the institution maintains iron discipline. Although the younger minors are segregated from older inmates, children and adults alike are locked in regulation prison cells at night and during much of the day. Dressed in prison garb, the inmates are marched to and from meals and other routines.

. . . dinner must be eaten in about ten minutes. There is a "hole" for disciplinary cases, with cells for about 50, including several cells with almost no light, and four cells with no furnishings whatsoever, not even a bed. . . .

In the opinion of ACLU lawyers the Defective Delinquent Act is hopelessly unconstitutional. Let us consider an adult convicted of a crime according to due process of law. Ordinarily he will be given a punishment to fit the crime, as prescribed by statute, e.g., a maximum of two years for assault and battery. But if, pursuant to a "commission finding" he is found "defective," he may be put away forever—not in a "training school" or "mental hospital," but in a prison. There is no definition in the law of what a "defective" is—the court or the commission can define it as it likes. For a juvenile, the situation is even more dreadful. He need never have been accused —much less convicted with due process of—of a criminal act; "deliquency" is enough. He may well have been found delinquent at a five-minute hearing at which he did not know the specific charges against him, at which hearsay evidence was admitted, at which no cross-examination was allowed, and at which he could not produce witnesses for himself. Almost certainly he was not represented by a lawyer, and may have been told he didn't need one. This boy, under the Defective Delinquent Act, can spend his life in prison on the grounds that he is "defective" and has "criminal tendencies." . . .

As usual, it is the poor who are the victims of the system. If a family has money, their retarded son will be sent to a private institution. Dallas is a dumping ground for the unfortunate children of the poor and inarticulate.

—Spencer Coxe, Executive Director, American Civil Liberties Union, Greater Philadelphia Branch

PUNISHMENT WITHOUT CRIME: "CRIMINAL TENDENCIES"

Armando Beltrante is 44 years old but seems much younger, almost boyish. He is plump and gregarious and talks almost incessantly, using phrases like "deprivation of civil rights" that sound oddly out of place in his fractured discourse.

Armando Beltrante spent 22 years in prison, starting in 1944, when he was 16 years old, after he had allegedly broken a store window near his home in Philadelphia.

For that offense, which displayed "criminal tendencies," and because he had suffered brain damage as a result of meningitis as a child, he was ordered to jail under a Pennsylvania statute that required neither a trial nor a definite sentence.

"They said I have an I.Q. of 89," he says. "That's not so bad, is it? Eighty-nine is higher than a lot of people. And it's no reason for deprivation of your civil rights."

DAMAGE SUIT FILED

The phrase no doubt recurs because it is partly on the basis of his civil rights that a sympathetic lawyer has sued the state on his behalf for damages "in excess of $10,000," a formula that is used in Pennsylvania for suits that involve more than that amount.

The suit, filed in Harrisburg by Martin Heller of Philadelphia, the lawyer, contends that in addition to depriving Mr. Beltrante of his freedom, the state, by keeping him in jail for 22 years, aggravated his mental condition and that he also developed a form of Parkinson's disease, a serious nervous disorder. . . .

In the seven years since Mr. Beltrante was freed, he has held menial jobs as a dishwasher, doorman and bootblack. He runs errands, and goes along with lawyers to courtrooms to watch the proceedings.

He usually carries a copy of the United States Constitution and calls his courtroom visits "studying law."

—Wayne King, *The New York Times*, February 23, 1973

BEFORE THE LAW

Before the law stands a doorkeeper. To this doorkeeper there comes a man from the country and prays for admittance to the Law. But the doorkeeper says that he cannot grant admittance at the moment. The man thinks it over and then asks if he will be allowed in later. "It is possible," says the doorkeeper, "but not at the moment." Since the gate stands open, as usual, and the doorkeeper steps to one side, the man stoops to peer through the gateway into the interior. Observing that, the doorkeeper laughs and says: "If you are so drawn to it, just try to go in despite my veto. But take note: I am powerful. And I am only the least of the doorkeepers. From hall to hall there is one doorkeeper after another, each more powerful than the last. The third doorkeeper is already so terrible that even I cannot bear to look at him." These are difficulties the man from the country has not expected; the Law, he thinks, should surely be accessible at all times and to everyone, but as he now takes a closer look

at the doorkeeper in his fur coat, with his big sharp nose
and long, thin, black Tartar beard, he decides that it is
better to wait until he gets permission to enter. The
doorkeeper gives him a stool and lets him sit down at one
side of the door. There he sits for days and years. He
makes many attempts to be admitted, and wearies the
doorkeeper by his importunity. The doorkeeper frequently
has little interviews with him, asking him questions about
his home and many other things, but the questions are
put indifferently, as great lords put them, and always
finish with the statement that he cannot be let in yet. The
man, who has furnished himself with many things for his
journey, sacrifices all he has, however valuable, to bribe
the doorkeeper. The doorkeeper accepts everything, but
always with the remark: "I am only taking it to keep you
from thinking you have omitted anything." During these
many years the man fixes his attention almost continuously on the doorkeeper. He forgets the other doorkeepers,
and this first one seems to him the sole obstacle preventing
access to the Law. He curses his bad luck, in his early
years boldly and loudly; later, as he grows old, he only
grumbles to himself. He becomes childish, and since in
his yearlong contemplation of the doorkeeper he has come
to know even the fleas in his fur collar, he begs the fleas
as well to help him and to change the doorkeeper's mind.
At length his eyesight begins to fail, and he does not
know whether the world is really darker or whether his
eyes are only deceiving him. Yet in his darkness he is
now aware of a radiance that streams inextinguishably
from the gateway of the Law. Now he has not very long
to live. Before he dies, all his experiences in these long
years gather themselves in his head to one point, a question he has not yet asked the doorkeeper. He waves him
nearer, since he can no longer raise his stiffening body.
The doorkeeper has to bend low toward him, for the

difference in height between them has altered much to the man's disadvantage. "What do you want to know now?" asks the doorkeeper; "you are insatiable." "Everyone strives to reach the Law," says the man, "so how does it happen that for all these many years no one but myself has ever begged for admittance?" The doorkeeper recognizes that the man has reached his end, and, to let his failing sense catch the words, roars in his ear: "No one else could ever be admitted here, since this gate was made only for you. I am now going to shut it."

—Franz Kafka, "Before the Law"

3.

THE PRISONERS

Every society has the criminals which it deserves.

—Jean-Alexandre Lacassagne

Murderer, Prostitute, Rapist, Homosexual, Embezzler.
Apart from the pronouncements of law, a prisoner exists
with an identity separate from that imposed by the courts.
Prisoners, unless entirely broken, are persons who experi-
ence a range of emotions and express a variety of attitudes
and interests—they are individuals: neither the embodi-
ment of particular evils nor the remote shadowy figures we
might think them to be.

For some, prison becomes a natural—even necessary—
way of life because they have never seen, heard of, nor
imagined an alternative except for "someone else"; it is a
conscious choice, born of self- or social hatred, the final
rejection of a world that long ago rejected them. Others,
elitists of a kind, welcome imprisonment as society's long-
delayed recognition of "talents" that were too great for
the outside world to contain. If there are those few for
whom prison is merely a risk of the game, for more, after
years of despair and lives that no longer work, imprison-
ment is merely the final insult.

Why were there no alternatives?

ARCHIE
(A way of life)

—Oh, to me when I'm out crime is a way of life, a profession. At times it can be exciting, at times it can be some-

thing you're quite proud of. Not you personally of course, you couldn't, because you're not a criminal, at least not in society's eyes. You work for your living, and what you do is socially acceptable; and for all I know, where you live, in your own community, you might have a certain amount of prestige.

It's difficult for people like you to understand that I too, in my own community or what's the word, *milieu* is it—in that setting, I too have a certain amount of prestige. What's more, I don't want to lose it, anymore than you would yours. If you were caught embezzling the local cricket-club funds or whatever it was you were connected with, you'd take a sudden drop; people would look sideways at you when you went in the local for a drink, your friends wouldn't send you Christmas cards, even your wife would get the cold-shoulder. Because suddenly you'd no longer be considered reliable. Exactly the same thing would happen to me, in my world, if—well, let's be quite frank about it, even if it was generally known for instance that I was prepared to sit here like this and talk to you. It wouldn't matter how much or how little I was actually telling you: the mere fact that we were acquaintances would start doubts in people's minds. The code is that you don't mix with straight people. It's a very necessary law too, for self-preservation, my own and everyone else's. No matter what happens, what goes on, you don't know anything and you don't talk.

If it's a big robbery that six of us have pulled off, say, and there's been just one small error somewhere which brings the Law round to see me, the other five know—they have to know—that not only am I not going to let out a word about having anything to do with it, but even if by some incredible misfortune I'm so stuck with it that I'm obviously going to get ten years, I'll never so much as hint with a pause who the others were who were in it too. 'Joe Smith?' 'No, I don't know him.' 'Sam Brown?' 'I've never heard of him.' 'Jack Jones—you can't say you don't know him, he's married to your sister.' 'Is he really? That's funny, I've not heard from her for five years.'

You see, this is the only thing the criminal fraternity have got. It is a fraternity, though of course it doesn't operate down among the petty larcenists and what you might call the thoughtless one-man crooks who never plan anything. But amongst the firms, amongst the teams who work on a large scale and plan everything down to the last detail, which is what you have to do if you're after the big money, it does. Because all the other advantages are on the side of the Law. The radio-controlled cars, the forensic scientists, the squads of fifty or a hundred men on call at any one time, the legal experts, the barristers, even the judicial system—they're on the side of straight society. So the only thing we've got when it comes to the show-down is this absolute certainty, one with another, of a hundred-percent reliability.

And if you haven't got that reputation, you're finished: you won't be asked to join in, you won't get a proposition, you won't even know a job's under consideration. The first you'll hear about it is when you read about it in the papers after it's over, like everyone else.

That's the number one thing: reliability. It's expected of you while you're outside prison—and just as much while you're in. Things get around fast: there's a man up in Durham prison now, I've never met him, and I don't know him except by name. But he was one of the boys —until about three months ago. He wanted to get his parole, so he passed-on a bit of information to the prison authorities: something quite trivial, a prisoner had got something in his cell he wasn't supposed to have. That man now, he's finished for the rest of his life: there's not one respectable criminal, inside or out, who'll ever trust him, take him in on a job with them, recommend him to someone else, or would even point out a sixpence to him if they saw it lying in the gutter.

—Tony Parker, *The Frying-Pan*

PAT
(... any other person...)

Sometimes I feel as low as sixpence on the ground I'm so depressed: I feel like that outside too, but once I've got a few pints and a couple of rums inside me I start to pick up. One day becomes more or less the same as the next when you're drinking, they run-on into each other, and that's the way I prefer it to be.

I ought to do something for my kids, I suppose, having brought them into the world. But they're not mine, they're hers; and I can't persuade myself it isn't better it should be any different. The only future I see for me is keep on coming back to prison again. You don't want it to be like that, but you know it always will be, so what can you do?

If I was starting my life over again, there isn't one point in it anywhere I could look back and say 'That was the moment when I ought to have stopped and taken a step in the other direction instead; that was the turning-point, I'd like to go back and have a fresh start from there.' There's nothing, no, no time ever which I see in that sort of light.

Only except perhaps right back at the beginning, when I was actually born—no, even further back than then, in the very second I was conceived. That would be the only time I'd wish to change: I wish it had been some other cell and some other sperm or whatever it is, that'd come together—and what'd been given life then had grown and been born, and come out into the world another human being. I wouldn't mind if it had been a conquering general, one of the world's great statesmen, or the meanest humblest labourer you can think of, digging for peat in Ireland or sweating his guts out at the bottom of a coalmine in Nottingham. Any one, any other person, important or completely ordinary and unimportant, it wouldn't matter in the slightest. But whoever it was, I'd sooner be that person. I'd sooner be anyone else there was than be me.

—Tony Parker, *The Frying-Pan*

MOLLY McGUIRE
(The same. The same.)

Molly McGuire was born in County Mayo, Ireland, where she lived for the first eight years of her life in a two-room shack with her father, mother, grandmother, two older sisters tunefully called Noreen and Doreen, an elder brother named Michael, an emaciated cow originally designated Sean and nicknamed Slimy, a variety of pigs and chickens which bore no appellation, and a roistering, ruffianly dog named Bridie.

. . . She enjoyed life in spite of the hunger and cold and poverty, until the terrible night when she was seven and, wide awake, saw her father, Fluther, whom she'd always known to be a "bummer," return from a binge with two of his close friends—a roaring, hell-raising spree under the stars during which he and his companions quarreled and yelled most of the night. When at last he came into the house, he passed out with his feet in the fire. He awoke, shaking his bloodied head like a sick hound and in a bawling uproar. That night he became a permanent cripple.

And it was as a cripple that he gathered up his family one day just after Molly's eighth birthday, thumped his hand on the table and said, "We're going to the proper place, the only place, America." . . .

In New York, Molly McGuire learned that her father and most other Irishmen couldn't get proper jobs even if they were equipped to hold them. Irishmen, in Molly's early days in New York, occupied the same position Negroes and Puerto Ricans do today. They were the last hired and first fired. Indeed, the only jobs open to them, regardless of their abilities, were the lowly, menial jobs the natives would not have—bootblacking, hodcarrying, longshoreman's work, chimney-sweeping—and, for the fortunate ones Tammany picked out to utilize for its own ends —saloonkeeping. And so, like it or not, they had to live in the grimy houses of the Five Points alleys and other such dishonored places. . . .

Molly says, recalling her early childhood in New York, that she was never devastated by it because she lived in hope of becoming a prostitute and earning money enough so she could eat decently and have a place to sleep. She "prayed to the good Gawd" for many years, and then, when she was twelve, her prayers were answered and she was hired to work as a waitress-hostess in a combination restaurant-bagnio on Minetta Street in Greenwich Village that was called De Vito's Minetta House. She remembers the place as in a constant uproar, loud, clamorous, overpowering. She describes poor men, some Irish but mostly Italian, coming there and behaving like nabobs with her and the other girls, who ranged in age from eleven to sixteen. She remembers that the men came not only to sleep with the girls, but also to drink with them. She maintains that she and the rest consumed gallons of ale, porter, beer, and stronger stuff, in a front room of the house adjoining the restaurant—the only room not used for sleeping. . . .

But always, from the time she was sixteen and even while she felt herself at the height of her success, she lived in constant anxiety. She was sixteen. Soon she'd be seventeen. And eighteen. And how long would the Glad House want her once she was past eighteen? She recalls, and this may be the last recollection she expresses with vitality and sufficient logic so that fact follows orderly fact, a dreadful day after she'd had her eighteenth birthday when the owner and manager of the Glad House, a man known as Handsome Haggerty, . . . came splendidly to her defense. He said, "It's nothing turrible being a ould lass of eighteen, Molly. Don't you torment yourself. Be the all-pitiful Gawd, no matter how ould you get to be, nineteen, twenty even, yez ain't going to get shoved out of no job so long as Handsome is here."

All the same, when she was twenty he told her she was too old to continue working, and her life as a vagrant began. For a while, she tried streetwalking, but the competition was keen and there were younger girls soliciting. Besides, she had no confidence any more. So she went from bad to worse. From drinking in the good saloons and bars, she degenerated to the bad ones. She frequented them, as she does today when she can afford it, more for companionship than for drink. Not that she doesn't want and need to drink, of course. Anyone who'd been sold her first three pennies' worth of rum when she was a little over eight—by an entrepreneur who turned children into customers—would want to drink. But it is generally true, and was certainly true when she was younger, that she never minded commitment to jails or hospitals where liquor was unavailable to her so long as she was surrounded by people and had enough to eat.

The saloons and bars Molly recalls from her earlier days along the Bowery—not to be compared to the anemic ones on the Block today—included such places as The Black and Tan, where gang fights were the order of the day, and Suicide Hall on the Bowery and Houston Street, serving, in lieu of whiskey, colored camphine and rectified oil of turpentine.

"I still see me there in Suicide Hall," she says, "drinking and feeling a fire burning in me blood. Ay, and then the police come and take me out of there and I come before the judge with the sweat rolling down me and he talks a great streak, you know, and I'm hoping he'll send me to the hospital. But he don't. Nor will he send me to jail either, although I beg him.

"'It is winter, Your Honor,' I say, reminding him, 'and I can't live out in the street in the winter—and what am I going to do? I ain't so different from the other people who want to stay warm. I want to stay warm too.'

"But he only sends me out again. The same then and all of these years as today. The same. The same."

Molly McGuire and the other elderly vagrant women in the House of Detention are as much the victims of our prejudice as the large mass of Negro and Puerto Rican House of Detention inmates are. They are living examples out of history that our inhumanity toward minorities can help drive any people, not Puerto Ricans and Negroes alone, to the revolving door of the Women's House of Detention. . . . Molly McGuire is a symbol of the shame of our past. For it is a fact that, while Negroes and Puerto Ricans comprise the majority of today's inmates of the

Women's House and of every county jail, male and female, in the county, Irish and Italian immigrants were in the majority before 1912. Between 1845, when the New York City Police Department was first created—primarily as a means of coping with Bowery derelicts—and 1855, the number of drunk arrests, mostly of Irish men and women, was 100,000. By the 1870's, the number exceeded 40,000 Irish derelicts a year and one out of every three arrested was a woman. Irish children as young as eleven years old were arrested in the 1870's. . . .

Molly McGuire's present life is typical of the whole group of vagrant inmates off Skid Row, if you include the younger Skid Rowers, mostly Puerto Ricans and Negroes, along with the Irish and Italians of Molly's generation. She and they live on the Bowery—when they are not either in a hospital or the House of Detention—alongside respectable old people living on their pensions or old age insurance, insane and feebleminded people, cripples, blind beggars, prostitutes called "fleabags" because they are inclined to be syphilitic, and a few elderly, egocentric Hobohemians. They all live today as Bowery derelicts lived as long ago as 1892, when, during his memorable anti-vice campaign, the Reverend Dr. Charles H. Parkhurst, touring through several Bowery flophouses, exclaimed: "My God, to think that people with souls live like this."

—Sara Harris, *Hellhole*

BERTHA GREEN
(". . . you just drift along.")

There are other House of Detention repeaters like Bertha
Green . . . who certainly must have been treated, one way
or another, as she says her madams treated her. They, like
Bertha, say that of course they were overwhelmed by the
small pay and the long hours and the hard work. But
these alone might not have tipped the scales and made
them turn to prostituting. The literal straw that broke
their backs was the attitude their employers took toward
them. Bertha, like the majority of the inmates of her generation, recalls—with more emotion than anything else
elicits from her—the insults and snubs, conscious and unconscious, to which she was subjected.

Bertha says, "No trick, no matter how he dirty and hurt
you, can treat you worse than some madams you housework for do. Many of them are what you call these nervous and excitable women. And no matter how hard you
work, they tell you you lazy and are laying down on the
job. And sometimes they stand around while you doing
you work and make funny faces like they feel you can't
be right in what you do. Or they sit there and watch you
work, looking at you till you think you go crazy with
feeling they hate you. And you can hear they voices going
tch, tch, tch, as they watch you. They talking to you in
voices that say they hate you and still not saying any
words you can make out. Or sometime they talk to you
but don't look at you. You ever see somebody lean back
in they chairs and rub they eyes and look out the window
like they gonna talk to it? Then they do talk to the window. Like you ain't even around. They say to the window,

'This gal is just as lazy as all the rest of them people.
They all the same. They lazy and liars and cheats.'

"And sometime, most of the time in fact, they act like
I am a crook. Some of them only examine in my bag to
see if I toting things. But a couple examine me all over
like I am in court or in the House of D., and they one
madam, she make me take off my dress and show her if
I got anything hid underneath. And to shake out my shoes.
And I got all shook up while shaking out my shoes and I
say to myself, 'All the prostitutes I know ain't no worse
off than I who try to do a honest job to take care of me
and my baby.' So with everything, I just don't care. I
mean what I remember about my first trick is I remember
he pay me $1.25 to go up on a roof and he a white man
all dressed up in a blue suit and wearing a tie and if he
ever tell a white woman to do what he tell me for $1.25,
she kill him.

. . . you get to a time after you know nothing's no good
that you just don't care any more and you say to yourself:
'What the hell, why worry?' And then you just drift along,
and you take you first trick and he make you feel dirty,
sure, especially if he a white man. But then you got to
think how all men is the same, no matter what they color.
And how dirty it make you feel when some madam want
to examine you underwear to see if you crooking her or
something. . . ."

Bertha Green speaks for all the prostitutes of her generation . . . when she compares the two realities, her life as
a prostitute and her life as a domestic worker, and finds
one as bitter as the other. It is hard to blame the women
for having chosen the life they have, in view not alone
of their circumstances but also of the lack of their preparation for coping with them. Certainly, the fact that there
are not many more Bertha Greens than there are in the
House of Detention is a miracle and a tribute to the moral

strength of the vast majority of Negro refugee women from the South who did not engage in prostitution or other illicit activities despite their abundant and destructive disillusionment with New York, the "promised land."

—Sara Harris, *Hellhole*

ALFRED HASSAN
(. . . in prison all my life.)

Don't be telling me what is right. You talk that right jive, but where was you when my old man and the neighbors was teaching me how to steal and shoot dope? Where was you when me and my brothers and sisters was crazy and blind from hunger? Where was you when my mama was gambling away the welfare check? Where was you when the World was calling me a dirty nigger and a greasy Mexican and a poor white peckawood? Where was you when the cops was whipping me upside my head just because my skin was dark? Where was you when I was losing respect for your law and your order? Where was you when Wrong was my only salvation? I'll tell you where you was. You was clear across town—Y'know, over there living in them big, fine houses—talking that trash about right and wrong. But check this out: There ain't no such thing as right or wrong in my world. Can you dig? Right or wrong is what a chump chooses to tell himself. And I chose to tell myself that stealing is right. I had a choice: to be a poor-ass, raggedly-ass, mathafukker all my life or to go out into the streets and steal me some money so I could buy me a decent pair of shoes to wear, or shoot me some dope so I could forget about the rat-

and-roach infested dump I live in. Yeah, I got a chip on my shoulder. But it didn't get up there by itself. And it's gonna stay up there until you eliminate the funky conditions that breed cats like me. Yeah, you gonna send me to the pen. But that ain't no big thing because I've been in prison all my life. And if you think you can rehabilitate me by sending me to prison, then you are sadly mistaken. How do you rehabilitate a cat who has never been "habilitated"? There ain't nothing to rehabilitate. I know why you're sending me to the pen. You're sending me there to be punished, to do some A'ems and P'ems. But, fool, don't you know that you can't get nothing down by throwing salt into my open wounds? And I want you to know one thing before I split. I ain't ashamed of what I did or who I am. I'm me—dig. I've talked that talk, and now I'm ready to walk that walk . . .

—Eve Pell, ed., *Maximum Security, Letters from Prison*

THE LONG NIGHT

From somewhere on the other side of the long thicket of shrubbery, Larry could hear the shouts of children playing in the park. The bright, sunlit air seemed to trap their laughter like some sleeping insect, holding it quivering in the afternoon and folding it inward so that it was a thing divorced from the coolness in which he and Shirley lay.

"I love the park," Shirley said lazily. "I come here a lot when you're away at Stanford."

"Alone?" Larry asked. His face, much too young for his nineteen years, grew serious.

Shirley looked at him from the corner of her eye. "Sometimes. But most of the time I come with a girl friend."

"No boys?"

"Well, once." She sat up, dusky blonde hair disarrayed and floating about her pretty, triangular face. "Why, jealous?"

"No," he snapped. "Of course not!"

There was a suggestion of a pout about his too full lower lip as he rolled onto his stomach. He glared at a blade of grass. She was laughing at him, he knew this, and the thought angered him even more. Suddenly, he jumped to his feet.

"What's wrong?" she asked.

"Nothing. I'll be right back."

"Where are you going?"

He gestured up the path to the building that housed the park restrooms. The building was set back in a clump of shrubbery punctuated with several dispirited rosebushes.

"Oh, that." Shirley rolled onto her stomach. "Don't be gone too long."

Larry glared down at her back. His fists clenched and opened. Whirling, he marched toward the restroom building. He didn't really have to go up there. It was just an excuse to hide his anger, to get away from her and collect his temper.

The door to the men's side stood ajar behind a reed-paneled fence. The rosebushes that halfway hid the fence looked even more unhealthy at close range. Their summer blossoms were brown and dead. Larry pushed through the door and wrinkled his nose at the stench of ancient urine permeating the stagnant air of the restroom. The back wall carried a long urinal with ugly, dark splotches where the porcelain had been chipped away. The bottom of the trough was stained rust brown. There was a man standing at the trough. He was well dressed with a sport coat and an open shirt. Probably in his late thirties, Larry thought.

Larry wished the man wasn't there. He had always had trouble urinating in public restrooms when some stranger was standing next to him. It had always taken a major muscular effort on his part.

Larry purposely didn't look at the man as he positioned himself at the trough. He tried to urinate but he couldn't. He just stood there straining and becoming more embarrassed by the moment. Then he realized the man was taking too long, deliberately prolonging his stance. Larry could feel the man looking down at him from the corner of his eye.

He began to tremble and he tried to stop himself but he couldn't. He'd heard of other guys being approached by homosexuals, but this was the first time it had happened to him. He was suddenly sick and afraid, but it was compounded with a kind of strange excitement which he couldn't at first identify. The reality of the moment slapped him and he had a vision of the man bowed before him.

I'm no queer, goddam you! he wanted to scream. But he couldn't. He had to get out of there! He couldn't move though.

The man moved closer. Larry felt the man's hands turn him away from the trough and again he tried to move, to throw up his arms, to run, but he couldn't. He watched in horror as the man knelt before him. The man's eyes were glazed, hardly acknowledging that Larry even existed. He might have been performing some arcane rites before a lifeless idol instead of . . .

"All right!" a voice commanded.

Larry jumped with fear.

There were two men in the doorway. They were dressed in suits, but from their manner there was no doubt they were police detectives. The man sprang to his feet and looked wildly about for some way to escape. The tallest, youngest detective rushed into the restroom proper while the shorter, gray haired one blocked the doorway. The man in the sport coat bolted past the taller detective and tried to shove his way past the gray-haired detective standing in the doorway. That detective grabbed the man's collar and shoved him back against the wall. The man stumbled and fell, hitting his head against the urinal trough. He sat there shaking his head and moaning softly.

"You have no right," he kept saying. "You have no right!"

"You're both under arrest," the older detective said.

"Oh, no, please. I didn't do anything!"

"Sure," the taller detective said, sneering. "Sure, we know."

The older detective produced a pair of handcuffs and leaned forward over the man in the sport coat. He grabbed the man's hands and snapped the cuffs onto his wrists.

"Oh, God," the man said. "What will people say? What will my wife say!"

"Frisk him," the older detective told his partner, nodding at Larry.

"Let me go," Larry pleaded. "My girl is down the path. I wasn't doing anything. I've never been in trouble before. Jesus! Please!"

"I'm sorry, son," the older detective told him. "We have to take you in." He nodded to the younger detective and the younger detective produced a pair of handcuffs.

"Uhn-uh," Larry mumbled, staring at the handcuffs and shaking his head. "Oh, Jesus, don't do that. I'm not a queer."

But the detective snapped the cuffs on Larry's wrists. The older detective helped the man onto his feet and the two detectives shepherded Larry and the man out into the late afternoon. Larry heard the children's laughter and the squeak of a swing from somewhere behind the restroom house. Down the path, Shirley still lay on her stomach on the grass with her back turned. Larry stared down at the cuffs glistening in the late afternoon sun and then at the stern faces of the detectives. He looked at the bowed, defeated face of the man in the sport coat and he knew all this couldn't be real.

The four of them were joined by a uniformed policeman. The policeman, a stocky, red-faced man in his early forties, looked at the man and then at Larry. "What have you got here?"

"A couple of tearoom queens," the young detective answered.

"That's enough!" the older detective said. He looked down the path at Shirley. "That your girl, son?" When Larry nodded dumbly, the detective said, "We can take you down that way and let you tell her."

"No! I don't want that."

The older detective spoke to the uniformed policeman. "After we leave, go down and tell her that her boyfriend got himself into a little trouble and we had to take him downtown. Don't tell her what for."

The patrolman shrugged. "Okay, but she'll find out soon enough."

Larry fought back threatening tears as the older detective took his arm. The four of them started toward a light blue unmarked car parked along the driveway.

"This will kill my wife," the man in the sport coat said. "If this gets out I could lose my job. I could—" His eyes pleaded with the older detective, then the younger one. "You must believe me! This is the first time I've ever done anything like this."

"Bullshit," the younger detective said and shoved the man toward the police car.

In the police station, they had to wait while the desk sergeant finished booking a seedy looking man in faded blue jeans and a dirty tee-shirt. The man in the sport coat, still pleading and protesting his innocence, was booked first and then led away down a long corridor. Then Larry was booked and led away to be fingerprinted and photographed. After that he was led into another room where he was told to strip and shower.

He finished and was then given a pair of pin-striped coveralls. There was a huge "P" on the back of the coveralls and they were too big and there was a hole in the left leg, just above the knee. His hands began to sweat, but when he wiped them on the baggy legs of the coveralls the course material stuck to his skin which was already sweating from the heat and moisture generated by the shower.

The older detective led him through two electrical gates that opened and shut with a clank behind them. The smell of antiseptic cleaner was too strong and Larry thought he might vomit. As he was being led down a short corridor with bars on either side, it was as if the bars were telephone poles flashing by on each side of a car he was riding in that was speeding toward some terrible destination. But he couldn't stop the car; the brakes wouldn't work.

"How about your folks?" he dimly heard the detective ask. "You want me to contact them?"

"No," Larry mumbled. Again, he had to fight back the tears.

They reached the end of the corridor and another gate. An officer in a glass enclosed cage pushed a button and the gate slid open. A guard was waiting for them. . . .

The long night had begun.

—Jim Roberts, *IN, A Magazine About Prisons*

CARL PANZRAM
(". . . I have lived as you taught me.")

This is a true statement of my actions, including the time and places and my reasons for so doing these things, written by me of my own free will at the District Jail, Washington, D. C., November 4, 1928.

I was born June 28, 1891, on a small farm in Minnesota. My parents were of German descent. Hardworking, ignorant and poor. The rest of the family consisted of five brothers and one sister, all of whom are dead except three of us brothers and our sister.

All of my family are as the average human beings are. They are honest and hardworking people. All except myself. I have been a human animal ever since I was born. When I was very young at five or six years of age I was a thief and a liar. The older I got the meaner I got.

My father and mother split up when I was about seven or eight years old. The old man pulled out one day and disappeared. This left my mother with a family of six on a small worked-out farm. As fast as the older boys grew up, they also pulled out. One died. This left me, my sister, one older brother, and my mother. My sister and I were sent to school during the days, and as soon as we came home in the evenings, we were put to work in the fields where my older brother and mother were always at work, from daylight until long after dark sometimes. My portion of pay consisted of plenty of work and a sound beating every time I looked cock-eyed or done anything that displeased anyone who was older and stronger and able to catch me and kick me around whenever they felt like it, and it seemed to me and still does now that everything was always right for the one who was the strongest and every single thing that I done was wrong. Everybody said so anyway. But right or wrong I used to get plenty of abuse. Everybody thought it was all right to deceive me, lie to me and kick me around whenever they felt like it, and they felt like it pretty regular. That is the way my life was lived until I was about eleven years old.

At about that time I began to suspect that there was something wrong about the treatment I was getting from the rest of the human race. When I was about eleven years old, I began to hear and see that there were other places in this world besides my own little corner of it. I began to realize that there were other people who lived nice, easy lives, and who were not kicked around and worked to death.

I decided that I wanted to leave my miserable home. Before I left I looked around and figured that one of our neighbors who was rich and had a nice home full of nice things, he had too much and I had too little. So one night I broke into his home and stole everything that to my eyes had the most value.

Those things were some apples, some cake, and a great big pistol. Eating the apples and cake and carrying the pistol under my coat, I walked to the railroad yards where I caught a freight train going to the West where I intended to be a cowboy and shoot Indians. But I must have had my wires crossed because I missed my connections somwhere. Instead of going out and seeing the world, I was caught, brought back home and beaten half to death, then sent to jail and from there to the Minnesota State Training School at Red Wing, Minnesota. Right there and then I began to learn about man's inhumanity to man.

. . . The manager's name was John Moore. The matron's

name was Miss Martin. And a fine pair of Christians they
were to have in charge of a lot of young boys to train.
My first reception at the school was to be met by Mr. John
Moore who told me the rules. Next day he called me into
his room to take my pedigree for an oral and physical
examination to be put on the records of the institution.
He began the oral examination by asking me my name,
parents, habits, schooling, home life and history of my
associations. He asked me if my father was insane, was he
a drunkard, was he lazy or industrious. He asked me if
my mother was a prostitute or a drunkard, was she educated or ignorant. After asking me all these questions and
explaining in detail just what each question meant and
all about it, he then stripped me naked and began my
physical examination, looking to see if I was lousy or had
any kind of sickness or disease. He examined my penis
and my rectum, asking me if I had ever committed forni-
cation or sodomy or had ever had sodomy committed on
me or if I had ever masturbated. He explained in detail
and very thoroughly just what he meant by these things.
That began my education. I have learned a little more
since.

This Mr. Moore was a Christian, very much so. I was
taught to pray when I got out of bed in the mornings, to
say grace at each meal and give thanks to the Lord after
it. We sang a hymn at each meal. A Bible lesson every
evening before bedtime, and then just before bedtime to
say another prayer. On Sundays we were sent to Sunday
school in the morning and church in the afternoon. Oh,
yes, we had plenty of church and religion all right. I
used to be pretty ignorant and not able to read very well
so I always had a hard job learning my Sunday school
lessons. For failure to learn these lessons I was given a
whipping.

. . . Naturally, I now love Jesus very much. Yes, I love

him so damn much that I would like to crucify him all over again.

At that time I was just learning to think for myself. Everything I seemed to do was wrong. I first began to think that I was being unjustly imposed upon. Then I began to hate those who abused me. Then I began to think that I would have my revenge just as soon and as often as I could injure someone else. Anyone at all would do. If I couldn't injure those who injured me, then I would injure someone else. . . .

I started doing time when I was eleven years old and have been doing practically nothing else since then. What time I haven't been in jail I have spent either getting out or getting in again.

What you have done and are doing to me, you are also doing to others. What I have done to you, many others also do to you. Thus, we do each other as we are done by.

I have done as I was taught to do. I am no different from any other. You taught me how to live my life, and I have lived as you taught me. If you continue teaching others as you taught me, then you as well as they must pay the price, and the price is very expensive. You lose your all, even life.

. . . I have no desire whatever to reform myself. My only desire is to reform people who try to reform me. And I believe that the only way to reform people is to kill 'em.

I may leave here at any time for some big house, mad house or death house, but I don't give a damn where they put me. They won't keep me long because no power on earth can keep me alive and in jail for very much longer. I would kind of like to finish writing this whole business in detail before I kick off so that I can explain my side of it even though no one ever hears or reads of it except one man. But one man or a million makes no difference to me. When I am through I am all through, and that settles it with me.

In my lifetime I have murdered 21 human beings, I have committed thousands of burglaries, robberies, larcenies, arsons and last but not least I have committed sodomy on more than 1,000 male human beings. For all these things I am not the least bit sorry. I have no conscience so that does not worry me. I don't believe in man, God nor Devil. I hate the whole damned human race including myself.

If you or anyone else will take the trouble and have the intelligence or patience to follow and examine every one of my crimes, you will find that I have consistently followed one idea through all of my life. I preyed upon the weak, the harmless and the unsuspecting.

This lesson I was taught by others: might makes right.

—Thomas E. Gaddis and James O. Long, *Killer*

MARIE
(. . . there was nothing else.)

1926: "Ugly! Ugly! Marie's ugly!"

"Mommy, the kids say I'm ugly. I'm not, am I?"

"No dear, you're just big for your age. You're only six after all."

1929: "Marie, I have to tell you something. Your Mother's dead, there's just you and I now. Bring me that glass like a good girl. Dead, your Mother's dead. No, you're too young for this stuff. Rotten stuff anyway, kill a man. Killed your Mother even though she never drank a drop . . ."

1937: "You're a big girl now. Going out with boys even. Your Aunt told you about that, didn't she? About boys and the things they want to do and stuff like that . . . Keep your legs crossed you hear! Hey, don't cry, honey, don't cry. I know you're a good girl, always was . . . hand me that bottle, huh."

1939: "What for you want to marry that guy? He's fifteen years older'n you? Ah what the hell, you haven't had much of a life with me . . . He's got money, I gotta admit judging from that car and those fancy suits. But why you? I mean face it, honey, you're no looker . . . Ah don't cry, kid. Sure he loves you. Know what? I'm gonna give you the best wedding a girl ever had—the kind your mother would have liked. Hell with the money, the railroad's got a credit union. I should be good for it after twenty-five years."

1940: "Jack, I'm nervous. I mean with boys I never did any of those things . . . But now it's our wedding night and I guess . . . Jack? Why don't you answer me? Jack, don't you want to kiss me or anything? I paid twenty dollars for this nightgown, don't you like it? Jack . . . you're sleeping!"

The police found Marie roaming the streets in the twenty-dollar white nightgown, half frozen, hysterical, and incoherent. The impotent older man she'd married to escape her alcoholic father had made no attempt to consummate their marriage, and for the sensitive homely girl this was the final rejection, the final proof that she could not succeed as a woman. The paradise promised by the slick women's magazines, and the instant beauty guaranteed by the manufacturers of every type of bottled cream, paint, and powder had failed her. For Marie there was nothing else, and by the time the police brought her to the state mental hospital early that morning, she had retreated as far as possible from reality.

Within a week her husband had been to see the hospital authorities. He secured their cooperation in getting an annulment and deposited two thousand dollars with them to be given to Marie when she recovered and left the institution. She was released after a year. In place of the nervous timid young girl was a relatively more stable woman with a veneer of indifference and a rapier sense of humor that had become her defense for the pain and frustration produced by her circumstances.

With the money supplied by Jack, whom she never saw again, Marie went to New York and took a one-room and kitchenette apartment in Greenwich Village. She didn't work regularly but began frequenting various bars where there was always someone to talk with to ease the loneliness of her empty life. Marie made another discovery during those days. In spite of her lack of good looks, she could always have male company as long as she was willing to end the evening in bed. In addition, many of the men were generous and helped to keep her in clothes, food, and rent. This was not prostitution in the strict sense of the word; as yet she didn't set a price beforehand or consider that she was being paid for services rendered. Finally, in another grasp at happiness and normalcy, she married one of her "friends."

The second husband was a complete contrast to the first. He was a "wheeler-dealer" in every sense of the phrase, fast talking, shallow, and capable of vicious outbursts of temper. Marie and Don traveled the New York–Miami–Chicago circuit, and as his wife she came to know intimately the world of vice and crime that she had only skirted free-lance.

Her drinking was becoming a serious problem and gradually built into a major source of tension with her husband. Like most men of his ilk, he was totally lacking in compassion, and a lush was the lowest thing he knew.

"I didn't mind the beatings," Marie told me one night. "He was always real sweet afterwards. But I couldn't stand it when he tore me down or bawled me out in front of other people." Once more she was being rejected and humiliated. All the sensibilities and self-respect on which she had never had more than a tenuous hold were finally squeezed out of her, and when Don left after six years of marriage, Marie turned to professional prostitution in earnest. . . .

For the next ten years the pattern remained pretty much the same—drinking, hustling, and short-term arrests first in New York then in Connecticut. For the last three of those years she was living with a much younger man whom she supported and whose mother finally reported them to the police. Now the authorities had her on a cohabitation charge, and in view of her record she was sentenced to the State Farm for Women for three years. There she again received psychiatric help and established a relationship with the Catholic chaplain that brought back echoes of early training she hadn't thought about for decades. After one unsuccessful parole attempt at the end of eighteen months, she returned to the farm to complete her sentence, and during this period she met a sister of the Dominican Sisters of Bethany who was visiting the prison.

Marie blossomed under the guidance of the priest and the nun who had become her closest friends, and the deep unfulfilled hunger in her for love and acceptance seemed to direct itself toward religion. Later she expressed some interest in entering the convent. It was with this in mind that she was brought to Lataste House [a halfway house] upon her release. . . .

. . . In the constant round of talk that was our life, and in a sense our therapy, at Lataste House, it was difficult if not impossible to get her to admit that the old life had failed to bring her happiness. In spite of the fact that she had a fairly good job in a hospital and as happy a home life as we were able to provide for her, we watched her slipping back into old attitudes and nurturing old desires, and we were powerless to stop the downward drift. She refused to see another psychiatrist and to face the one truth without which an alcoholic can't make it—the simple fact that she could never take another drink.

All our urgings resulted in merely a desultory attendance at A. A. meetings and a sporadic contact with a Matt Talbot group conducted by the Religious of the Cenacle. The help was there and even a degree of motivation but it wasn't strong enough. One night she just disappeared. She left behind all her clothes and personal belongings as these women usually did, and when I found her in a bar on Boston's lower Washington Street, I was forced after an hour's fruitless talking to admit that the jungle had reclaimed another victim.

—Beverly Byrne, *The Love Seekers*

CARYL CHESSMAN (The reason)

Yes, in a sense, I became a criminal and an outlaw by choice, but that doesn't detract from the fact there was a reason. When a youngster, whether with justification or not, I reached the point where I believed it was better to be anything than afraid. I gladly traded fear for guile and hate. My psychopathy became a shield, and the more those in authority tried to hound or pound it out of me, never attempting to learn why it was there in the first place, the thicker I built its walls.

And that is what, in my opinion, must be understood— such a rebellious, secondary personality would never be formed or forged if there wasn't a strongly felt need for it. Certainly it is never the result of spiritual spontaneous combustion. Moreover, however falsely, such a personality offers not alone protection but integration as well, and the opportunity to grow, to know purpose, to be "free," to have and retain individuality, to be a quantity that must be given social recognition and reckoned with.

It seemed to me, just as it usually seems to my kind, that society was simply trying to strip or rip off my shield, that it was willing to do so ruthlessly, that it didn't care about me personally, or the amount of humiliation or degradation it might inflict in the process. I stubbornly balked at being manipulated, regulated, or being compelled to conform blindly through fear or threat or punishment, however severe. Indeed, I came to question the validity of a society that appeared more concerned with imposing its will than in inspiring respect. There seemed to me something grossly wrong with this.

"We'll make you be good!" I was told, and I told myself nobody should, would or could *make* me anything. And I proved it.

—*Caryl Chessman's Own Story*

Biographical Notes

ARCHIE. Inmate of H.M. Prison Grendon, England's first and only psychiatric prison, built in 1962. Little is known of Archie other than that he was (according to author Tony Parker, who knew him well) "softly spoken, widely-read and highly intelligent, and serving a long sentence for an offense involving violence, but which was not murder."

PAT. Also a prisoner at Grendon, he is the illegitimate son of an Irish waitress. He emigrated to England at twenty, after serving terms at the reformatory and industrial schools. Arrested several times for shopbreaking and assault.

MOLLY McGUIRE. Age seventy-four, Education, none, Number of times in the House of Detention, forty-four by 1960. Molly McGuire is a pseudonym.

BERTHA GREEN. Age forty-six, Education, partial Elementary School. School dropout, Marital status, single, Number of times in the House of Detention, twenty-eight by 1960. Bertha Green is a pseudonym.

ALFRED HASSAN. Prisoner at Folsom, in California.

JIM ROBERTS. Inmate at Folsom Prison, California.

CARL PANZRAM (1891–1930). Imprisoned for most of his life, from the age of twelve, Panzram was hanged at the Fort Leavenworth Federal penitentiary.

BEVERLY BYRNE. Free-lance writer. Without any previous experience she became director of Lataste House, a halfway house for women prisoners, located in Massachusetts. Lataste House closed in 1965, after an existence of eighteen months.

CARYL CHESSMAN (1921–1960). During his twelve years on Death Row, his books gained him worldwide support in his fight for life. Despite an IQ of 172 that enabled him, while in prison, to master the study of law, his legal efforts to gain a retrial on charges of which he claimed to be innocent—charges that no longer carry the death penalty—proved finally unsuccessful. Guilty on seventeen counts for kidnapping, robbery, and sex offenses, he was executed at San Quentin.

4.

THE OTHER PRISONERS

Prison life is just hell, man—grey, lonely, cold, and a heartbreaker for everyone concerned—for the keeper as well as for the kept.

—John McCluney, inmate,
Auburn State Prison,
New York

The relationships between the keepers and the kept are often a dramatic replica of those in the outside world: the struggle against, acquiescence to, or use of, unreasonable authority. In our own lives, this struggle may relate to the government, society at large, family, friends, or work— but unlike the prisoners, we have some degree of freedom to protest, or to move on. There is even the possibility of a change in personal attitudes, as there is a possibility of a change in the powers that confront us. Unlike the prisoner, we do not move in an entirely closed world.

The people who represent these powers are familiar: the bureaucrat—often the recipient of political patronage, ill-equipped, simply "doing the job," as blind to his own identity as to those whose lives he controls; the altruist— his humanity trapped in the prison setting, his well-meaning and sometimes short-lived innovations not infrequently leading to demotion or dismissal; the authoritarian—satisfying an urge for dominance either by pushing the law to its extreme or by inflicting physical punishment as a gratification of sadistic desires.

According to The Official Report of the New York State Special Commission on Attica: "In the 1930s, New York State had a 90-day training course for prison guards. The program was progressive for its time, and older officers spoke highly of it. Between World War II and the late 1950s, however, there was no formal training for officers. More than one-third of the officers at Attica on September 9, 1971, began their jobs during that period. Those who started after that were given two week's training."

The Message is clear: We get what we pay for. Or, to reinterpret Lacassagne: Every prison reflects the society it serves.

BREAKING IN

The appearance of a new officer sheds hope into the dismal lives. New guards—unless drafted from the police bureau—are almost without exception lenient and forbearing, often exceedingly humane. The inmates vie with each other in showing complaisance to the "candidate." It is a point of honor in their unwritten ethics to "treat him white." They frown upon the fellow-convict who seeks to take advantage of the "green screw," by misusing his kindness or exploiting his ignorance of the prison rules. But the older officers secretly resent the infusion of new blood. They strive to discourage the applicant by exaggerating the dangers of the position, and depreciating its financial desirability for an ambitious young man; they impress upon him the Warden's unfairness to the guards, and the lack of opportunity for advancement. Often they dissuade the new man, and he disappears from the prison horizon. But if he persists in remaining, the old keepers expostulate with him, in pretended friendliness, upon his leniency, chide him for a "soft-hearted tenderfoot," and improve every opportunity to initiate him into the practices of brutality. The system is known in the prison as "breaking in": the new man is constantly drafted in the "clubbing squad," the older officers setting the example of cruelty. Refusal to participate signifies insubordination to his superiors and the shirking of routine duty, and results in immediate discharge. But such instances are extremely rare. Within the memory of the oldest officer, Mr. Stewart, it happened only once, and the man was sickly.

Slowly the poison is instilled into the new guard. Within a short time the prisoners notice the first signs of change: he grows less tolerant and chummy, more irritated and distant. Presently he feels himself the object of espionage by the favorite trusties of his fellow-officers. In some mysterious manner, the Warden is aware of his every step, berating him for speaking unduly long to this prisoner, or for giving another half a banana,—the remnant of his lunch. In a moment of commiseration and pity, the officer is moved by the tearful pleadings of misery to carry a message to the sick wife or child of a prisoner. The latter confides the secret to some friend, or carelessly brags of his intimacy with the guard, and soon the keeper faces the Warden "on charges," and is deprived of a month's pay. Repeated misplacement of confidence, occasional betrayal by a prisoner seeking the good graces of the Warden, and the new officer grows embittered against the species "convict." The instinct of self-preservation, harassed and menaced on every side, becomes more assertive, and the guard is soon drawn into the vortex of the "system."

—Alexander Berkman, *Prison Memoirs of an Anarchist,* *1912*

THE SYSTEM

Civil Service was an attempt to rid the prisons of corruption, eliminate the politicians, and raise the standards of the employees. In a large measure it accomplished those short-range goals. But what it also created was a constipation in the system that has allowed mediocrity to become the dominant force. Creativity in the individual employee is not encouraged; in fact, it is stifled. The system has become the all-important factor, and in order for the system to survive, it must be self-perpetuating. Each employee, upon joining the system must make a personal decision. He has three alternatives. He can either work against the system and try to bring about some change, with possibly his only reward being ulcers or a series of psychosomatic illnesses; or, he can give the system what it wants and climb the ladder to an administrative position, with the resulting realization after twenty years of indoctrination that change is impossible; or, more likely, he can stay in the system, be quiet, and collect a paycheck.

As a result of this, the prison has become a haven for employees who are content with the status quo. Moreover, they become seriously threatened when a member of the staff turns against them and becomes a maverick, trying to initiate change in the system. Consequently, what has evolved is a paralyzed structure with the opposing forces complementing each other: the staff doesn't want change and the inmates don't want change.

—Anthony J. Manocchio and Jimmy Dunn, *The Time Game*

FAMILY AFFAIR

Q: Suppose for a minute that you had the authority, a free hand, to make changes in the prison system, to do almost anything you wanted to do—what would you do, and what do you think it would accomplish? . . .

A: I would arbitrarily, capriciously, and without exception pension off every administrator and guard with more than twenty years' service, give them their pensions whether they are qualified or not, and get them to hell out of the system. I would lose a few good men that way, but more importantly I would have gotten rid of the old-timers, many of whom have been in the system for thirty or more years. These old-timers have, for the most part, penological mentalities that are inadequate in this day and age, mentalities that make it difficult if not impossible for them to accept radical change. Rehabilitation does not begin at the end of a blackjack, and neither brutality nor animal-like treatment has ever made a better man out of anyone. Efforts to improve the penal system, to reform it significantly, will be resisted as long as the system is administered by old-timers who see the reformers as enemies, threats to the little walled kingdoms in which the old-timers are more at home, feel more secure, than they do in their own homes.

Q: Do you really think the old-timers look upon reformers as enemies?

A: You'd better believe it. Remember, each time we point out a failure in the prison system, we are pointing out *their* failures, the failure of *their* system, of *their* old-time method of doing business. They feel that any effort to interfere with the way things have always been done, any suggestion that things could be done better some other way, is in effect saying that their past, their record, has been a failure. There are many like the captain of guards who once told the men on Death Row: "This is my prison, and no goddamn lawyer or judge is going to tell me how to run my prison." Hell, there are whole families working in these prisons, fathers and sons working as guards, other sons working in civilian capacities, daughters and sisters and wives working in the offices, all looking out for each other, all covering up for each other. The prison becomes a sort of family business.

Q: It is difficult to see these men having such a stake in what is, after all, only the place where they work.

A: It's a hell of a lot more than that. This place gets in their blood; it's their world, has been for twenty or thirty years, and this is where their friends are, where they feel comfortable. You would be surprised at how many of them come in on their days off, perhaps to take some of their friends on a tour of the place, perhaps simply to *be* here. We have men in here who willingly work the night shifts, who probably haven't slept with their wives except on their days off for twenty years, and they love it. This *is* their home.

Q: Who would replace those you pension off?

A: No problem. In every prison, including this one, there is a small but growing cadre of highly motivated, well-educated, bright young men who have come along in the last ten years or so and are on their way up. Some of the old-timers resent them and refer to them as those "smart-ass college kids," but in a competitive civil service system, they can't be stopped, and they are the hope for the future as far as prison reform is concerned.

Q: Can they accomplish what the old-timers have not?

A: They are a good bet. They will at least have what the old-timers will never have—the support and respect of the inmates. As far as the inmates are concerned, the best-liked, most respected supervisors are, invariably, the "smart-ass college kids." They care, they are dissatisfied with the record of the past, and they show genuine concern for the inmates. The inmates recognize and respect this.

—Edgar Smith, *A Pre-posthumous Conversation with Myself*

THE FUN BEGINS

I know of at least one associate warden in the system who has left express orders that he is always to be informed, even if he is away on vacation, whenever there is an escape. As soon as he hears of an escape, he runs home (he lives on the grounds) and changes into tall leather boots, large Western hat, leather jacket, and completes the regalia with a riding crop—along with his heavy holster and gun, of course. And then, for him, the fun begins. I would love to talk with him about some of the feelings he has while tracking a man down. Naturally I suspect the obvious, a degree of sexuality involved. But then I guess there is that element in all prison work anyway, though few of us will admit it.

—Anthony J. Manocchio and Jimmy Dunn, *The Time Game*

OVERTONES

"I started out as a line staff. I worked in one of the cottages. After I had been here six months a supervisor came up and asked me what was wrong—I had been here six months and I hadn't written out a disciplinary report. I told her I didn't see any reason to be writing disciplinaries when I was talking to the individuals and we were preventing the problems from happening. They just didn't understand at that time that the best method of control is to know and understand the individual.

"I made it through that six months and worked my way up through custody rank to program administrator . . . that's through five levels of supervision. It took me three years to make my first promotion—that has a lot of overtones!!

"I have to admit I'm still biased against people in uniforms myself—why do they need them? Are they a crutch?"

—Kathryn Watterson Burkhart, *Women in Prison*

IN THE BAG

Something happened today that had its comic overtones. I noted in here a few weeks ago my resentment when the guard at the entrance to this cellblock, after asking me the contents of the paper bag I had brought back from commissary, then required me to show him that I was telling the truth. I made it a point, while he looked in the bag, to remark on what such a job would do to him.

"You know perfectly well I won't lie to you," I said. "You know as well that I would not try to smuggle in dope or other contraband. But you have so conditioned yourself to distrust that you are unable to take my word even when you know you can. That kind of attitude will have its effect on you."

He handed the bag back to me with a smile, and we said good night.

The following week, by some whim of officialdom, we went from commissary directly to our cells instead of going first to the office.

Last week, however, we returned to the previous routine.

As a result, a few minutes after four o'clock, when the work day ended, I came trudging down the corridor toward D-block with another paper bag clutched in my hot little fist. Holland, the guard, had a grin on his face while I was still thirty feet away. I walked up to his desk.

"Good evening."

"Good evening," he said. "Commissary again today?"

"Uh-huh."

He motioned at the bag.

"What you got in there?"

"Oranges. Apples. A bag of potato chips. Couple bars of candy. Package of razor blades." I looked at him and smiled. "Want to look?"

He hesitated a moment; then he held out his hand.

"Let me see."

When he opened the mouth of the bag and peered in, I said, "You open your wife's mail at home?"

"Of course not!" He looked up, startled.

"You will," I promised him. "When you make suspicion the determining factor in your relationship with a whole group of other human beings, for a full working day, you won't be able to slough it off with other human beings when the working day ends. You'll start to suspect them of lying, too. It's in the nature of the job. You ought to get out."

The smile left his face.

"Better go upstairs," he said quietly. "Supper soon."

Today was the third time we went to commissary during the afternoon. At four o'clock I came through the gate on to the main floor corridor and looked toward D-block. Holland was there, and had seen me. The grin on his face was wide and, it seemed to me, sheepish.

We talked for a few minutes when I reached him, mostly about his school work and his wife. Then, after a pause, he motioned to my little brown paper bag.

"Been to commissary again, I see."

I nodded wordlessly. His lips twitched.

"What's in the bag?"

I looked at him squarely and solemnly.

"A gun," I said. "Two hacksaws. A stick of dynamite. And three oranges. Want to look?"

The grin spread over his face.

"Go upstairs," he said. "And don't show me that bag again!"

—Alfred Hassler, *Diary of a Self-Made Convict*

THE OTHER PRISONERS

Like the policeman, the prison guard is a much-maligned man. To prisoners, they are all "pigs"; to many others they represent everything brutal and insensitive in American society. No doubt that view is warranted, in many cases; but as a general indictment it is grossly unfair.

As a result of the uprising at Attica, and the bloody crushing of it, the prison guard is at the moment more in the public eye than ever before. In fact, school children in the once placid town of Attica—where the prison is the primary employer—have been complaining to reporters that it is untrue that their fathers and brothers are cruel and brutal to prisoners.

Actually, the worst faults of the Attica prison can hardly be laid to its guards; at worst, they are the instruments of an inhuman system, and at best—as many showed in the aftermath of the uprising—they may understand more of the prisoner's grim plight than do high state officials.

Statistics show that most guards have a low level of

general education, with 16 percent of them not having completed high school. They are paid commensurately, with 79 percent earning less than $8,000 a year. Thus, it is too much to expect that many of these men will have a sophisticated understanding of social issues, or that their handling of prisoners will reflect sensitive psychological approaches; society just doesn't seek out men of those qualities to guard its prisoners.

Moreover, the prison guard's job is highly dangerous and many of these men—particularly in a time like the present, when there is widespread unrest among prisoners —spend their working days and nights in something near terror. They know that prisoners almost anywhere, if led by determined men, can stage the kind of revolt that erupted at Attica; so guards are constantly subject to being held hostage, as well as to the hourly dangers of working among desperate and hostile men.

At the same time, of course, prisoners are substantially in the power of guards at most times, and since many guards are insensitive and brutal, the prisoners, too, live in fear. Men who fear other men usually come to hate them, so in these vast and gloomy fortresses, where everything is largely hidden from the public, fear and hatred mount in an ever-tightening circle. This hideous atmosphere can almost be touched and felt, as if it were tangible, in many prisons. . . .

. . . ample history from the earliest times shows that a master-slave relationship is more corrupting for the master than for the slave. To have absolute power over another human being can bring out the worst in a man—just as, in some cases, abject slaves have been known to rise to heights of character and nobility. When guards have nagging fear for their own safety, when they are irritated and frustrated by the conditions in which they work, when they find prisoners in their power, with no one to see—in such cases, even good family men and churchgoers can be corrupted into physical brutality. . . .

. . . if American society is going to tolerate a prison system designed primarily to cage animals, and if the men who operate it are going to be recruited from the lowest educational levels, paid the minimum and pitted physically against the inmates in Darwinian struggle for survival, then nobody should expect much in the way of "corrections" or "rehabilitation."

We get from our guards, that is, just about what we ask and just about what we pay for.

—Tom Wicker, *The New York Times,* September 28, 1971

". . . THE SCREW TOO IS ALL ALONE."

The screw has an extremely dangerous job: double doors, spy-holes, passkeys, and, if necessary, straitjackets are visible weapons; while the prisoner is sly. The screw has a public-welfare job, which, if it does not bring him big pay, at least gives him a certain importance, which is also gratifying. A kind of aura travels with him wherever he goes: "That's So-and-So—you know, the Prison Guard."

The heartless watchdog is a myth, a popular print: the severity, the harsh voice, the arrogant strut . . . That is all appearances; actually the screw is not a bad guy. Except that he has been taught that the basic equation of his profession is: being nice = getting into jams.

Oh, those jams! He is just getting ready to take a little

break, half-duty, half-rest, in the warmth of the office; and a "jam" comes up and stirs things up; he risks losing the good opinion of his superiors and the food on his children's table if he doesn't immediately restore order. His children . . . who, with breakfast still on their faces, kissed him in the morning, "Daddy"; the captive kid brought here in the last paddy wagon . . . no, there's no comparison, my kids are kids, not thugs.

Daddy has to work with bad men.

The screw wears stripes and gives orders: "So-and-So, straighten the place up fast, get a rag and a broom, an inspector is coming."

He wants to get promoted and therefore he obeys: a sardine lying between two layers of his brain like an unheard-of sandwich. He watches the big shots go by, he opens doors for them deferentially; out of the corner of his eye he inspects the copper pots and pans and scouts for cobwebs, while the inspector wanders through the entire prison, bored and eager to get it over with.

In short, the screw too is all alone.

That is why he associates with us. Even when we're resting, our fingers merely dreaming, he has to look at us. Yes, the toughest part is at night. We toss in our beds, our mummy-like bodies mutter and snore; and the solitary keeper waits for us to return to him.

In the guardroom his colleague has finally corked off, having nothing more to gossip about; the screw on duty looks over the day's accounts, does sums in the account book, everything in proper order right up to the end of the month; and then he puts his head in his hands . . .

"Now you can send that fat Polish woman, God, you can show pity or not, whichever you like . . ."

"Oh God, send me good prisoners."

Not one of those crummy little hoods that have to be

cleaned up and calmed down with the shower treatment, no, not that! A good one: not crafty, not a troublemaker, one that can be depended on . . .

. . . whose nice underwear it is a joy to search through in the suitcase marked "Clean Linen" that a girl friend brings him every week; one who canteens a lot and writes little; who will be respectful, willing and compassionate toward us. Who will take us into rich and horrible worlds, or who will simply talk to us.

But it is not just in the nice clothes but "in everything" that the screw has his hands; he yawns as he counts the strokes of the bells.

The blessed knell of retirement drowning in the toasts of a testimonial dinner: an apotheosis.

O God, do not blame him.

—Albertine Sarrazin, *The Runaway*

Biographical Notes

ALEXANDER BERKMAN (1870–1936). Born in Russia, Berkman emigrated to the United States in 1888. An anarchist, he hoped to commit what he thought would be the first terrorist act in American history. The occasion was the Homestead Steel Company strike; the victim, industrialist Henry Frick. Frick was only wounded and Berkman was sentenced to twenty-two years in Western Penitentiary in Pennsylvania. He served fourteen years. With his great friend and fellow-anarchist Emma Goldman he was deported to Russia in 1919, as a result of antiwar activities. Sick and despondent, Berkman committed suicide in Nice.

ANTHONY J. MANOCCHIO. Studied criminology at the University of California, and is a former counselor of the California Prison System. Because of dissatisfaction with the California State Prison System, Manocchio left to participate in experimental community correctional programs. He is still searching for more efficient ways to treat offenders.

JIMMY DUNN. A pseudonym. The prisoner described spent fourteen years, between the ages of thirteen and thirty-two, in confinement. Dunn, a pimp, heroin addict, and dope peddler, and Manocchio were residents of the same prison.

EDGAR SMITH (b. 1934). Convicted in 1957 for the killing of a fifteen-year-old girl, Smith spent fourteen years on Death Row in the New Jersey State Prison. Although Smith maintained his innocence during that time, he later admitted his guilt before a judge in an open court, and was finally freed in 1971. He is married and lives in Southern California.

KATHLEEN ANDERSON. The subject of "Overtones," she was formerly a teacher of the deaf. She is now ombudsman (in charge of self-help groups and of volunteers) at California Institution for Women.

KATHRYN WATTERSON BURKHART. A free-lance writer who lives in Philadelphia. As a newspaper reporter for the *Philadelphia Bulletin,* she won national recognition for her coverage of the criminal justice system. Miss Burkhart lectures frequently on urban problems and has hosted an NET special on women in prison.

ALFRED HASSLER (b. 1910). Editor, newspaperman, and pacifist, Hassler was imprisoned as a conscientious objector during World War II. He did time during 1944–1945, in the federal penitentiary at Lewisburg, Pennsylvania. He was a former executive secretary of the Fellowship of Reconciliation.

ALBERTINE SARRAZIN (1937–1967). Born in Algiers, she was interned by her adopted parents in a reformatory for girls. Later escaping to Paris she became a prostitute, lesbian, thief, and drunk. *The Runaway* and *Astragal* were written during confinement, and inspired Henri Charrière to write his *Papillon*. Mme. Sarrazin, later married, died after an operation just a week before her thirtieth birthday.

5.

CASTE AND CLASS

There is a White line . . . and a Black line . . .

—Charles McGregor

For most of white America, caste is a concept associated with India. But speak to the blacks, Puerto Ricans, Chicanos, and Indians, and you find that, despite small gains in race relations, America, too, has its own class system. Formerly, class was a matter of birth, but these social barriers are gradually being overcome by acquiring education (status) and by accumulating wealth (power). The old aristocracy has given way to the new moneyed class that gives us—and them—whatever privileges we have.

Black against white, white against brown, rich against poor; inside and out, equality is only a dream—even as education-equals-job-opportunity is still a dream for most of the minorities of this country; only wealth secures the rights theoretically due to all. And always in the background, officialdom encourages class differences to maintain and to strengthen its control.

Besides the standard racial prejudices, prison inmates establish "class" roles of their own: rapist against wino, child molester against thief, superpatriot against the CO.

Inside or out, we are all victims of a need for caste and class.

WORLD IN MICROCOSM

The societal tensions and conflicts which affect the nation as a whole likewise affect prison communities. Thus racial strife is duplicated and perhaps even exaggerated in prison. The white prisoner, unlike white Americans on the other side of the prison gate, cannot dissociate himself from the problem by the simple expedient of fleeing to the suburbs; he is trapped and has no place to flee. Close living conditions, such as exist in all prisons, tend to foster petty animosities under the best circumstances. And when there is added to these personal frictions the catalytic agent of racial discord, a highly combustible situation results.

In virtually every prison the proportion of nonwhite to white prisoners is twice that of the general population of the United States. As a rough and unofficial estimate, nonwhite prisoners account for between twenty and twenty-five per cent of the Federal prison population. The usual explanation given is that these figures merely reflect the fact that nonwhite Americans commit more crimes than do white Americans. The explanation misses the point, to wit, that typical white middle- and upper-class crimes are rarely punished (i.e., tax evasion and underhand business dealings), and crimes committed by white middle-class youth are frequently overlooked and never come to trial; furthermore, even when they do, prison sentences are less frequently imposed. Thus, crime statistics which purport to show a racial etiology are more a reflection of a white, racist, bourgeois-oriented law-enforcement and judicial system than they are of actual incidences of criminal activity. Many of the crimes which result in Federal convictions of nonwhites are really nothing more than the business activities of men for whom other avenues of "legitimate" business are closed. (Of course, we do not condone the drug trade in the nonwhite—or for that matter, in the white—community. As these communities become politicized, the curtailment of the activities of pushers will certainly be accorded high priority in any radical program. Nevertheless, we must realize that pushers are merely employing the techniques of capitalism in order to earn enough money to feed their own habits and stomachs.) We find in prison men who have had no choice but to hustle for a living in order to support themselves and their families. Many black prisoners (as well as a very substantial number of white prisoners) are, in effect, doing time for society's crimes.

—Howard Levy and David Miller, *Going to Jail*

THE LINE

The most difficult thing to discuss is racism in prison, because when you have been exposed to it as a member of the minority group, it is so arduous not to be influenced by your own anger, resentment and frustration. When I first entered prison, there were three times as many Whites as Blacks, but as the years passed this situation dramatically reversed itself. White jobs in prison are still selective for whites with token assignments of special jobs for Blacks. In some cases, if the administration assigns a White prisoner to a job and he refuses it, they give it to a Black prisoner to anger the Whites and show the White prisoners what can happen if they don't accept the special jobs. I heard remarks made by the administration, "That if you want the niggers to take over the joint just keep turning down these jobs." There is a White line to the mess hall and a Black line—a White line to the movies and a Black line . . .

—Charles McGregor, *Fortune News,* March 1970

HATE WITHOUT CAUSE

Racism in prison is just like a reconstruction of the whole struggle for equality—the separation of human beings because of color. The whole idea of white supremacy as opposed to black supremacy . . . the lack of interest on the part of the administration—but more, the awareness of racism by the administration and the way they use it to control the population of already anti-social people. This means that they only contribute to the inmate's negativeness. It affected me because it taught me to hate people for a color and to divide my feelings for people in general. To top it all, the hate was without cause—and sanctioned by the administration.

—Melvin Rivers, *Fortune News*, March 1970

RACISM IN REVERSE

At Cook County Jail in Chicago, where 85 per cent of the staff is black, women say the policies and jobs and discipline favor blacks—who are 80 per cent of the prison population.

"A girl from a southern state came in here and three of the women were gonna beat her up," said Maria Fisher, an inmate in Cook County. "She was from Alabama or Mississippi or one of those states. It was three against one and I told them, 'If you wanna fight one by one, that's okay. But three against one ain't fair.' I had just been sick and didn't feel too good, but I told them they were forcing me into it. 'She's a whitey, you gonna fight for a whitey?' I said, 'I don't care if she's a greenie, three to one ain't fair.' The officer was there but she wasn't doing anything. She was just sitting at her desk pretending nothing was happening 'cause she wanted to see the white girl get licked, too. Anyway, it was really wild in here; I got hit in the chest with a wastebasket and hurt pretty bad.

"But I'm not gonna beat her just because she came from a southern state. She can't help where she comes from any more than anybody else can. The officer locked her up after the fight and spit on her and threw water in her cell. I used to think it was whites against blacks in America, but in this jail it's blacks suppressing whites and blacks."

—Kathryn Watterson Burkhart, *Women in Prison*

A CONCENTRATE OF RACISM

. . . racism is scattered, diffused throughout the whole of America, grim, underhanded, hypocritical, arrogant. There is one place where we might hope it would cease, but on the contrary, it is in this place that it reaches its cruelest pitch, intensifying every second, preying on body and soul; it is in this place that racism becomes a kind of concentrate of racism: in the American prisons, in Soledad Prison, and in its center, the Soledad cells.

If, by some oversight, racism were to disappear from

the surface of the United States, we could then seek it out, intact and more dense, in one of these cells. It is here, secret and public, explicable and mysterious, stupid and more complicated than a tiger's eye, absence of life and source of pain, nonexistent mass and radioactive charge, exposed to all and yet concealed. One might say that racism is here in its pure state, gathering its forces, pulsing with power, ready to spring.

—Jean Genet, from Introduction to *Soledad Brother*

MAGNATES AND COUNTRY CLUBS

Westbrook Pegler once called Danbury a "country club." He was writing about Joseph P. Schenck, the movie magnate, who was jailed on an income tax rap in 1942. Danbury was in fact a country club for Schenck and it still is for other members of the privileged classes.

When I arrived, Schenck had been gone for a couple of months but the inmates were still talking about his special treatment. The man was not unpopular for he bought generously from the commissary for other inmates. He worked more or less when he felt like work and often made extended visits to the warden's home outside the prison, a rare favor. His wife contributed to the civilities by inviting the warden's wife to the Schenck's estate on Long Island. Of course Schenck was released on the day he became eligible for parole.

The reports on Schenck were secondhand but I was able to observe the favoritism shown to other bigshots, notably corporation officials convicted of defrauding the government on war contracts. First, these men got short sentences, out of all proportion to the penalties imposed on other prisoners for less serious offenses. Second, they always made parole, and they were the only inmates paroled on the first day of eligibility. The ordinary prisoner considers himself lucky to be paroled two weeks to four months after becoming eligible. Third, the company officials got preferential treatment within the prison. They were assigned to the few desirable white collar jobs, usually in the education department but sometimes as clerks in the parole office or hospital. The more I observed this uniform pattern of favoritism, the stronger became my resolution to write an article exposing it as soon as I got out. By naming names, I felt I could make a convincing case.

Screws and even the higher officials treated these prominent felons with respect. Some of the screws sucked around them for jobs. An official of the Sullivan Dry Dock & Repair Company used to advise the screws to see him when he got back to the plant, but he assured his fellow inmates that if any Danbury applicants turned up he would have an attack of amnesia.

Minor violations were overlooked when committed by the industrial aristocrats. These men were never ordered to sit silently on the bench and none was ever put in solitary.

—Jim Peck, *We Who Would Not Kill*

DAVID

During the ten years that I have been in prison, I have seen only one youngster protected by the administration when he first entered the prison. This sixteen-year-old, whom we will call David, was kept in the Admission and Orientation section of the prison for almost a year and then went to work in the Seclusion Unit for a few more months. In both places he was separated from the general population. Then he was placed in the Education Department but still kept under official surveillance. From there he was assigned to the Warden's residence. Finally, after almost two years, he came back inside to finish his schooling and was placed in the general population. By this time David was able to take care of himself and the "wolves" had gotten the administration's message of "hands off!"

David was not a homosexual who needed protection from his own emotions. He was a young, good-looking boy who needed protection from other cons' uninhibited emotions. He got this protection—but why him and not others who came in as young?

David came from a middle-class family. His parents were intelligent people who were concerned about what might happen when he entered prison. Concerned enough to come here and talk to the warden before David even arrived. One visit from two concerned middle-class parents was enough to insure this boy's protection. Unfortunately, most young cons' parents are neither intelligent nor middle class.

—Mike Misenheimer, *An Eye for an Eye*

CASTE BEHIND BARS

County Jail
November 20, 1951

Dear Nelson:
Thank you very much for the welcome deuce, the stamps and the postcards. Loot is pretty hard to come by here for those who don't have visitors, and they resort to a variety of means to raise it, one of the most popular the lifting of it from one another . . .

Another institution that has filtered through the bars is the caste system. ("All animals are equal, but some are more equal than others.")

At the top are those who are alumni of the state pen. The other inmates regard these eminences much as a Lawrenceville boy might look at a Princeton man.

The gradations continue all down the line to the "winos," chronic drunkards who are regarded frostily as 30-day interlopers and not true criminals at all. Maybe the winos are disconsolate with nobody to look down upon, or maybe they just settle contented and cozy at the bottom.

I cannot tell—the light is rather dim down there.

The Indoor Ward McAllister, B.

—James Blake, *The Joint*

Biographical Notes

HOWARD LEVY (b. 1937). Born in Brooklyn, New York, Levy, a dermatologist, entered the army in 1965 as a commissioned officer. In 1967 he was court-martialed after having refused to instruct Special Forces troops at Fort Jackson, South Carolina. Released on bond in 1969, Levy served twenty-six months of his three-year sentence. He is now back in New York City where he works for a medical research group and continues his anti-war activities.

DAVID MILLER (b. 1942). Born in Syracuse, New York, Miller after being graduated from college became a member of the staff of the Catholic Worker. In 1965, he publicly burned his draft card and was the first person to be sentenced after the law prohibiting this act was passed. He served twenty-two months in Federal prisons, most of them prisons in which Levy at various times had also been confined—Allenwood Prison Farm Camp, Lewisburg Federal Penitentiary and Farm Camp, and the United States Disciplinary Barracks at Fort Leavenworth.

MELVIN RIVERS. A former president of Fortune Society, an organization of ex-convicts and other interested persons, dedicated to helping released prisoners and advocating change in the criminal justice system, Rivers served four years in various New York state prisons.

MARIA FISHER. Born in Jamaica, West Indies, is a revolutionary, and was closely associated with the Black Panthers. She was arrested on a homicide charge, and was still in prison in 1973.

KATHRYN WATTERSON BURKHART. See biographical notes, chapter 4.

CHARLES MCGREGOR. Spent twenty-five years in the New York prison system and is now released.

JEAN GENET (b. 1910). Famous novelist and dramatist was born in Paris. At ten, he was sent to a reformatory for stealing, and therafter he spent the next thirty years in prisons throughout Europe. Condemned to life imprisonment after his tenth arrest for theft in France, he was finally pardoned by President Vincent Auriol, thanks to the efforts of many of France's greatest literary figures —Sartre, Beauvoir, et al.

JIM PECK (b. 1914). For refusing to bear arms during World War II, Peck was sentenced on November 26, 1942, to the Federal prison at Danbury, Connecticut. He was released on April 2, 1945. He is still engaged in antiwar activities as a staff member of the War Resisters League.

MIKE MISENHEIMER. Born in North Carolina, he joined the paratroopers during World War II, when he was seventeen. Two years later he was arrested for robbery after which he did time in the North Carolina penitentiary. For "inflicting an injury during the commission of a robbery" he is now serving a life sentence in the Indiana State Prison.

JAMES BLAKE. Pianist and writer, Blake attended two universities, but because of a craving for pot and because he was, as he himself describes it, the "world's most inept burglar," he has spent almost half of his adult life in prison. His book, *The Joint,* is composed of letters, some of which were discovered in Nelson Algren's home, others, in a shoebox of Blake's personal effects stored in a Bowery mission.

6.

SLAVE LABOR

**To pay a man fifty cents
a day for his work in a
prison shop is to tell him
. . . just what you think
he is worth. You had
better hope he does not
come to believe you.**

—Joseph Whitehill,
Friends Journal

*Each generation contends with its own nightmares. Politi-
cal and social activists, born in the 1950s, study the
lessons of My Lai, Laos, and Cambodia, too preoccupied
with the present to concern themselves with the past.
Mention of the slave-labor and concentration camps that
spread throughout German-occupied Europe during World
War II evokes only the vaguest response; Buchenwald,
Auschwitz, and Dachau are already forgotten, like the
men, women, and children who died there.*

*At the height of the war, in the early 1940s, there were
thirteen major German concentration camps controlling
at least nine hundred labor camps from which vast armies
of political dissidents, Jews, and prisoners of war were
recruited to work—and die—on road construction gangs,
on the building of fortifications, and in the factories of
Farben and Krupp. Despite the scope of the operation
and the terrible destruction of lives (equaled only by the
Stalinist labor camps of the 1930s), the goal of the Nazi
program can be compared to that of our prison industries
today: reduction of people to chattel, for private and state
gain.*

*Within the United States, the system of chain gangs is
appallingly similar. During the period of their greatest
use as forced labor, the mortality rate was as high as 25
percent. In the early history of this country, forced labor
was largely used in the construction work of our various
state capital buildings. Even today these same conditions
exist in the South, as so clearly described by Tom Murton.*

*The prisoners of the Germans were rewarded by death;
ours, by ten cents an hour "incentive pay."*

AUSCHWITZ

. . . the sale of labour was a part of the plan to commercialize the prisoners until such time as they became too weak to be worth preserving. Throughout German-occupied Poland, to take the special case of this molested country, the labour of the Polish Jews was sold to commercial bidders and the ghettoes were turned into labour camps controlled by the S.S. The ordinary labour camps for non-Jews deliberately exploited the physical strength of the prisoners who were contracted out to the firms, while some camps specialized in providing labour for road-construction or the building of fortifications.

Gangs were often sent from the camps to work on long-term secret projects in distant places; prisoners were sent from Buchenwald to work in the Channel Islands, for example. Factories were built by means of forced labour, and gradually the S.S. penetrated into normal industry with the sale of labour at a vast profit. Firms could apply for the use of prisoners to the S.S. Main Economic and Administration Office. Daily rates ranged from four to eight marks according to the relative skill, or lack of it, in the labour force required. . . .

[Rudolph] Hoess [commandant of Auschwitz] testified at Nuremberg that the thirteen major concentration camps spread across German-occupied Europe controlled no less than 900 labour camps, housing from 100 up to 10,000 prisoners according to need.

—Roger Manvell and Heinrich Fraenkel, *The Incomparable Crime*

ARKANSAS

There was another basic reason for much of the hostility toward our attempts to reform the Arkansas prison system. The success of reform meant the death knell of profitable exploitation.

The state prison farms had long been self-supporting. Traditionally, they were run for the profit of the state and of a few selected individuals. In 1966 the penitentiary system made a profit—for the state—of $300,000. The profit in 1967 was $220,000. The profits that went to individuals have not been tabulated.

The state, fond of its profits from what amounted to slave labor, was not willing to relinquish more than a little of those prison profits for operating funds for the maintenance of the prisoners. The prison, therefore, functioned with a minimum of money. There was little mechanization. The bulk of farm work was done with mules and convicts who labored in the fields ten to fourteen hours a day, six or seven days a week. Within the prison, the needs to maintain discipline and meet work quotas were the immediate causes of the brutality which sometimes resulted in murder. Nothing was to get in the way of production for profit—men were beaten for minor infractions. . . .

Most prisons in the United States have vocational training projects. Arkansas didn't. The work programs used in the institution were designed for two ends: profit, for the state and individual freemen; and for the inmates, degradation. There was absolutely nothing an inmate could learn in the Arkansas prisons that he could ever put to use in the freeworld, unless he planned to be a sadist or a criminal. . . .

This whole system of exploitation began in the days after the Civil War, when the farmers and plantation owners who were forced to free their slaves looked for a new source of cheap labor and found it in the prisons. The same thing happened intermittently in other states, but it became a way of life in Arkansas.

State records show that on May 5, 1875, "the entire penitentiary, its buildings, equipment and the labor of all convicts confined then or after," were leased to a Mr. Jno. Peck for ten years. State supervision of such an arrangement was minimal, and anyone who submitted critical reports would be dismissed by the Penitentiary Commission. During this period, up to 10 per cent of the prison population might die during one year.

As early as 1890, the prison board did attempt to abolish corporal punishment, but pressure from the lessees of the penitentiary was too strong. The board was, however, able to establish rules limiting the use of the strap and requiring that only wardens that the board had specifically authorized could administer punishment.

In 1892 the penitentiary lease earned the state a profit of $32,128.42. The next year, the highest bid for a ten-year lease was $31,500 a year. As a result, the state decided to eliminate the middle man and lease individual prisoners and groups of prisoners. In the one-year period from 1898 to 1889, over two hundred inmates died in mines, quarries, and turpentine camps.

A public scandal ensued, and the prison board had to restrict the type of labor for which a prisoner could be leased. The leasing of prisoners was formally abolished in 1912, when the governor, George W. Donaghey, pardoned more than four hundred prisoners and broke the back of the system.

—Tom Murton, *Accomplices to the Crime*

SLAVE LABOR: A KALEIDOSCOPIC VIEW 1911–1913

In 1911 the State of Texas enacted a law which provided for the payment of ten cents per day to prisoners or their families. The law was in operation from June, 1911, to June, 1913, during which time $136,905.64 was paid to prisoners or their families. It was found that the prisons were not self-sustaining and in 1914 the Attorney-General declared the law unconstitutional. Since then nothing has been paid.

—*Star-Bulletin*, Sing Sing, January 1920

1961–1965

Incentive Pay

The Administration of this Department recently instituted an Incentive Pay Program for inmates in certain job assignments. It is the hope of the Commissioner and the Warden that all inmates will eventually be included in this pay scale.

Unskilled Category
$.03 per hour—5 hour day,—5 day week

Semi-Skilled Category
$.06 per hour,—5 hour day,—5 day week

Skilled Category
$.10 per hour,—5 hour day,—5 day week
The purpose of the above Pay Schedule is to give a
man an incentive to develop better work habits.

—From *Progress Through Crisis,* 1954–1965, The City of
New York Department of Correction

1970

Today, Federal Prison Industries, Inc., is far and away the
most profitable line of business in the country. Profits on
sales in 1970 were 17 percent (next highest is the mining
industry with 11 percent)—the average for all U.S. industries is 4.5 percent. The board of directors' annual
report summarizes the success story: over a thirty-five-
year period, 1935 to 1970, the industries grossed $896
million, increasing their net worth by $50 million and con-
tributing $82 million in dividends to the U.S. Treasury—
thus, like it or not, we are all shareholders in the proceeds
of captive labor. Because the Army is a major customer
(the industries supply it with everything from military
dress shoes to electronic cable), the war years have been
especially good to prison industries. A chart in the report
depicts successive peak periods under the headings "WW
II," "Korea," "Vietnam," the latter responsible for a spec-
tacular rise in sales from $38 million to $60 million over
a seven-year-period.

The secret of this immense profitability is not hard to
discover; in fact it is laid out for us in the board of
directors' report. Pay rates for inmate workers in the federal industries range from 19¢ to 47¢ an hour . . .

In 1970, 5,478 inmates earned $3 million for an average wage of $547 a year. In the same year, the report informs us, annual production for each inmate worker was $12,168, and the average profit per worker stood at $2,350.

—Jessica Mitford, *Kind and Usual Punishment*

1973

Gary Krist, with a long sentence in Reidsville Prison in Georgia, observes:

"No prisoner in the Georgia Department of Corrections is paid for his work. The idea of working to maintain your own tomb is dehumanizing and counterproductive."

Krist, interestingly, notes that prisoners provide the state with a cheap labor force and "if no inmate would work for less than a minimum standard wage, there would be fewer prisons. If the state had to meet the cost of food, clothing, and maintenance of quarters (with no labor force to produce), the costs would be so astronomical that the public would weigh their priorities and decide that they wanted lower taxes more than costly revenge."

—*Fortune News*, January 1973

Biographical Notes

TOM MURTON. A professional penologist and former assistant professor of criminology, Murton became head of the Tucker Prison Farm in Arkansas in 1967. Later, appointed head of the state's department of correction, by Governor Winthrop Rockefeller, Murton attempted to humanize primitive prison conditions throughout the state. His attempts at reform were resisted by corrupt political forces and Murton was dismissed from his post after having served for little more than a year.

FORTUNE NEWS. A publication of the Fortune Society, a self-help organization in New York City comprised of ex-prisoners who are helping other prisoners upon their release, and working for changes in the criminal justice system.

7.

FAMILIES AND FRIENDS

> The husband is inside the
> iron bars.
> The wife is outside the
> iron bars, looking in.
> . . . .
> Who could stand here
> and watch their meet-
> ing, unmoved?
>
> —Ho Chi Minh

The prison experience is the severest test of faith for prisoners and their families and friends.

For the one inside, there will always be doubts and self-recriminations; for those outside, anger, pity, and the shock of disbelief. And for both, there is the knowledge that life, having been irrevocably altered, can never be the same.

Too often, when the prisoners question loyalties, families counter by accusations and distrust. In this way insecurities of both are strengthened, and, for both, "doing time" is that much worse.

For the prisoners and their families, visits, letters, and photographs are the bridge between the inside world and out: the prisoners and their families remember, as each wonders whether the other will forget.

The prison experience calls for understanding on both sides; only then will both survive.

THIS ALL TEARS AT MY HEART . . .

It's not easy to be married to a man in prison. We survive the financial hardships, the lonely isolation, frustrations, guilt feelings, etc.—but we are prisoners in our own little world. We, who have never committed a crime—are kept prisoners when we sentence ourselves to wait for our loved ones.

But why does the state of New York add to the burden we carry by insisting on the most dehumanizing conditions for a visit to an institution. I'll go even farther—the counties and the cities, as well as the State, stand accused. It is such that I share equally the punishment the court meted out to my husband. Each time I try to visit him, archaic rules and regulations, screens, glass windows, unreasonable visiting hours, telephones that seldom work (the only means of communication in county jails), being kept waiting, being searched, rude correction officers—this all tears at my heart.

The same bad conditions do not exist at all institutions. Some have one, some have another and a third may have both. In New York State, Sing Sing visiting conditions are much more human than others which only makes me wonder why others cannot implement that which is used at Sing Sing. At Sing Sing, no screen is used to separate a man and his wife. I was able to bring my children there to visit their father so they could be assured that he was not dead.

My husband is kept in a cage during most of his imprisonment. But when I go to visit him, why must I visit a zoo? Do my children have to equate their father with the monkey they saw at the Central Park Zoo?

Please don't answer my questions with "security." I'll answer that one into the ground. Don't answer me "no coddling the criminal." I am not asking for coddling. I ask for me to be treated as a human and for my children to be given that. We have not been convicted of committing a crime.

Do not alleviate overcrowding in city jails by sending my husband to an institution 300 miles away. How can I afford to go visit him? And I *need* to visit him. That's all I have left in my life.

How can you talk rehabilitation? What is more important to rehabilitation than family stability. I will try to do your job of rehabilitation through "love"—if you'll allow it. I'm not asking for conjugal visits and I'm not asking for weekend passes. I'll start by asking you to tear down the screens, have more realistic visiting hours for the wife who must work to hold her family together. Don't force me to go on State welfare so I might have a day per week to visit my husband. One Saturday or Sunday visit per month will not suffice.

My husband must be reassured that his family is surviving, that his wife is being faithful, that his children remember him. Without that, you can take your schooling, your job training and your other token programs and junk them. You will not begin to rehabilitate the man unless you understand the key words in rehabilitation are human contact and love. I can give him that.

You worry about security. My husband will be less apt to cause you any trouble if he knows that his children are going to be up to visit him. If you are worried about him receiving contraband, I think you'll find your correction officers are more likely to be the carriers than the wife who does not want to endanger her visiting privileges.

We should have a common goal—to rehabilitate my husband. Try for some continuity. I'll help you if you'll let me.

—Barbara Allen, *Fortune News*, April, 1970

SEARCH AND DESTROY

What most visitors didn't know—at least they never knew it unless the prisoner told them—was that immediately after such a visit, many of us were subjected to a strip search. And I saw so often its impact upon the younger prisoners, when they would come out of a high with someone they loved and then were stripped to the bone in the next room; and this not a half-hour after the visit, but *immediately* afterward. That is, they were immediately being reminded that they were nothing more than a piece of meat available for inspection.

And that was the price of having a visit at all—that was the way you came out. To walk out of the visitors room with a smile on your face and an inner glow because you had just shared at least some measure of love, and then to go into that utter denial of your humanity and of what had just taken place between two or three persons was a species of degradation that was, I would say, memorable. A memorable incursion of the state against the human being. Search, that is, and destroy. I would say that there were two things that were most difficult for most prisoners. One was coming out of the visiting room to the strip search. And the other was the threat that always overlay your mail and your letters.

—Daniel Berrigan, *Absurd Convictions, Modest Hopes, Conversations after Prison with Lee Lockwood*

FEAST DAY

The feast day of Our Lady of Carmel finally came. For days and days the women had scraped their savings together and carefully prepared the meal for their visiting children, a meal worthy of princes. Some of the children would come from the schools where they had been placed, others would come directly from their homes.

The prison changed its aspect with all that preparation, and still more when the day came and with it swarms of children. And if the visitors weren't the children of the inmates, then they were the grandchildren or the nephews and nieces. Up to the age of fourteen they were admitted. Young voices echoed within the walls, and those basketball posts perhaps served some purpose.

I did not expect my sons, considering it wiser not to see them that day. Perhaps it was for this reason that I had time to observe the happenings.

Long before the hour the women gathered in clusters at the door of the front office. They were combed and brushed, powdered and rouged, dressed up for the occasion —and could have served as models for Goya's *Caprichos*. The youngsters arrived singly or in groups, their eyes wide with terror. They were frisked just before entering the yard, and they were not used to this. Nor did they like the look of that gray crowd of mothers, who were offering their best smiles. Unfamiliar arms clasped them. Kisses rained down on them from all sides—the only caress allowed the inmates in the whole year.

The mothers of some of the children had to be identified for them. Many could not recognize their mothers; such a long time had passed since they had last seen them.

The women, my comrades, moved about restlessly. Until their young visitors arrived, they were afraid that an accident or a punishment would deprive them of the expected encounter. After the children arrived, the women exhibited them with pride, introducing them to everyone. The children also were wearing their best clothes. Their families or teachers had dressed them up for the occasion.

A few of the women lingered until suppertime, hoping

in vain to see their offspring arrive. Distrustfully they stood near the front office, silent and motionless. Finally, when the bell rang, they dispersed. Now there was no need to wait: the children would not come. Swallowing their tears, they went off by themselves.

Then there were the inmates who had expected no one. They lingered at a distance, contemplating the scene. Some of them approached a woman whose son was a visitor, asking if she wouldn't lend them the child for a moment and let them hug him.

A little girl was surveying us with evident distaste. Her mother caught her and held her close. The child broke into loud weeping.

"But, my child, I'm your mother, your very own mother!"

The little girl stuck out her tongue. "No, you're not my mother! And I'm scared, and I want to go. My mother is pretty, but you're ugly."

The woman forced a smile, pressing the little body close. We finally managed to convince the child.

—Isabel Alvarez de Toledo y Maura, Duchess of Medina Sidonia, *My Prison*

THE IMAGE

Under the glass top on my desk is a photograph of a smiling, lean-faced boy—proud and young and aware and about to become a teen-ager. His tanned image stares out at me in reminder of the hurt and bewilderment I burdened him with as heritage.

His mother tells me he does well in school, "an honor

student," the letter said. "He likes to write things, and draw, and has a most amazing memory," she adds.

As I read her words, I am moved to wonder if he can remember those times he expressed an interest in "doing the things Dad does." He was only seven then, a sensitive and self-aware seven, bursting at the seams with curiosity about the Nature of things. (Dad, how do trees grow?)

I wonder, too, if he can recall how eagerly I rushed out to buy all the paraphernalia for a small fisherman— miniature rod and reel, dip net, waders, flies—exactly the way I recalled my father had made certain I learned the "man things" every paternal generation is charged with passing along.

Did I completely hide the bitter disappointment I felt when he cried at seeing a fish hooked and dangling from his line as I coaxed him to put it in his creel. How could I know that his interest—and satisfaction—lay in watching a speckled trout flash across a creekbed, not in hooking it on a line? Months later he would carry a woefully cat-mangled sparrow and ask, "Can you make it well, Dad?" and cry himself to sleep when I couldn't. About this time his fishing gear was relegated to a cluttered corner of the garage, never to be used again.

I never got to really know my son, nor he me. Our time together was too short. But our blood bond still remains. In his memory, like mine, are the weals of disappointment at the ties which should have been, but now, tragically, are lost. And we shall both be poorer for the loss. I because he shall become a man without my counsel; he because I cheated him of his rightful kinship.

When I came to prison I walked from his life and, as his mother once wrote, he walked into manhood years ahead of his time. (Don't worry, Mother, now that Dad is gone I will care for you.) Once he was confused, bewildered by the turn of events which deprived him of his father. (Mother, why did the policeman take Dad away?) Now he sees with clarity, although the maturity for understanding the vagaries of man is not yet his.

Sometimes, too, I plumb my thoughts for some long-forgotten sign which I might have missed, a sign which now I might seize upon desperately and twist to interpret as added assurance to his mother's "Don't worry, he will grow up to be a fine man."

But this, also, is denied me. Our man-boy relationship is unable to reach across the time of prison years. What were once very real qualities of my son have, with the passage of the years, faded beyond recall.

So he smiles out at the world from my desk—in prison—and I look at his image, and hope for him, and speculate upon his potential—and pray.

—Art Powers, *An Eye for an Eye*

LETTER FROM ATTICA

March 18, 1971

My Jocko

I know it's been a long time since I wrote and I have certainly neglected you. But I do not like to write letters. I have to work very hard at relating to your life now. The small boy I remember is not you anymore—nor am I the same person I once was. Your mother tells me beautiful things about you and what you are doing and I am very glad and happy for you. But to participate so remotely in your life is not easy.

Really, to think of you, I want to be with you and part of your existence—share your experiences, and *see* you grow and change. That's the only real excitement and meaning between people no matter if they are father and son or whatever. I read your mother's words and wonder is she just saying things that don't have a reality—it's hard to imagine you thinking about me at all now. Soon perhaps, your mother will tell you some things about me and then I will not have to feel so dishonest when I try to write to you.

You see I'm in a very strange position: I could write to you and make comments about your activities, perhaps attempt some instruction here and there and sound just like the fool I would be if I did so; or, if you understood my circumstances, I could try to relate my life honestly to you—and then I would have much to tell you. I don't know how much of it you would benefit from but at least it would be honest and you could pick and choose as you like. It's not that I'm not interested in your activities; I'm more than interested; I'm envious! A nine-year-old youth with so many interests and accomplishments!! Judo, music, biblical history, geography, science, magic. . . . . ! ! Instead of an absentee father you need several fulltime secretaries.

About your opening move in our chess game: P-Q4 is a very aggressive beginning. (Your mother says it's a *yellow* belt you're trying for, not a *black* one.) Well, alright, let's see if you know this response: I move P-KN3.

I've been working on "small space exercises" and maybe you'd be interested in this one (if you're ever in a small space): Kneel on the floor, sit back on the bottoms of your feet, hands on stomach and touch your head to the floor *behind* you. If this is too easy try putting your arms folded across your *back* and do it.

I don't know Hebrew at all but if you ever get into

Spanish maybe I can be of some help. Spanish is a good language to know these days, especially in Nueva York. Keep working and studying and growing. I love you much.

Dad

Sam Melville
#26124
35-28

—Samuel Melville, *Letters from Attica*

SLOWLY I AM LEARNING ...

July 28, 1968

My first visitors—members of my family—arrived for three hours this afternoon. Seeing them had special significance, because even some close friends have repeatedly been turned away. In any event, their visit communicates to me a blessing of freedom from my family, and a reminder of how ties of respect and love have deepened from that freedom. Given the need, I suppose that we would die for one another. But more importantly, we would die first for others who need us more. Given the need.

I have made my family suffer—not once or twice, but repeatedly. And in doing so, I have taken repeated cues from my brother, also a priest, and without reserve the greatest man I know. My parents, my brothers, and their families have by American standards a powerful right to something better. My family has made generous, if not extraordinary, concessions to the mystical union of God and country. Four sons went to war during the second world conflict—three of us served abroad in the Mediterranean and European theaters. Two sons are priests, another an outstanding educator and family man, two others the heads of superb families. And now this—one priest in jail and the other on his way. A paradoxical justice for my parents and the others.

Yet whatever one sacrifices conscientiously to justice is restored and renewed. So it has been with my family. There has never been a hint of reproof, much less of rejection. Only a strenuously loving effort to understand. And the result of this effort has often been to lead *me* toward deeper awareness of my special responsibilities.

That is why I say that our love for one another grows in intensity even as it grows in freedom. As we said our good-byes, disconsolate parents and relatives were parting from their young men—criminals and inmates, as classified by the federal system. It was a moment sobered by the unmentioned possibility that I would never see my aged and feeble parents again. But we managed to preserve the essence of parting—refreshed by the strength we lent one another, and gladdened at the thought of the work yet to be done. Sadness and a sense of loss were clearly out of place. We left one another grateful for the mercy given us.

I am neither a sensitive nor a sentimental man. My background, experience, and discipline, the service that must be always available for others, have forced me to keep a tight rein on sentiment, to learn to master fear, and to adopt an attitude toward life which many would even consider reckless. A compromise with truth fills me with loathing, and an inability to conceal my position has sometimes made *my reality* painful to those I most love. But my family has smoothed the rough edges of arrogance, and their love leaves me a failure in love, and a debtor to it. Slowly, I am learning, and will continue to learn, that without love a passion for justice can fashion a demagogue and a brute. "Love takes no pleasure in other's sins, but delights in the truth; it is always ready to excuse, to trust, to hope, and to endure whatever comes." I Corinthians 13:6.

—Philip Berrigan, *Prison Journal of a Priest Revolutionary*

A WASP WOMAN VISITS A BLACK JUNKIE IN PRISON

After explanations and regulations, he
Walked warily in.
Black hair covered his chin, subscribing to
Villainous ideal.
"This can not be real," he thought, "this is a
Classical mistake;
This is a cake baked with embarrassing icing;
Somebody's got,
Likely as not, a big fat tongue in cheek!
What have I to do
With a prim blue and proper-blooded lady?
Christ in deed has risen
When a Junkie in prison visits with a Wasp woman.

"Hold your stupid face, man,
Learn a little grace, man; drop a notch the sacred shield.
She might have good reason,
Like: 'I was in prison and ye visited me not,'—or some
   such.

So sweep clear
Anachronistic fear, fight the fog,
And use no hot words."
After the seating
And the greeting, they fished for a denominator,
Common or uncommon;
And could only summon up the fact that both were human.

"Be at ease, man!
Try to please, man!—the lady is as lost as you:
'You got children, Ma'am?' " he said aloud
The thrust broke the damn, and their lines wiggled in the
    water.
She offered no pills
To cure his many ills, no compact sermons, but small
And funny talk:
"My baby began to walk . . . simply cannot keep his room
    clean. . . ."
Her chatter sparked no resurrection and truly
No shackles were shaken
But after she had taken her leave, he walked softly,
And for hours used no hot words.

—Etheridge Knight, *Black Voices from Prison*

COMMON DENOMINATOR

August 14, 1968

Billie is what I would call a street savage, and what jailhouse veterans would call a hustler. Out "on the street"—
prison parlance for freedom—Billie is a small-time con man
living by the craft and ethics of the small-time underworld.

Jet black, with a head massive and handsome, features shifting graphically from suspicion to cunning, a body kept lean and muscular by hyperactivity, he lives here as he lives outside, a professional in deals and dupes. But Billie also is a parasite, created by black-white syndromes and by that species of larceny we call profit motivation; pressed, he will admit being a small-time thief—he wants a piece of the national action.

Billie is, I'm convinced, a casualty par excellence of our white supremacist, hedonist, and manifest-destiny Great Society. If he is redeemable (I'm sure he is), he may very well be irremediable. Illiterate, ignorant, yet profoundly sensitive, he knows little except the tools of his trade, and the survival they supposedly guarantee. On the street, he pimps for white or black "Dudes," pushes narcotics or numbers, plays assorted con games with unwary tourists, gambles with cards or bookmakers. He loves life outside as passionately as he hates it here, perfectly unconscious that his profit schemes are played by respectable fellow countrymen with far greater impunity and success.

My coming opened new doors for Billie's trade. He introduced himself by offering labored and absurd evidence of devout Catholicism. When this was solemnly accepted, he swept into fond reminiscences of the old home town, after which he generously offered himself as my prison patron and bodyguard. "Don't nobody mess with Pop," he would scream to anyone within earshot.

Such security, however, came with a price tag. Soon he was confiding his financial embarrassments—this one or that one at home failing him, or money forever on the way. I believed him—as far as it went, he spoke the truth. (And of course there are many men here with neither families nor friends. Some do hard and valuable work for the institution, with little or no recompense.)

Soon Billie began to ask for cigarettes—jailhouse currency—and I responded by buying him a carton every other week at the commissary. (No easy trick, with other men in need, and a twenty-dollar monthly limit.) The arrangement proceeded happily, with enrichment to our friendship. One morning, however, Billie came to me in a rage. Someone had stolen his cigarettes, and because he is a heavy smoker, the theft had left him in painful circumstances. He was a consummate actor, ranting with such conviction and energy that he convinced me thoroughly. It was easy for me to feel sympathy for him, because with men largely defenseless and commonly poor, stealing in jail is a particularly despicable crime. It is, in fact, the capital offense, taken more seriously by inmates than an unjust attack, or even knifeplay.

Billie vowed to kill the thief and announced at large the traps that he would set for him. This should have made me suspicious—he was obviously protesting too much. But to my relief, his fury subsided after a half-hour, and I proceeded to think no more of it.

Tranquillity was short-lived. Coming in from the farm that evening, I discovered that I had become Billie's partner in fate, two cartons of cigarettes having disappeared. (Prior to their loss, I remember feeling guilty about such wealth, but men had returned loans, leaving me the lot of the rich, and ripe to be plucked.)

Events took a more rapid pace. The loss was of no great importance to me. I reflected that a type of justice had been served, since I had more cigarettes than I could possibly use, while others around me had none. Yet I compounded previous mistakes by mentioning the theft to Billie, who publicized it with evangelical fervor, taking special pride in his being a fellow victim. In an hour's time the news had penetrated to all quarters—apparently even to the administration. People came by to express their shame and regret. A few offered cigarettes, others brought locks and advice to use them.

My embarrassment and feeling of inadequacy poorly prepared me for what followed. Jailhouse justice began to take over. A delegation approached me with the stolen cartons, and one member, a huge black, confessed that he had won them gambling with Billie, and that news of the theft confirmed his suspicions that my friend had stolen them. I insisted that he take them back, but he vehemently and somewhat ominously refused. My sense of foreboding suggested that the violence so senselessly begun might produce new victims.

My suspicions were not unfounded. When Billie returned from work in the kitchen, he faced a committee of justice that charged him with theft, sentenced him, and promptly executed sentence. Tender sensibilities like mine could only regard the proceedings with amazement and aversion. Nevertheless, although it was a kangaroo court enforcing vigilante law, in its own setting it was vested with a certain legitimacy and force. Billie was given a thorough beating, which was accompanied by fearful expressions of derision and contempt. The whole affair was over very suddenly, violently, and effectively—before I could even get on the scene. Perhaps it could be compared to the branding of Cain.

But Billie was resilient. He rushed over to see me, and it was clear that he blamed me more than his judges. He demanded to know who it was that had framed him. When I refused to tell him anything, he stormed away, still protesting his innocence. Since then, he has been more subdued and remote, having little to say to me. Or I to him.

A staunch believer in human rights and compensatory treatment for blacks, I had contributed to their affair, unfortunately, more presumption than wisdom. In my paternalism I had judged Billie by an updated version of the white man's burden: Since he was ignorant, brutal, and neurotic, I would help him by an overwillingness to condone his failures, and an overavailability to his needs. In all honesty this is simply going one notch better than sitting in a rectory parlor dispensing sympathy, advice, and alms to "deserving Negroes."

I had forgotten that prison provides a common denominator for us, that previous credentials evaporated before that fact, or faced reevaluation and acceptance. And because I had forgotten, for Billie I became nothing more than another white "dude" ready for fleecing. Accordingly, his appraisal of me had been immeasurably more accurate than mine of him. He had set me up with relish; his only mistake was to gamble with the loot too soon.

—Philip Berrigan, *Prison Journals of a Priest Revolutionary*

PRISON ALPHABET

Suddenly they stopped summoning me for interrogation. The empty prison days fell into a kind of regular routine, marked by the issue of hot water in the morning, the fifteen-minute walk in the prison yard (during which we were followed by guards with rifles and fixed bayonets), the meals, the washroom. The interrogators seemed to have forgotten my existence.

"They do it on purpose," said Lyama. "It's three weeks since I was last called. They hope prison life will drive you crazy, so that, in sheer desperation, you'll sign any old nonsense."

But I was so shaken by my first experience of Black Lake "justice" that I was glad of the unexpected respite.

"Well, let's make sure we don't go crazy," I said to Lyama. "Let's use our time to find out all we can about our surroundings. You said yourself that the great thing was to establish contact—and he's still tapping, isn't he?"

The prisoner in the cell to our left was still tapping on the wall, regularly, every day after dinner. But I had been too exhausted by the interrogations to listen properly to his knocking, and Lyama despaired of ever getting the hang of the prison alphabet.

One thing, however, we had noticed. On the days when our neighbor went to the washroom before us—this we could tell by the sound of the footsteps in the corridor— we always found the shelf sprinkled with tooth powder and the word "Greetings" traced in it with something very fine like a pin, and as soon as we got back to our cell, a brief message was tapped on the wall. After that, he immediately stopped. These knocks were altogether different from the long sequences our neighbor tapped after dinner, when he was trying to teach us the alphabet.

After two or three times it suddenly dawned on me:

" 'Greetings'! That's what he's tapping," I told Lyama. "He writes and taps the same word. Now we know how we can work out the signs for the different letters." We counted the knocks.

"That's right!" Lyama whispered excitedly. "The tapping comes in groups with long and short intervals. And he tapped out nine letters in all: g-r-e-e-t-i-n-g-s."

During the long months and years I spent in various prisons, I was able to observe the virtuosity that human memory can develop when it is sharpened by loneliness and complete isolation from outside impressions. One remembers with amazing accuracy everything one has ever read, even quite long ago, and can repeat whole pages of books one had believed long forgotten. There is something almost mysterious about this phenomenon. That day, at any rate, after deciphering the message "Greetings" tapped on the wall, I was astounded to find a page from Vera Figner's memoirs whole and fresh in my mind. [Vera Figner, 1852–1942, famous woman revolutionary who took part in the assassination of Alexander II and was imprisoned in the Schlüsselburg fortress in St. Petersburg for twenty years. The memoirs are about her experiences during this time.] It was the page in which she gave the clue to the prison alphabet. Clutching my head, myself astounded by my own words, I recited as if talking in my sleep:

"The alphabet is divided into five rows of five letters each. Each letter is represented by two sets of knocks, one slow, the other quick. The former indicates the row, the latter the position of the letter in it."

Wild with excitement, interrupting each other and for once forgetting the guard in the corridor, we tapped out our first message. It was very short:

"W-h-o-a-r-e-y-o-u?"

Yes, it was right! Through the grim stone wall we could sense the joy of the man on the other side. At last we had understood! His endless patience had been rewarded. "Rat-tat, tat-tat-tat!" He tapped like a cheerful tune. From then on, we used these five knocks to mean "Message understood."

Now he was tapping his reply—no longer for a couple of idiots who had to have the word "greeting" repeated a hundred times, but for intelligent people to whom he could give his name:

"S-a-g-i-d-u-l-l-i-n."

"Sagidullin? Who's that?" The name meant nothing to Lyama, but it did to me. Much more boldly, I tapped:

"Himself?"

Yes, it was he—Garey Sagidullin, whose name for years past had not been mentioned in Kazan without an "ism" tacked on to it: Sagidullinism.

It was the heading of a propaganda theme. "Sagidullinism," like "Sultan-Galeyevism," stood for the heresy of Tartar "bourgeois nationalism." But he had been arrested in 1933. What on earth was he doing here now?

Through the wall my bewilderment evidently was sensed and understood. The message went on:

"I was and I remain a Leninist. I swear it by my seventh prison"—and startlingly: "Believe me, Genia."

How could he know my name? How could he, through the wall, in spite of all the strictness of our isolation, know who was next door? We looked at one another in alarm. We had no need to speak out loud. The thought was in both our minds. He might be a *provocateur*.

Once again he understood and patiently explained. It appeared that in his cell, too, there was a chink between the window boards, and for a long time he had watched us walking in the yard. Although we had never met, he had once caught a glimpse of me at the Institute of Red Professors in Moscow. He had been brought back to Kazan for re-examination on additional charges. It looked like the death sentence.

From then on, though outwardly nothing had altered, our days were full of interest. All morning I looked forward to the after-dinner hour when the guards were changed and, as they handed over their human cattle, were for a while distracted from peeping through spy holes and listening at doors.

Garey's brief messages opened a new world to me, a world of camps, deportations, prisons, tragic twists of fate —a world in which either the spirit was broken and degraded or true courage was born.

. . . I had mastered the technique of tapping so thoroughly, by the end of a week, that Garey and I could recite whole poems to each other. We no longer needed to spell everything out. We had a special sign to show that we had understood, so we could use abbreviations and save time. A blow of the fist meant that a warder was about. I must confess that he used this signal much more often than I did, and I would surely have been caught if it hadn't been for him. However interesting the conversation, he never ceased to be on the alert.

I was never to set eyes on this man. He was eventually shot. I disagreed with many things he said and I never had a chance to discover exactly what his political views were. But I know one thing for certain: he endured his seventh prison, his isolation, and the prospect of being shot with unbroken courage. He was a strong man, a man in the true sense of the word.

—Eugenia S. Ginzburg, *Journey into the Whirlwind*

PEACHES AND ME

It all started in early May, 1970. I was serving a six month sentence for breaking and entering into a house. One afternoon about one o'clock a new inmate came into the jail at which I happened to be, to await an appeal of a two-and-one-half year sentence for using a motor vehicle without proper authority and various other charges. After he had changed from street clothes to prison dungarees and striped shirt he was put on the tier directly above me; that is when I found out his name was Ray.

When he was in jail prior to this time he said everyone

called him Peaches. I couldn't understand why a person in jail would be called Peaches, but I found out why after talking to Ray, who was 18 years of age and very good looking. It seems that Ray has very soft skin (just like a peach). A person like that has to be very careful in jail. He told me that he had just been in another jail in Salem ten days before he arrived here. During his three months stay there other inmates tried to force him into homosexual acts; he refused naturally. He was finally released into his own custody, but once again he was in trouble with the law and he went back to jail.

It turned out that when they put Ray above me it was really a good thing, for when we got together we started to become friends. Of course, Ray hesitated at first because of what the other jail inmates tried to do. After talking to him for a week he got to trust me some. He told me his father was in a state prison and that his mother did not really care about him, so Ray didn't have anyone. He seldom received letters or visits from anyone. Seeing this, I felt sorry for him; it's hard enough doing time without being alone. I said to myself, "I'm going to help Ray as much as I can". But the most I could do was talk to him as often as possible and see to it that he had cigarettes and enough books to read. I told him I would try my best to get him a radio. It wouldn't be easy because usually you would have to buy one from another inmate. I happened to be lucky. I got one off a friend of mine who was going home, and gave it to Ray. He was really happy. He trusted me after that, and finally realized that I wanted to help him and be his friend, and was not seeking sex acts. After that our friendship increased. At first I wasn't sure if Ray cared for me or not, or if he was using me to satisfy his wants and needs. He told me many times that he really cared but I still wasn't sure. . . .

. . . People probably wonder what two men can talk about everyday. Most of it is about the jail, but we talked about sports, girls and getting out which for me was to be soon. One day after the mail was passed out, I found Ray crying in his cell and I didn't know why. I tried to talk to him but to no avail, except that he showed me a letter he had just received from his mother. After reading the letter I found out why Ray was so upset. It seems his mother didn't want anything to do with him. She told him not to bother writing or coming home when he got out. I tried to comfort him. After awhile he stopped crying and we started talking about the letter. There wasn't much I could tell him except that it might turn out alright and maybe I could talk to my mother about the possibility of Ray coming home to live with us and become part of our family. I told him not to count on it but that I would talk to my mother next time she came up to see me and that I would try and explain the situation to her and find out if it was possible. Two weeks later, I received my visit. I was never happier in my life to see my mother as I was that day and she really couldn't understand why I was so happy. I explained to her all about Ray being my closest friend, in fact he was more of a brother to me and it would mean a lot to me to have Ray in the family. After she thought for awhile she said she didn't want to say yes or no just yet, but that she would think it over and I agreed with her. I asked her about visiting both of us next time she came up so that she could meet Ray and find out what kind of person he was. I said, "I think you'll like him. I do. In fact without any doubt in my mind I can say I've grown to love him very much and I'm very fond of him."

But, good things don't last. After being together for so long, the jail master thought that something was going on as far as sex between Peaches and myself so he separated us. I went to talk to the jail master to find out what was going on and he told me that he had heard stories about Peaches and myself and that it would be best to keep us apart, for the benefit of the jail. In what way he meant 'for the benefit of the jail' I'll probably never know. I didn't give up though. I kept trying to get moved back with Ray but to no avail. Every time I talked to the master he said, "I'll never put you back on the same tier for as long as you're here." Every time he said that I felt like crying because I couldn't see how a man with so little understanding or knowledge of any kind of needs of a prisoner could get the job he has. Everyone in jail has a friend that he can tell anything he wants to without it getting back all over the jail. I think you know how I feel. There are some things you can tell a person and he understands and other people wouldn't or couldn't. This is how Ray and I were. We could tell each other anything without worrying about embarrassment or it getting back to the wrong people. I talked to a lot of the inmates and most of the guards about the way the master kept Peaches and me apart; most of them felt the same way I do about the need of a friend, especially Ray because he didn't have anyone on the outside and he depended on me to be with him when he needed me. For one man to stop Ray from being with the one person that really cares for him was a crime in itself.

Don't get me wrong, I really care for Ray. I love him very much and I'm going to help him in any way I can to become a good citizen, but I can't help thinking that what happened between Ray and me is probably happening in other jails, to other kids, young kids that need help, who need the love from a friend because they never got the love from their family. They are asking us for help and love, and the judge and probation officers put them in reform school or jail; and when they get there a lot of them find a friend they can trust and a friendly, brotherly love that everyone needs but the masters keep them apart because they think sex is involved. I know that in some cases sex is involved but to condemn everyone for a minority of the friendships is wrong. And it's about time someone told people about how politicians run our jails and guards and masters of our penal system. I don't think they care about our young people. I don't want you to think I'm a radical or something but I'm only 20 years old and this was my third time in jail—and it will be my last. I found the love and trust I need in a fellow human being and I thought that even if Ray and I didn't get back on the same tier it would not really matter because we would always have the love and trust for each other no matter where we were.

—Joseph La Bonte, *The Boston Phoenix*, May 22, 1973

My friends, or at least those persons I had thought were my friends, ceased to exist at the moment of my arrest. With a single exception, that of my former high-school football coach, not one person I had regarded as a friend made even the smallest effort prior to my trial to send me a card or a note, or to contact my family, to wish me luck; nor have any of them done so during the eleven years that have elapsed since my conviction. The attitude of those people may cast a dreary reflection on the quality of the friendships I had formed, but I have never permitted myself to become demoralized by it. Rather, it has enabled me to better appreciate, and to value more highly, the very few genuine friendships I have found in recent years. Today, I can count the number of my friends on the fingers of one hand, and all but one of these persons were completely unknown to me prior to my arrest; yet each in his or her own way means more to me than all my former friends combined.

—Edgar Smith, *Brief Against Death*

Biographical Notes

BARBARA ALLEN still waits with her children for her husband's release.

DANIEL BERRIGAN (b. 1921). Priest, educator, poet, and political activist, Berrigan was ordained in 1952. He and his brother, Phillip, were the first priests to receive Federal prison sentences. Arrested in Catonsville, Maryland, following the burning of draft records, Berrigan was sentenced in 1968 to a prison sentence beginning in April 1970. He escaped, went underground, and was finally captured. Sent to the Correctional Institute in Danbury, he did time from August 1970 until his release in February 1972.

ISABEL ALVAREZ de Toledo y Maura, Duchess of Medina Sidonia. Advocate of land reform, political revolutionary, and opponent of Franco and American influence in Spain, she bears one of Spain's most illustrious names. Imprisoned for eight months in one of Franco's jails for her political activities, she managed, upon her release, to escape to France; her three children, after a long and bitter court fight, had already been taken from her, and placed in the custody of their father.

ART POWERS (b. 1927). Born in Indiana, Powers was convicted at twenty-one to a ten-to-twenty-year term for burglary. A high-school dropout, during imprisonment he received his high-school diploma and earned twelve semester hours of college credits through correspondence courses. He is still in Indiana State Prison.

SAM MELVILLE. In 1970, after pleading guilty to a series of bombings in New York City, Melville was sentenced to from six to eight years in prison. From Sing Sing he was finally sent to Attica, where he helped lead the rebellion of September 9, 1971. He was shot four days later, age, thirty-six.

PHILIP BERRIGAN (b. 1923). Ordained in 1950, Father Berrigan was arrested in 1967 for throwing blood on draft files in the Baltimore Customs House. After serving a term of imprisonment, Berrigan was returned to jail following his participation in the Catonsville raid. He did time in the Federal penitentiaries at Lewisburg and Allenwood, Pennsylvania, as well as at Danbury, Connecticut, with Daniel.

ETHERIDGE KNIGHT (b. 1933). Black poet and former drug addict, Knight was arrested in 1960 for robbery and given a ten-to-twenty-five-year sentence. He had resorted to theft to supply the habit he had developed as a result of a wound sustained in the Korean War. He was released from Indiana State Prison in 1968.

EUGENIA GINZBURG. The wife of a high official of the Communist Party, she was a victim of the Stalinist purge of 1934. In 1937, after three years of harassment she was imprisoned for eighteen years, charged with political deviancy. From prisons to labor camps and finally to exile in Siberia, Eugenia Ginzburg was determined to survive. She did, and was able to write her remarkable book, *Journey into the Whirlwind*. She now lives in Moscow.

JOSEPH LA BONTE. Both La Bonte and Ray are now out of jail. Though they live in different Massachusetts towns, they remain good friends.

EDGAR SMITH. See biographical notes, chapter 4.

8.

SEX IN PRISON

**People have to be close
to other people . . .**

—Preston S. Smythe,
San Quentin

Caught in a world of men without women, or of women without men, the prisoner can either engage in homosexual relationships, cultivate a gift for fantasy, or else retreat into a life of celibacy.

Outside, homosexuality and masturbation are expressions of sexuality, even as celibacy may be a deliberate choice. But in prison, what is natural soon becomes grotesque: fantasies that were once a means of pleasure become its end; celibacy by choice is changed to enforced self-denial. Homosexuality is generally turned into a form of barter—a medium of exchange, for cigarettes or protection from those who are stronger—even though some homosexual relationships in prison are based on affection and trust, these are the exception; rape and assault are the rule.

According to the 1969 Davis Report on Sexual Assaults in the Philadelphia Prison System, during a twenty-six-month period approximately 2,000 sexual assaults were committed by 3,500 aggressors against 1,500 prisoners. As usual after such reports, there was a brief cry for prison reform, but public interest gave way to public apathy and conditions throughout the Federal and states' prison system remain the same.

Our indignation is selective: it stops at prison walls. Newspapers, radio, and television ply us with accounts of rape and we are quite properly incensed—but toward the prisoners we show little concern at all. Although we have removed individuals to a world where they must suffer (as a matter of course) the very crime that so shocks our sensibilities—when it victimizes others—we are content to believe that in such a world the prisoners will be rehabilitated.

UNTITLED POEM #1 (by Juno Bakali Tshombe/ Craig Dee Anderson)

got me a hard on.
    a goddamn black/blown-up/throbbin/
    ass-bustin/for-real hard on.
    i ain't found nothin' to calm
    this monster down,
    because it ain't where you think
    it is,
    and it ain't what you think it
    is.
    but.
    you can dig it if you look for it.
    it's everywhere.
    even in your troubled sleep
    it's there,
    alive and kickin'.
    like
    some kind of gnawing madness
    chewing at your bones,
    and sucking on your brain,
    biting on your nerves.
    mmm-mmm-mmm-mmm.

got me a hard on.
    its a motha
    and it's swelling up my thighs
    and teasing my toes.

making my calfs bulge
with great expectations,
and this urge is getting next to meeeeeeeee,
ooooooooweeeeeeeeee.
got me a tiger by the balls.
i got the greatest hard on
in the world.

got me a hard on
for some
CRACKER/JACKS.

—Norfolk Prison Brothers, *Who Took the Weight*

ELSIE

I lie on my bed, staring at Elsie. Elsie is the name I have
given to the print which rests on the towel-rack against
the wall. It is a reproduction of Lautrec's 'Back of a Girl'.
It is a grey print, sad as a prison. It shows the naked back
and black-stockinged legs of a girl seated on the floor, her
rounded, tantalising buttocks wrapped in a towel. I have
spent hundreds of hours looking at her. She was a present
from my prison visitor. I had a very good reason for
naming her Elsie, but already I have forgotten what it
was. One always has a good reason for everything one
does in prison, although the reasons seldom stand up to
a close inspection.

Her skin looks grey and unhealthy, and surely smells
sweetly of sour sweat. At first it put me off, but I have
grown to live with it for she is all I have. Of course she
is a tart, but then most of Lautrec's models were. This I

don't mind—I have always found tarts to have a quick wit, an ability to laugh at themselves, and Elsie is no exception. Sometimes, when I have stared at her back for a long time, she turns round and wrinkles her nose at me suggestively.

Her posture is relaxed as she gazes musingly into the background of the picture. I feel she is supple, and this knowledge is an added fuel to my desire for her. A stiff, frigid beauty would not appeal to my contorted fantasies.

In the world outside, fantasies are limited by the lack of time to indulge in them. Here we have no reins or checks, and no desire for them. Our fantasies are all we have. When the doors are banged for the last time at eight o'clock, the bolts shot, the metal disc over the Judas Eye slid to one side, and our bodies noted as present, then we are alone, free to withdraw into the world of our choosing. Three hundred and thirty of us under one roof—three hundred and thirty private worlds. How distorted are they? I wonder. How unreal?—in what way different from the real world? How different from the fantasies of those not imprisoned? Perhaps not so dissimilar. I try to remember my old fantasies, those other fantasies of eight years ago. I cannot recall them. Perhaps there weren't any, or perhaps they were uncomplicated and not too improbable. Those I have now are out of this world.

I stare hard at Elsie, my eyes fixed and unblinking. It requires a lot of concentration to break through the barrier which separates the animate from the inanimate. There is a fine down on her shoulders and thighs which Lautrec overlooked, or deliberately didn't portray. It is fine and fair, and salty to the taste-buds of the tongue. Her arms are down, hiding the tight nests of hair in their pits, but if she obeys my will and makes her only move, I shall see one of them.

At last. She moves slowly, raising her right hand up over

her head till the tips of her fingers rest lightly on her left
shoulder, her arms forming a grey, triangular halo across
the back of her hair. Her head lowers till she is looking
back at me under her arm, her lips parted and pressing
against the wet warmth of the hair, auburned by sweat.

She wrinkles her nose and cat-slits her eyes at me. My
loins move and my testicles press suddenly heavy against
my thighs. I hear my breath, newly loud and harsh in the
silence of the cell, and I feel my own sweat run free, a
faint trickle against my ribs and in the hollow of my back.
Faustus sold his soul that he might see the face that
launched a thousand ships. I would sell mine if this dead
whore would come to life.

—Zeno, *Life*

WE NEVER
SAW HER AGAIN ...

Stadelheim 1919

Dear ——,

We are a hundred men here in prison, separated from
our wives for months. Every conversation between any two
men always ends in the same way—women.

The high walls prevent any view. Within the walls is
a small hut. It was, we heard, some sort of wash-house,
which was not used. One day one of us saw that the
shutters of the hut were opened. He saw two women at
work. One stayed in the wash-house, the other went
away and locked the door. Soon we knew all. The two

women were a wardress and a prisoner, who was to be released in a short time. She had been sentenced to eight years' imprisonment for child-murder. She had already served five years; in a few weeks' time she was to be pardoned.

It would be too complicated to tell you how we contrived to exchange notes with the girl. First playful and harmless ones, then feverish, passionate and confused ones. Everything which, in that closed-in existence, had come in dreams, wishes and fantasies went out to that woman. One morning she gave us a signal. We were to stand near the window at a certain hour.

Impossible to describe what happened. The woman opened her dress and stood naked at the window. She was surprised and taken away. We never saw her again. But we learned that the pardon had been annulled.

Never has a woman moved me so much as that little prisoner, who, in order to make men happy for a few seconds (in a very questionable way) suffered with unsophisticated wisdom three more years in prison.

—Ernst Toller, *Look Through the Bars*

THE RACKET

If you listened to a majority of the prison women, you would think there was not a sexually normal officer in the whole House of Detention. Although it is certainly not true that everyone so accused is a lesbian, anyone who has given any thought to the subject realizes that some officers doubtless are. This place they have chosen to work in is, in the last analysis, manless, and so if their interests and

feelings had not been centered on women, whether overtly
or not, they—at least those among them capable of earning
similar salaries elsewhere—might not have elected to come
here at all.

Despite what they say about their officers, there are few
House of Detention women who claim to have had actual
relationships with them. They talk about friends and friends
of friends who were in the House of Detention three, four,
ten years ago, who were intimate with officers. And what
they say, when you pin them down, is that, three years
ago, an officer I call Knocky Nelson had an affair with an
inmate I call Lucky Lopez and went further in her les-
bianism, although she was an officer, than many inmates
would have gone.

[When] I first met Knocky, she looked to me, until I
came to know her, like any hopelessly addicted inmate
out of the House of Detention, sick, weak, unreachable,
and altogether unable to delve into herself. She turned out
to be entirely opposite to what I'd conceived her—a lost
person, admittedly, but nevertheless wise and rational
about people, including herself. "I guess," she said, the
first time I went to see her in her dingy furnished room in
East Harlem, "that, although I was an officer, I am so
much a weak sister as any of the inmates are."

She said, "Well, you know, most of the inmates of the
House of D. had tragic childhoods and that's one reason
why they ended as they did. Well, my childhood was as
tragic as that of the inmates. They didn't overcome their
childhood tragedies, and although it seemed for a while
that I did, I didn't either." . . .

Knocky was ten going on eleven when she was declared
a neglected child, taken away from her mother, and sent
to the Lowell School in upstate New York. It was supported by Baptist Church women and prided itself on its
"missionary-type teachers who live and work among the

colored children in our school." The high brick wall at the Lowell School made it look like a prison from outside. . . .

Knocky could have gone home when she graduated from elementary school if it hadn't been for the fact that her father's whereabouts were still unknown and her mother had gone from bad to worse. She was a vagrant as well as a prostitute. So Knocky stayed on at the Lowell School, attending the high school in town and helping the matrons with the younger children. She passed her next four years in uncomfortable monotony, working hard at the Lowell School, making good grades in the high school, but having little or nothing to do with the other high school students. She read. . . . Books filled her mind with ideas which gave scope to her imagination.

After she graduated from high school, Knocky worked at the Lowell School for almost five years. She grew more religious with the years. There were times, after the children she oversaw were in bed, when she was seized with a mystical rapture, and she wanted to surrender herself entirely to God—to be a missionary in His behalf, perhaps. She forgot, during the time of her religious rapture, her longing for an earthier life, for contact with other people, for love even.

Sometimes, though, religion wasn't enough to keep Knocky from becoming gloomy. She was wasting her youth here at the Lowell School (and youth doesn't last forever, after all), throwing her life away. . . .

She dipped into the savings she'd accumulated while living in at the Lowell School and rented a room in an interracial boardinghouse near Columbia University. Most of the other boarders were young students, freshmen at Columbia, and elderly schoolteachers who were depressingly like many of the matrons at the Lowell School. . . .

About six months after she came to New York, Knocky, having taken a Civil Service examination for city prison officer, was high on the list of appointments to be made to the House of Detention for Women.

On March 4, 1963, Knocky Nelson dressed in her trim, navy blue Correction Officer's uniform with the stiffly starched shirt and the smart-looking tie, and rode herself up in the jail elevator to Floor Seven, her work assignment on the four-to-twelve P.M. shift. . . .

If you're trying to blame someone else for your being what you're fated to be, Knocky says, then Lucky Lopez is responsible for having changed her from an officer into an inmate—worse than an inmate. . . . There was something about Lucky. Her face, from the time Knocky first saw her, stood out among the tough young hood faces and the tough old outcast faces. She looked, with her skin stretched taut over broad facial muscles and her hair cut short as a man's, like a dark James Dean. She talked with zest and enthusiasm and an assurance (at least outwardly) Knocky envied. She talked colorfully about her past life. She said she was born restless. She never could stay in school when she was a kid, not even when she went there in the morning with the best of intentions. . . .

Knocky doesn't know when Lucky ceased being another inmate and became the most colorful, the most intriguing, the most fascinating person in her otherwise drab life. She was like a character out of the novels Knocky had read during her early days at the Lowell School. She seemed, even in jail, to have the only things that made life worth living—pride in self, love (to Knocky who's never related to a single person in her whole life, Lucky's sordid sexual affairs appear love-inspired), and companionship. She seemed not even to know what loneliness was and so Knocky was bound to be enthralled by her.

Lucky came on to Knocky's floor after Knocky had been working at the House of Detention for seven months. Knocky was regarded, at that time, as a fine, even dedicated officer with a good potential for success. Lucky had been transferred to Knocky's floor from the sixth floor. She came with four others, and one night the five of them were sprawled on the floor—it was Recreation time—and Knocky passed them and Lucky "made a thing" out of coyly peeping under her skirt.

"Hey, officer," Lucky said, "I don't know your name. What is it?"

"Nelson."

"I mean your first name."

Knocky "knew that officers weren't supposed to give inmates our first names but—I don't know—already then, I didn't think of Lucky as an inmate. I told her Knocky. And is was funny—the girls sitting with her began laughing and kidding me about my name.

" 'Jocky, did you say? Is your name Jocky?'

" 'No. It's Knocky.'

" 'Oh! Pocky!'

" 'Not Pocky! Knocky!' " Knocky laughed and so did everyone. Lucky summoned Knocky to join her friends on the floor and she sat down in spite of the baldly disapproving look on Rita Malone's face. Lucky and her friends continued the conversation they'd been holding before Knocky came. They talked of a thousand things—of "tricks" and how to interest them, of narcotics and where to "cop" it, of the floors in the specialty and department stores which were easiest to steal from. They gossiped about other inmates on their corridors, vituperatively and violently. They used a peculiar imagery Knocky had never been exposed to before to emphasize their ribald scorn. All the names they mentioned were, of course, unfamiliar to Knocky but she listened attentively anyhow. That night, she thinks now upon reflection, was "the beginning of the end, the beginning of my downfall. I began looking on the inmates as my friends and myself as less than their equal."

Knocky says she honestly tried to stay away from Lucky and her group but that she felt irresistibly drawn to them from the beginning. Only with these women, out of everyone she'd ever met, could she be giving and affable because not fearful of rebuff. Only with them could she hope to attain the popularity she'd always desired above everything. . . .

Knocky and Lucky began spending many nights on Recreation, keeping as apart from the other women as they could. They'd sit and talk together by the hour or, rather, Lucky would talk and Knocky would listen. Bragging, exaggerating her "big scores" on the outside, Lucky would tell of the women with whom she'd been and how well she'd satisfied all of them.

And one night Lucky held Knocky against a more or less inconspicuous wall of the Recreation room and pretended she was a police officer frisking her. "The fuzz frisks you like this, Knocky." She let her hands slide intimately between Knocky's legs until Knocky could hardly breathe, and then, once she'd gauged her effect, she asked, "Is this kicks, baby? Huh, is it? Is this kicks or is it kicks?" She prevailed upon Knocky, without too much urging, to open a darkened shower room and sneak in there with her. She slipped out of her clothes in an instant and then undressed Knocky. After they made love, she asked—it was the first and last time she ever worried about Knocky—"Are you all right now, baby? Was it good? Did I make you happy, man?"

One night, after Knocky and Lucky had been intimate for some time, a new young girl was assigned to Floor Seven. She was perhaps seventeen or eighteen years old and very pretty in the overly tight garment. She smiled as she walked by Lucky and Knocky, coy, aware of her attractiveness to all the bulldykes on the corridor, including Lucky. She walked over to where a couple of inmates were playing cards and bent over, ostensibly to see somebody's hand. She stayed bent a long time, casting surreptitious glances at Knocky and Lucky—to see her effect upon them. Then, shaking her hair which was vibrantly blond and long to her shoulders, she straightened up and stood in posed bewilderment, as if wondering where she would go next.

"Oh, man," Lucky said, jumping up from the floor. "Oh, man!" And pushing her hand toward her mannish-cut hair, she walked toward the girl who was slowly making her way out of the Recreation corridor and back to her cell. . . .

One Saturday afternoon a week after the young girl—Eloise Reiber was her name—had first appeared on Knocky's floor, Knocky saw Lucky and Eloise, arms clasped around each other's waists, walking toward the corridor in which Lucky's cell was located. Her heart sank as she watched them go, and as soon as she could decently do so, she followed them. When she came on to the cell block, she saw two of Lucky's trusted friends standing squarely in front of her cell and shading from view all that went on. They refused to move away from the cell when she ordered them to. When Lucky came out of the cell and back on to the Recreation corridor, Knocky told her she "was through, finished, and I didn't want any more to do with her. . . . Then come tomorrow night, and she asks me to go into the shower room with her. And I went. And, you know, she gave up Eloise for me or they had a fight—but Eloise was out of our lives. So Lucky and I made it together every night until her time was up and then I knew I couldn't give her up. I wanted to make it with her on the outside."

All this happened within perhaps a week. . . .

Knocky was with Lucky in The Bird in Hand in Harlem —a huge, dirty "gay bar" with harsh lights and ornamented with faded travel posters from Italian and Japanese airlines—when a skinny, drunk, black-faced femme perched like a crow on a stool next to Lucky and began stroking her. Knocky, watching, turned in fury, ready to slap her. The woman hurled her beer at Knocky in a stream. Knocky slapped her and she fell off her stool. A police officer in uniform came and took Knocky and the woman to the police station, booked them both on charges of disorderly conduct. Knocky, on trial, received a suspended sentence, but the Department of Correction heard about the incident and issued her a stern warning. Two days later, Knocky was again arrested for disorderly conduct—another fight in another "gay bar" with another femme who was interested in Lucky. This time a surly Department of Correction official said, "You're wearing our patience a little thin."

Knocky was fired, finally, after she stole, forged, and cashed a check made out to another officer in the House of Detention. "I knew I had to get caught," she says, "but when I did it, I wasn't thinking about tomorrow or anything except getting some money Lucky had to have. I couldn't help it." Knocky says Lucky is an obsession with her; she's a slave to Lucky. They fight and she tells Lucky she doesn't want anything more to do with her and Lucky shrugs her shoulders and says, "Suit yourself, man." And then Knocky cries and begs Lucky to forgive her. She's glad to lie down on the ground for Lucky to walk over. . . . But today, Lucky doesn't even walk over her. Lucky doesn't want her now that she's a cheap prostitute with an oil-burning junk habit. She taunts her by saying, "You're just a screw, man; it's all you are and all you'll be. . . ." And she tells her she's a fool ever to have fallen for her or any other bulldyke king in the House of Detention. She tells her that she and other dyke kings, the dykes who matter, that is, use femmes like her—who get all involved in sex and fall in love and want to live happily ever after like squares—to advance their own ends, and it's a pity that the femmes don't know it. It's a pity that the femmes don't know that sex is a racket in the prison. And she says, along with Rusty, that "jerked-up femmes" like Knocky Nelson don't belong outside, that they deserve to spend the rest of their lives in the House of Detention, "hellhole" though it is, because "they're too weak and sick to live on the outside."

—Sara Harris, *Hellhole*

FOR FRECKLE-FACED GERALD

Now you take ol Rufus. He beat drums,
was free and funky under the arms,
fucked white girls, jumped off a bridge
(and thought nothing of the sacrilege),
he copped out—and he was over twenty-one.

Take Gerald. Sixteen years hadn't even done
a good job on his voice. He didn't even know
how to talk tough, or how to hide the glow
of life before he was thrown in as "pigmeat"
for the buzzards to eat.

Gerald, who had no memory or hope of copper hot lips—
of firm upthrusting thighs
to reenforce his flow,
let tall walls and buzzards change the course
of his river from south to north.

(No safety in number like back on the block.
two's aplenty. three? definitely not.

four? "you're all muslims."
five? "you were planning a race riot."
plus, Gerald could never quite win
with his precise speech and innocent grin
the trust and fists of the young black cats.)

Gerald, sun-kissed ten thousand times on the nose
and cheeks, didn't stand a chance,
didn't even know that the loss of his balls
had been plotted years in advance
by wiser and bigger buzzards than those
who now hover above his track
and at night light upon his back.

—Etheridge Knight, *Black Voices from Prison*

Homosexual arrangements in prison are made almost exclusively on the basis of force (threatened or actual), not
on the basis of free choice. The strongest, most aggressive
inmates "cop" the available "homos." And unless he has
adequate protection, the passive homosexual will be pres-
sured into unwanted sexual relations by various inmates.
The facts of life for most imprisoned, passive homosexuals
are demeaning stares, ridicule, social ostracism, and constant seduction.

—Howard Levy and David Miller, *Going to Jail*

BOBBY

The Queen of the Rock, a really beautiful faggot, was Bobby—a feral, venal, coldly poised and enameled creature who filled me with awe. It was said she extracted staggering prices from her lovers for her favors.

One Saturday afternoon, Bobby and her current lover were discovered flagrante in an upstairs two-man cell, and taken to the Rock Lieutenant, known to cons as Uncle Ben. An old weary, bored, sardonic Cracker, his legendary profanity was said to scorch the eyebrows and sear the brain. He could have sent the guilty pair to the Flat-Top, the sinister building where the rebellious were methodically starved. Instead, he procured a chain six feet long and fastened one end around Bobby's ankle, the other around the ankle of her lover. Saying: "You so goddam fond uh one anothah, ah'm gonna give you a chance to get fondah." For two weeks they went around the joint chained together. Their arrival in Mess Hall was always eagerly awaited. Bobby would come in the door, the chain looped around her wrist, the crestfallen lover following like a sullen bear. Then she would drop the chain with a loud clank on the concrete floor and sweep regally down the aisle to the steam tables. No time, nowhere in the world before or since have I seen poise to match.

—James Blake, *The Joint*

The prison "wife" is held in the same degraded and subservient position as are women outside of prison. But, as is also true of life outside of prison, the homosexual is afforded some of the same privileges given to women, or at least is given special favors which are thought of as privileges. They are objects upon which to bestow gifts and they are indulged in their occasional feminine fits of temper.

—Howard Levy and David Miller, *Going to Jail*

OUT OF THE VOID

For a moment George pauses. The veins of his forehead protrude, as if he is undergoing a severe mental struggle. Presently he says: "Aleck, I'm going to speak very frankly to you. . . .

"I'll give you my intimate experiences, and I want you to be just as frank with me. I think it's one of the most important things, and I want to learn all I can about it. Very little is known about it, and much less understood."

"About what, George?"

"About homosexuality. . . .

. . . as the months and years passed, my emotions manifested themselves. It was like a psychic awakening. The desire to love something was strong upon me. Once I caught a little mouse in my cell, and tamed it a bit. It would eat out of my hand, and come around at meal times, and by and by it would stay all evening to play with me. I learned to love it. Honetly, Aleck, I cried when it died. And then, for a long time, I felt as if there was a void in my heart. I wanted something to love. It just swept me with a wild craving for affection. Somehow the thought of woman gradually faded from my mind. When

I saw my wife, it was just like a dear friend. But I didn't feel toward her sexually. One day, as I was passing in the hall, I noticed a young boy. He had been in only a short time, and he was rosy-cheeked, with a smooth little face and sweet lips—he reminded me of a girl I used to court before I married. After that I frequently surprised myself thinking of the lad. I felt no desire toward him, except just to know him and get friendly. I became acquainted with him, and when he heard I was a medical man, he would often call to consult me about the stomach trouble he suffered. The doctor here persisted in giving the poor kid salts and physics all the time. Well, Aleck, I could hardly believe it myself, but I grew so fond of the boy, I was miserable when a day passed without my seeing him. I would take big chances to get near him. I was rangeman then, and he was assistant on a top tier. We often had opportunities to talk. I got him interested in literature, and advised him what to read, for he didn't know what to do with his time. He had a fine character, that boy, and he was bright and intelligent. At first it was only a liking for him, but it increased all the time, till I couldn't think of any woman. But don't misunderstand me, Aleck; it wasn't that I wanted a 'kid.' I swear to you, the other youths had no attraction for me whatever; but this boy— his name was Floyd—he became so dear to me, why, I used to give him everything I could get. I had a friendly guard, and he'd bring me fruit and things. Sometimes I'd just die to eat it, but I always gave it to Floyd. And, Aleck —you remember when I was down in the dungeon six days? Well, it was for the sake of that boy. He did something, and I took the blame on myself. And the last time— they kept me nine days chained up—I hit a fellow for abusing Floyd: he was small and couldn't defend himself. I did not realize it at the time, Aleck, but I know now that I was simply in love with the boy; wildly, madly in love. It came very gradually. For two years I loved him without the least taint of sex desire. It was the purest affection I ever felt in my life. It was all-absorbing, and I would have sacrificed my life for him if he had asked it. But by degrees the psychic stage began to manifest all the expressions of love between the opposite sexes. I remember the first time he kissed me. It was early in the morning; only the rangemen were out, and I stole up to his cell to give him a delicacy. He put both hands between the bars, and pressed his lips to mine. Aleck, I tell you, never in my life had I experienced such bliss as at that moment. It's five years ago, but it thrills me every time I think of it. It came suddenly; I didn't expect it. It was entirely spontaneous: our eyes met, and it seemed as if something drew us together. He told me he was very fond of me. From then on we became lovers. I used to neglect my work, and risk great danger to get a chance to kiss and embrace him. I grew terribly jealous, too, though I had no cause. I passed through every phase of a passionate love. With this difference, though—I felt a touch of the old disgust at the thought of actual sex contact. That I didn't do. It seemed to me a desecration of the boy, and of my love for him. But after a while that feeling also wore off, and I desired sexual relation with him. He said he loved me enough to do even that for me, though he had never done it before. He hadn't been in any reformatory, you know. And yet, somehow I couldn't bring myself to do it; I loved the lad too much for it. Perhaps you will smile, Aleck, but it was real, true love. When Floyd was unexpectedly transferred to the other block, I felt that I would be the happiest man if I could only touch his hand again, or get one more kiss. You—you're laughing?" he asks abruptly, a touch of anxiety in his voice.

"No, George, I am grateful for your confidence. I think it is a wonderful thing; and, George—I had felt the same horror and disgust at these things, as you did. But now I think quite differently about them."

—Alexander Berkman, *Prison Memoirs of an Anarchist*

Biographical Notes

JUNO BAKALI TSHOMBE/CRAIG DEE ANDERSON (b. 1947). Born in Boston, he is now a prisoner in Norfolk State Prison.

ZENO. A novelist, his identity unknown, Zeno has been a farmer, timber merchant, and served during World War II as a member of the British 1st Airborne Division. For murder, he was sentenced to life at thirty-eight. He was released after nine years.

ERNST TOLLER (1893–1939). German poet and dramatist, he became an ardent Socialist while still young. Arrested for political activities in 1919, Toller was imprisoned for five years in a fortress. He left Germany in 1932 and eventually came to the United States where he committed suicide in a New York hotel.

HOWARD LEVY. See biographical notes, chapter 5.

DAVID MILLER. See biographical notes, chapter 5.

ETHERIDGE KNIGHT. See biographical notes, chapter 7.

JAMES BLAKE. See biographical notes, chapter 5.

ALEXANDER BERKMAN. See biographical notes, chapter 4.

9.
SOLITARY

This way you don't have no outside vision of anything.

—George F. X. Lincoln, convict

In recent years, experiments have been made to determine the effects of sensory deprivation. Conducted by qualified scientists and physicians (not in prisons) and with volunteers fully informed of the objectives and speculated consequences, these experiments were performed under the best conditions. Though results were varied, it was concluded that total sensory deprivation can create a psychosis in even the most stable person.

Yet similar measures are standard practice in prisons— from three days to forty-three years. Depending on state laws, the warden, the staff, the prisoner himself, some are allowed to read, to write; others have nothing but the walls and the dark.

"Punitive segregation"; "solitary confinement"—called by whatever name, for the prisoner it will always be "cruel and unusual punishment."

LIVING ALL ALONE
(by Grandpa July 1919)

I cannot say it has been my good fortune to live a solitary life, but it has been my experience almost 43 years, from 1874, when I was 14 years old, up to 1917. A few details of that life may interest—the human element is indeed a surprise, in its utter absence. I have often been asked, "How could you live apart from men, all those years by yourself, without seeing or enjoying the association of others?" My answer has ever been that, I was so young, not realizing or knowing anything of life except as I lived it, it became, as it were, a natural way of living: though in truth it is a most unnatural life. The passing years flowed by without a change, and I grew up in boyhood, to be a young man; and then, as manhood arrived, and middle life, and finally the elderly life, solitude became my second nature, without on my part any noticeable change that I could remark. As a school boy, I was not much on books; sports, the active out of door life of a growing boy, were my attractions. In my solitary cell, without assistance or guidance of any sort, I found that the silence, the tiresomeness, the tedious, lonesome and weary sameness of the slow hours, little by little, induced me to devote my time to studious efforts; books, instead of men, became my constant companions, and, in time, a source of improvement, in the foundation of a useful life, in it might be a happier future. A day in solitary would begin about 8 A. M. as the increasing light penetrated the thick stone walls, by way of the narrow loopholes, 4 inches wide, 20 inches high. Unless the rats—numerous and big—had run off with some of my belongings, toilet was soon completed, breaking the ice in the water pail, maybe, for a wash, in winter, for the place was cold then, no heat at all; and cool in summer, unless several hot days slowly heated up the place; then it was a furnace for a long time. The rattle of the heavy 2 inch bars, 3 in number on each solid iron door, was the signal for our meals—3 per day—morning, noon and night. We hear today much of the simple life. Our menu in those days was simplicity itself: beans, hash, soup, bread, rice, molasses, rye burnt, camouflaged as coffee (?). Year in and year out, these were our staples—with white or brown bread—no fruit, and vegetables in our soup only—potatoes, onions, cabbage. After breakfast, as per my sentence of hard labor in solitary for life, I worked at my bench in my cell, making scrubbing brushes—a book propped before me to dip into as I could as the day went by, until about 3.30 P. M. dusk would creep in and very soon it was dark.

Finally in 1917 the solitary was changed to imprisonment for life, after being in the cell over 42 years. I cannot say I admire such a sentence on top of so many years there: but it is the order of the Governor and Council. Contrasting the old with the new, there is indeed a vast difference—the human element, so absent before, is now considered. Without much of a jolt, I fit into my new life thanks to the devotion, of my mother, and my wide reading. Under Divine Providence, what little mind is left me is due to my early efforts to steady myself, to study, to avoid the pitfalls, they are many—of solitude. The sympathy of my fellows "planted" near me, was ever mine. I owe them much in helpful kindness. "They were true friends to me." An invincible cheerfulness, and hopefulness in the future, has greatly tempered the hard spots in my solitude. My weak spot is bashfulness—due, no doubt, to solitary ways. It is a pleasure to see that while at one time "planting," for months of many was ordinarily the custom, today, very few are so treated. "It is not good for man to be alone"—solitary breeds disease, weakness, insanity, suicide. Hail to the brighter days.

—Jesse Harding Pomeroy, *The Mentor*, Massachusetts State Prison, 1920

DRY GUILLOTINE: DEVIL'S ISLAND

Solitary confinement . . . ! Entombed in a dark cell! The convicts call it *"La guillotine sèche,"* the dry guillotine! The convicts call these three cement cell structures, The Castle. Each of these is covered with a V-shaped, corrugated iron roof, and contains forty-eight cells arranged in two blocks of twenty-four. On the cell block of each structure is an iron walk where an armed guard paces night and day. The top of each cell is a grilled network, and he can gaze down and see everything which is going on inside. The cells are about twelve feet by nine, with a height of nine feet. The roof keeps out the sun and, also, the coolness of the rain. The only light which comes in is through the barred opening above the inmate's head: he is immersed like a fish in a clammy well.

In each cell there is a narrow wooden bench for the prisoner to sleep on and, during the day, he usually sets this up on end so that he can have more space to move. A small bucket for excrement is the only furnishing in the cell. An old blanket, and sometimes a piece of rag, and the prisoner—that is all. At the bottom of this semi-obscure pit the prisoner stays twenty-three hours out of each twenty-four. Each cell has a solid door; these open onto two walled passages that lead to an enclosed court. For an hour in the morning the prisoner is taken into this silent court where he can walk around in solitude, then he is taken back to his cell. It is the only time when he can see the sky. The rest of the day he lives in dim light; from dark to dawn—blackness and silence. He is alive in a tomb.

He has no work, nothing to read, nothing to write on—nothing to occupy himself with. In the dim obscurity his mind wanders while he paces back and forth or goes round and round, and at night he dreams of his piece of board. The only sounds he hears are those of the sea breaking on the rocks and the screams of the demented crying and howling in the third structure. And these elemental sounds which faintly reach his lonely ears in the depths of the cell block are of a kind which are horribly depressing to a man . . . the monotonous noise of the sea . . . the heavy splash of tropical rains on the iron roof when the wet season is on . . . the howls and piercing screams of the demented, are the only sounds which reach him vaguely from the outside world. The cells are damp, very damp, in that region where the atmosphere is already saturated with humidity. His teeth fall out with scurvy. He watches the green mold grow and creep along in the cracks, and passes his time away making tiny patterns and designs in it with one of his long nails which he has painstakingly worn into a point on the cement.

Thoughts . . . dreams. Of what? He is alone with whatever inner self he may have. The past is dead. For many the past was so sad that they have no pleasant memories to attach themselves to; for those who have something worth while in their former lives, it is even worse, this present emptiness. Most prisoners turn to the future, where things have not yet happened, and then become lost in great dreams, in fine plans. They dream of impossibilities, they foresee happiness. Life takes on the tone of a mirage, and they are soon blissfully going crazy.

After a while a prisoner in those cells has an ungovernable desire to go to the hospital: to see somebody, to talk with someone, to smoke a cigarette. It become overpowering, it is stronger than he: it becomes necessary that he get out of the solitary cell no matter what the price. The one way he can get out is to go to the hospital. So he finds an excuse for the doctor's visit, when he comes to the island once in the week. He must be sick, gravely ill; he knows that, and he makes himself sick! It is a voluntary and a desperate alternative.

Some find a way to wound themselves purposely, some smoke quinine to sham fever, some breathe sulphur to sham bronchitis or rub sperm into their eyes to induce a suppuration, others put castor beans in a cut so as to get a serious infection: they try everything. They impair their health, and often pay with a part of their bodies or with their lives. But when they are in the hospital they can talk, and read and smoke; and when they are brought back to Saint Joseph again, each will have on him a suppository made with paper or bread-dough, and full of tobacco!

When a prisoner has tobacco, and has almost finished his carefully rolled cigarette, he will wait for the guard's steps to get to the far end of the walk: he then throws the lit stub, tied to a precious pebble, up through the grill above his head; the butt falls into the next cell, the inmate draws a few puffs, then throws it in his turn into the adjoining one. The guard, if he pays any attention, has a hard time finding where the cigarette came from, for the long range of cell tops all look alike!

It is a miserable life, a life of horror where beings suffer inhumanly and are cared for like beasts. They are few, those who endure five years in the cells on Saint Joseph; yet this punishment of slow rot and death is inflicted on the condemned for their *évasions,* because they attempted to flee to life out of that Hell. *La guillotine sèche!* The dry guillotine! Albert Londres has found, better than anyone else, the name for the nerve-freezing cement structures on Saint Joseph.

"Fortunate are the simple in mind." But I do not think

the pitiful depraved, locked up in the third cell-block on Saint Joseph, are fortunate. When I was on Saint Joseph there were more than forty crazy men in the "Howling House,"—helpless, and treated and handled like so many rotting lumps of flesh. Their minds had been murdered but their bodies still hung together for a few more months or years. The guard in charge of them stole part of their food supply, the turnkeys stole another, and the little that was left for them was barely enough to keep them from dying of hunger. Most of them were naked, the clothes of the others were in shreds; they had nothing but part of a pair of trousers or a blouse made of old flour sack, and they chattered at night in their cells. Trembling from cold and physical exhaustion, they moaned and cried hoarsely to ears that were ever deaf; and, whenever one had a moment of lucidness and complained, a bucket of cold water thrown down on his head by a turnkey quickly calmed him—or started him off raving again.

Human derelicts prostrate in so many cages like frantic animals dirty and half-naked, their eyes bloodshot, their chins streaked with drool, they are forced to drink dirty water out of buckets that are filled whenever the turnkeys take a notion to do so. They are closed up just like the others and come out only for an hour, if at all. In the walled court some occupy themselves with their individual peculiarities. One man counted eternally, just as he had done for more than a year already, "27, 28, 29—27, 28, 29—27, 28, 29 . . ." Those who are as mild as he have a chance to exist longer than others, for their folly is inoffensive and does not annoy the guards too much. There was another who, every time he came out in the morning into the walled court, would throw pebbles, or whatever he could lay his hands on, at his enemy the sun; and, in the darkness of his cell, he would burble, staring at the dim light which reached him through the grill above his head:

this dim light was to him the sun's eye! Another used to have a wild fear of persecution, which was probably well founded, and would throw his food in the face of the turnkeys every time he had a chance, thinking always they came to poison him. It was not long before his cell had another inmate. There was another who scratched on his cell wall day and night, thinking his mother was in the other room, dying; in his frenzy, he thought he had to get to her. He would not stop to go out for exercise; sometimes the turnkeys, seeing his bleeding fingers, would take pity on him and drag him out into the court by force; but when they did, he would stand by the wall and scratch and mutter, without taking the time to eat his food. His fingers were worn, literally, to the bone, but this seemed not to bother him; I believe he finally bled himself to death.

Another, and he was an example of what is probably the most pitiful sort of inmate of all those locked into these rows of horror in the third cell-block, was constantly in the process of wording a letter of defense to the Director of the Administration. He was an intelligent individual, and I know for a fact that even the guards on the walk would listen, moved. He, like many others who have exposed how things are in the prison colony to the press and to the high authorities in France, had been classed as demented by the Administration and was kept there in the third cell-block out of pure revenge until he actually did go crazy. The Administration had seen to that, so that there could be no come-back in the future against its action. It may seem unbelievable, but this forcing of a sane man to become insane has happened time and again. Some of the most intelligent convicts in the colony have died, reduced to raving idiots, right there in the third structure cell-block of Saint Joseph, because they took it upon themselves to tell the people of their country how things are done in the French Guiana. Forgotten martyrs, all of them!

For they got no thanks for their humanistic endeavor, and
the press seldom sent them money for the revealing words
they smuggled out and which cost them their lives. They
were individuals who were civilized, who were educated
and reared in the ways of civilization,—who thought their
nation should know the atrocities which are done under its
flag. Their names are sent back to the Minister of Justice
in France with the citation: "gone crazy in the heat of the
tropics"—that is the end to investigation, hushed effici-
ently by the local Administration.

—René Belbenoit, *Dry Guillotine*

GEORGE F. X. LINCOLN

"Nineteen fifty-nine I was here for robbery and I came in
contact with Islam as taught by the Honorable Elijah
Muhammed. And at that time we were not recognized by
the prisons. Persecution was widespread. So we went into
court, filed a petition and what not, and over a period of
three years, we finally won the right to worship in prison.
Spent three years in solitary because of the court action.
    "Solitary is like a man in a room. It's like when you're
kids, your mother want to punish you, she says, 'Johnny,
I want you to stay in that room and don't come out.' You
can't play the radio. You can't play the TV. You jus in the
room. And if she really want to punish you, she pull the
shade down and tell you don't raise it up. This way you
don't have no outside vision of anything. And you only see
someone when they come by to feed you or see if you still
livin. An that's what solitary's like. And I went through
that for three years. And I think that I still have my sanity.

"You get a mattress. Sometime they let you stay fifteen days with no mattress—concrete and some water. It depends upon how angry they are with you. And at that time, of course, they was quite angry.

"I don't know if I coulda gone through it without my faith in my God, which is Allah."

—Leonard J. Berry, *Prison*

Biographical Notes

JESSE HARDING POMEROY (d. 1932). Child mutilator and killer, in 1874. Pomeroy was sentenced when he was fourteen, to life imprisonment. This sentence was later changed to life in solitary confinement. After having spent over forty years in isolation, Pomeroy was allowed to join the general prison population in the Massachusetts State Prison, where he was interned. He was later transferred to the state farm at Bridgewater where he died at age seventy.

RENÉ BELBENOIT (1899–1959). Born in France, Belbenoit was employed as a valet when a young man. Arrested for stealing the pearls of his employer, he was sent to Devil's Island. He escaped (one of the very few to do so), and later settled in California, where he died.

GEORGE F. X. LINCOLN. Sentenced to seven years for assaulting a police officer, Lincoln is a prisoner at the District of Columbia Correctional Complex, Lorton, Virginia.

10.

CAPITAL PUNISHMENT

Murder and capital punishment are not opposites that cancel one another, but similars that breed their kind.

—George Bernard Shaw

In general, capital punishment is reserved for the poor and the black. If we search long enough we can find white-collar criminals scattered throughout prisons or in the city jails. But on Death Row, most prisoners are black; almost all are poor. From 1930 to 1967, 2066 blacks were executed as opposed to 1751 whites. Since blacks comprised no more than 11.1 percent of the general population, the record speaks for itself: availability of funds for expert counsel determines innocence, poverty presumes guilt.

According to the late Lewis Lawes, warden at Sing Sing Prison during a forty-year period, 12.3 percent of the 406 persons sent to Sing Sing for execution were discovered to have been sentenced in error. So that aside from the racial and economic factors involved, there is always the danger of what Yale legal scholar Charles L. Black calls "the inevitability of caprice and mistake." Inadequate defense on the part of court-appointed lawyers and public defenders may mean the difference between death or the minimum sentence.

Now that the Supreme Court stands ready to review the question of the death penalty, demagogues of law and order are crying for its restoration. Though studies have proved "beyond a reasonable doubt" that capital punishment has never served as a deterrent against capital crimes, its proponents fail to see, what Beccaria observed, that "laws, which detest and punish homicide in order to prevent murder, publicly commit murder themselves."

DEATH AND DEMAGOGUERY

The Senate of the United States has voted 54–33 to restore the death penalty for a wide variety of Federal crimes, and the House of Representatives undoubtedly will follow suit—both at the urging of Richard Nixon. This would be one of the most astonishing and tragic turnabouts in history, were it not for the likelihood that it is more nearly another example of supine politicians pandering to the basest passions of their constituencies.

In 1935, 199 persons were executed in America. In 1950, 82 were put to death. By 1963 the number had fallen to 21. Since 1967, no execution has been carried out in this country. In 1971, nine states had abolished the death penalty by legislation. Others, like New York, had limited it to certain rare crimes. Elsewhere in the world, since 1922, 41 nations had abolished the death penalty. And in 1971, the Supreme Court of the most populous state, in one of the most brilliantly argued decisions of our time, made California the first state or nation to abolish capital punishment by judicial decision.

In 1972, in a far more limited ruling, the Supreme Court of the United States held that the death penalty, as then administered, was unconstitutional—not in itself, but because, as Mr. Justice Stewart argued, it was "so wantonly and freakishly imposed." But that was the high-water mark of the American movement against the death penalty —and in fact seems to have turned that movement around.

Since then, 21 states have restored the death penalty by legislation that they believe satisfies the Supreme Court ruling. The voters of California overturned that state's

Supreme Court decision and reinstated capital punishment. The highest courts of North Carolina and Delaware took judicial action to make death a mandatory sentence in certain cases. A handful of other states have sentenced people to death under old statutes that may or may not meet Supreme Court requirements.

All told, as shown by a study prepared by the N.A.A.C.P. Legal Defense and Educational Fund, 72 people now are on Death Row—31 in North Carolina, 17 in Florida, eight in Georgia, five in Massachusetts, three in Texas, two in Montana, and one each in New Mexico, Pennsylvania, South Carolina, Utah, Louisiana and Virginia.

What brought about the reversal? Crime rates are on the increase, including violent crimes, but not in a pattern that suggests the near-abolition of the death penalty had anything to do with the rise. Death-penalty states had rises as sharp as those without it, sometimes more so. Moreover, a chart in the Federal Government's new book, "Social Indicators 1973," shows that murder and negligent manslaughter occurred at a steady rate of about 10 per 100,000 of population in every year from 1933 through 1972, a period that included, first, a high number of executions, then zero executions for such crimes.

Yet, all the same tired and deceiving arguments are being made by death-penalty advocates like Senator McClellan of Arkansas—it deters murder, it protects society, it makes a rapist think twice. There is not a shred of statistical evidence to support any such claim, any more than there was five years ago, or ten. Capital punishment may be justified, by those who wish to do so, as sheer societal revenge; but those who maintain that it is a deterrent were shown up as the hypocrites they are by the "repulsive" amendment proposed by Senator Harold Hughes of Iowa.

Senator Hughes, a bold and humane man, would have required all executions ordered under the Senate bill to be carried out publicly, even televised. He argued that if there is any deterrence in death, surely that would emphasize it. But one of the arguments of the California Supreme Court in 1971 had been that the modern public, not accustomed to hangings in the town square, and however it might theoretically approve capital punishment, would rebel against having actually to watch the death sentence being carried out. Sure enough, the Senate rejected the Hughes amendment, 81 to 10, exposing the deterrence argument for the sham it is.

What, in fact, is happening is that politicians everywhere are selling out to the public's heightened fear of crime. Most of them are under no real illusion that capital punishment will actually prevent crime or protect the public. Given the absence of executions since 1967, and the likelihood of a new Supreme Court review of the matter, probably most of them do not really expect anyone to be killed by their legislation.

It can only be hoped that they are right, that this bloodthirsty posturing is only that although white Americans need not worry too much in any case. When 631 persons on the old Death Row were reprieved in 1972, 57.7 per cent of them were nonwhite. Of the 72 persons already on the new Death Row, 41 are black and one is an Indian —58.3 per cent nonwhite. No change there, either.

—Tom Wicker, *The New York Times*, March 15, 1974

"I HAVE NEVER SEEN A RICH MAN EXECUTED . . ."

I'm against capital punishment, not for emotional or moral reasons, but because it is unfair, inconsistent, and wasteful. It's unfair because it usually hits the poor man, rarely the rich one. It's inconsistent because the ground rules vary from state to state, even from court to court. And it's wasteful because it deprives society of manpower that could be useful.

Clinton Duffy, the former San Quentin warden, who presided over ninety executions and witnessed many more, has often pointed up the unfairness by saying, "I have never seen a rich man executed by the state." My husband Bill puts it less elegantly: "Only the poor slobs go to the gas chamber."

There are endless weapons of possible defense if a killer can afford them. But they may require costly investigation, lengthy witness searches, time-consuming research, heavy traveling expenses, and the help of a large staff of assistants. The gathering of evidence is never cheap.

The attorney with nothing to spend must keep his defense within his means. But the one with plenty of money can mastermind a campaign almost guaranteed to save his client's life. With the proper tools, he may be able to plant "reasonable doubt" in the mind of the jury. Perhaps he can show cause for a second-degree verdict, a recommendation for leniency, or even acquittal. Perhaps he can get a hung jury by convincing one member of the defendant's innocence, thus making a guilty verdict impossible. He can figure out various interpretations of the law to keep his client out of the gas chamber.

I don't remember a single person condemned to death in California who had unlimited funds for counsel at the time of his original trial. They were all forced to depend on court-appointed lawyers, whose resources were pitifully small. The only convict I knew who ever had a lot of money to spend was Chessman, and his funds came too late. The money helped keep him alive for years *after* his death sentence, but it didn't come in time to prevent him from being sentenced in the first place. Until *Cell 2455, Death Row* was published he had no money at all.

Yet there have been dozens of killers who never saw Death Row because they could pay for an elaborate defense right from the beginning. This had nothing to do with their guilt or innocence. They escaped death because their lawyers had the time and the money to uncover ways of saving them.

—Bernice Freeman Davis, *The Desperate and the Damned*

FIGHTING TO KEEP ALIVE

So, when brought to Death Row, my job was plain: establish, if I could, an illegal or unfairly obtained conviction. Fail and die. At bottom it was that simple, and yet I knew that job would take an awful lot of doing.

The staggering immensity of the task is best suggested by citing a few facts and figures. Thus far, originally based upon 2400 pages of trial record, litigation of the case has involved the preparation and filing of seven appeal briefs, four petitions for writs of mandate, two petitions for writs of prohibition, nine petitions for writs of *habeas corpus*, four petitions for rehearing, four petitions for a certificate of probable cause to appeal, five petitions for stays of execution, four petitions for writs of *certiorari*, with either supporting briefs or memorandums of points and authorities usually accompanying the petitions; two motions to augment and correct record, three motions for hearings, and a complaint in equity; plus numerous other incidental papers necessarily prepared and filed. These documents listed contain more than 450,000 words in all.

I estimate that at least three thousand hours were consumed in actual preparation, while I have spent, conservatively, another ten thousand hours in study. (Attorney fees are computed ordinarily at $20 an hour. At this rate, even assuming only one-tenth of the study and research I had made would have been necessary for an attorney, it would have cost me a minimum of $60,000 and probably closer to $100,000 had I paid counsel to litigate the case for me.)

My legal study and research has involved the partial or complete reading of some two thousand legal books, journals, reports, texts and the like. Notes taken from these total another half a million carefully organized words. Because I was unable to find texts bearing precisely on what I needed and wanted, I drafted for my own use a two-hundred-page text on *habeas corpus* and a four-hundred-page text on federal practice and procedure as it relates to state court convictions.

Opposing me at one time or another, either singly or in groups of from two to six, have been eleven different lawyers for the state. In addition to those, there are several more lawyers working for the state who have had a hand in opposing me but who have not formally appeared as counsel in the courts.

On several occasions since coming to the Death Row, I have been removed from the prison and personally appeared in the courts to prosecute habeas corpus proceedings in my own behalf. And I have been obliged to write and receive more than two thousand letters of a legal character while conducting the litigation and digging out facts and evidence from every imaginable quarter.

All this simply in fighting to keep myself alive!

—*Caryl Chessman's Own Story*

I'VE BEEN THERE BEFORE (by Joshua Hill)

We used to watch him strolling
Up and down the tier,
His lively footsteps falling
From the front back to the rear.

He'd look at everybody
With a grin upon his face
And it seemed like he was happy
To be here in this place.

And if you were to ask him
About that smile he wore
He'd say "I keep on smiling
'Cause I've been there before."

We'd ask him to explain himself
But all he'd do was grin
So no one knew the secret
Of where it was he'd been.

Well, he was executed
Just the other day
And I heard he kept on smiling
In that same familiar way.

I also heard he whispered
As they closed the Chamber door
"Death ain't nothing to me
'Cause I've been there before."

—Stephen Levine, ed., *Death Row*

A STORY
(by Clinton Duffy,
San Quentin warden)

Here is a story for those who may believe in capital punishment. It began when I was a young man growing up in a prison town. There was a man and his wife who used to come to San Quentin with their son, to visit their aunt and uncle who also had a boy my age. The three of us became buddies, a threesome. He used to come on the weekends when the executions were on Friday. And he would argue with me: "Get rid of these beasts. They're no good. Drown them all. Hang 'em. Shoot 'em. Get them out of our hair. No need of keeping them in these penitentiaries. Kill 'em all." And I would say, "No, it's wrong to kill." And as we grew up, we argued. He married; he was a little bit older. A boy was born. I used to play with the youngster. I used to ride him around San Quentin on my bicycle.

He grew up. He killed a merchant in San Francisco. He was sentenced to be executed. I was the warden. And this man who had been so adamant about capital punishment —a professional man—came and told me, "Clint, you have to help me save my boy. I used to say 'get rid of all these beasts; they're no good.' Here my boy is going to be executed. The only child we have—our own flesh and blood. You have to help me save him."

I had to lead that boy into the gas chamber. The man, within four or five months, died of a broken heart and alcoholism. Why didn't he stay with his belief in capital punishment for his own child? It was good enough for somebody else, but not good enough for him.

—Stephen Levine, ed., *Death Row*

HE WAS A...
WISP OF A MAN...

It was in Burma, a sodden morning of the rains. A sickly light, like yellow tinfoil, was slanting over the high walls into the jail yard. We were waiting outside the condemned cells, a row of sheds fronted with double bars, like small animal cages. Each cell measured about ten feet by ten and was quite bare within except for a plank bed and a pot of drinking water. In some of them brown silent men were squatting at the inner bars, with their blankets draped round them. These were the condemned men, due to be hanged within the next week or two.

One prisoner had been brought out of his cell. He was a Hindu, a puny wisp of a man, with a shaven head and vague liquid eyes. He had a thick, sprouting moustache, absurdly too big for his body, rather like the moustache of a comic man on the films. Six tall Indian warders were guarding him and getting him ready for the gallows. Two of them stood by with rifles and fixed bayonets, while the

others handcuffed him, passed a chain through his handcuffs and fixed it to their belts, and lashed his arms tight
to his sides. They crowded very close about him, with their
hands always on him in a careful, caressing grip, as though
all the while feeling him to make sure he was there. It was
like men handling a fish which is still alive and may jump
back into the water. But he stood quite unresisting, yield-
ing his arms limply to the ropes, as though he hardly
noticed what was happening. . . .

We set out for the gallows. Two warders marched on
either side of the prisoner, with their rifles at the slope;
two others marched close against him, gripping him by
arm and shoulder, as though at once pushing and supporting him. The rest of us, magistrates and the like, followed
behind. Suddenly, when we had gone ten yards, the pro-
cession stopped short without any order or warning. A
dreadful thing had happened—a dog, come goodness
knows whence, had appeared in the yard. It came bound-
ing among us with a loud volley of barks, and leapt round
us wagging its whole body, wild with glee at finding so
many human beings together. It was a large woolly dog,
half Airedale, half pariah. For a moment it pranced round
us, and then, before anyone could stop it, it had made a
dash for the prisoner, and jumping up tried to lick his face.
Everyone stood aghast, too taken aback even to grab at
the dog.

"Who let that bloody brute in here?" said the superintendent angrily. "Catch it, someone!"

A warder, detached from the escort, charged clumsily
after the dog, but it danced and gambolled just out of his
reach, taking everything as part of the game. A young
Eurasian jailer picked up a handful of gravel and tried to
stone the dog away, but it dodged the stones and came
after us again. Its yaps echoed from the jail walls. The
prisoner, in the grasp of the two warders, looked on in-

curiously, as though this was another formality of the hanging. It was several minutes before someone managed to catch the dog. Then we put my handkerchief through its collar and moved off once more, with the dog still straining and whimpering.

It was about forty yards to the gallows. I watched the bare brown back of the prisoner marching in front of me. He walked clumsily with his bound arms, but quite steadily, with that bobbing gait of the Indian who never straightens his knees. At each step his muscles slid neatly into place, the lock of hair on his scalp danced up and down, his feet printed themselves on the wet gravel. And once, in spite of the men who gripped him by each shoulder, he stepped slightly aside to avoid a puddle on the path.

It is curious, but till that moment I had never realised what it means to destroy a healthy, conscious man. When I saw the prisoner step aside to avoid the puddle, I saw the mystery, the unspeakable wrongness, of cutting a life short when it is in full tide. This man was not dying, he was alive just as we were alive. All the organs of his body were working—bowels digesting food, skin renewing itself, nails growing, tissues forming—all toiling away in solemn foolery. His nails would still be growing when he stood on the drop, when he was falling through the air with a tenth of a second to live. His eyes saw the yellow gravel and the grey walls, and his brain still remembered, foresaw, reasoned—reasoned even about puddles. He and we were a party of men walking together, seeing, hearing, feeling, understanding the same world; and in two minutes, with a sudden snap, one of us would be gone—one mind less, one world less. . . .

We stood waiting, five yards away. The warders had formed in a rough circle round the gallows. And then, when the noose was fixed, the prisoner began crying out on his god. It was a high, reiterated cry of "Ram! Ram! Ram! Ram!", not urgent and fearful like a prayer or a cry for help, but steady, rhythmical, almost like the tolling of a bell. The dog answered the sound with a whine. The hangman, still standing on the gallows, produced a small cotton bag like a flour bag and drew it down over the prisoner's face. But the sound, muffled by the cloth, still persisted, over and over again: "Ram! Ram! Ram! Ram! Ram!"

The hangman climbed down and stood ready, holding the lever. Minutes seemed to pass. The steady, muffled crying from the prisoner went on and on, "Ram! Ram! Ram!" never faltering for an instant. The superintendent, his head on his chest, was slowly poking the ground with his stick; perhaps he was counting the cries, allowing the prisoner a fixed number—fifty, perhaps, or a hundred. Everyone had changed colour. The Indians had gone grey like bad coffee, and one or two of the bayonets were wavering. We looked at the lashed, hooded man on the drop, and listened to his cries—each cry another second of life; the same thought was in all our minds: oh, kill him quickly, get it over, stop that abominable noise!

Suddenly the superintendent made up his mind. Throwing up his head he made a swift motion with his stick. "Chalo!" he shouted almost fiercely.

There was a clanking noise, and then dead silence. The prisoner had vanished, and the rope was twisting on itself. I let go of the dog, and it galloped immediately to the back of the gallows; but when it got there it stopped short, barked, and then retreated into a corner of the yard, where it stood among the weeds, looking timorously out at us. We went round the gallows to inspect the prisoner's body. He was dangling with his toes pointed straight downwards, very slowly revolving, as dead as a stone.

The superintendent reached out with his stick and

poked the bare body; it oscillated slightly. *"He's* all right," said the superintendent. He backed out from under the gallows, and blew out a deep breath. The moody look had gone out of his face quite suddenly. He glanced at his wrist-watch. "Eight minutes past eight. Well, that's all for this morning, thank God."

—George Orwell, *Collected Essays, An Age Like This*

THE RIGHT TO LIVE

If, therefore, there is a desire to maintain the death penalty, let us at least be spared the hypocrisy of a justification by example. Let us be frank about that penalty which can have no publicity, that intimidation which works only on respectable people, so long as they are respectable, which fascinates those who have ceased to be respectable and debases or deranges those who take part in it. It is a penalty, to be sure, a frightful torture, both physical and moral, but it provides no sure example except a demoralizing one. It punishes, but it forestalls nothing; indeed, it may even arouse the impulse to murder. It hardly seems to exist, except for the man who suffers it—in his soul for months and years, in his body during the desperate and violent hour when he is cut in two without suppressing his life. Let us call it by the name which, for lack of any other nobility, will at least give the nobility of truth, and let us recognize it for what it is essentially: a revenge. . . .
. . . Without absolute innocence, there is no supreme judge. Now, we have all done wrong in our lives even if that wrong, without falling within the jurisdiction of the laws, went as far as the unknown crime. There are no just

people—merely hearts more or less lacking in justice. Living at least allows us to discover this and to add to the sum of our actions a little of the good that will make up in part for the evil we have added to the world. Such a right to live, which allows a chance to make amends, is the natural right of every man, even the worst man. The lowest of criminals and the most upright of judges meet side by side, equally wretched in their solidarity. Without that right, moral life is utterly impossible. None among us is authorized to despair of a single man, except after his death, which transforms his life into destiny and then permits a definitive judgment. But pronouncing the definitive judgment before his death, decreeing the closing of accounts when the creditor is still alive, is no man's right. On this limit, at least, whoever judges absolutely condemns himself absolutely.

—Albert Camus, *"Reflections on the Guillotine"*

Biographical Notes

CARYL CHESSMAN. See biographical notes, chapter 3.

JOSHUA HILL. Prisoner No. A–89495, Josh has been on Death Row in San Quentin since he was nineteen.

CLINTON DUFFY (b. 1898). Beginning his correctional career as a secretary to the warden of San Quentin, Duffy was appointed warden in 1940. He served in that capacity for eleven years. During that time, having witnessed over 150 executions, he became an avowed opponent of capital punishment; since his retirement, he lectures and writes on behalf of its abolition.

11.

ESCAPE!

**Lord, I'm trouble, trouble
Jail break due some day.**

—Josh White

Even in the outside world, many of us try to escape from the pressures of competitive life. We do this in socially acceptable ways: through excessive watching of television, meaningless sexual encounters, compulsive buying of useless objects—the ways are endless and varied.

But for those inside, escape is most often toward life. Some are lucky and make it over the wall. Others escape for only a moment; once caught, they will have more than enough time to remember that moment (in solitary). A few —devoid of hope—make the total escape: for them, suicide is the sure way out.

Whether escape is toward or from life, "rehabilitation" provides the motive of despair.

Lord, I'm trouble, trouble
Makes me weep and moan
Lord, I'm trouble, trouble
Since the day I was born.
Lord, I'm trouble, trouble
Sure won't make me stay
Lord, I'm trouble, trouble
Jail break due some day.

—Josh White, "Trouble"

THE HUNTED

Saturday, November 11—Today there was an escape attempt. Three men tried to break out the front gate, using hostages. They forced Dr. Rinck, the chief medical officer, and his secretary, to walk with them at dagger point to the inner door of the gate, where Dr. Rinck asked the guards to open up. The "daggers" were a scalpel and the two blades of a pair of scissors the men had secreted in the hospital.

I shall never forget the experience of the two hours this morning when the break was being tried and thwarted! One reads, with tongue in cheek, of times when the air is "electric with tension," suspecting that the electricity was generated by the author's own imaginative dynamo. Today the atmosphere was exactly that. From the moment the siren's wail rose for the third time, which confirmed it as an escape warning, the tension began to rise. You could feel it in inmates and guards alike, something entirely apart from the superficial excitement and chattering going on.

We were rushed back to our quarters and the cell doors double-locked, while members of the staff ran for their assigned spots in the prison's prearranged plan to deal with escape. And the tension kept rising, paced by the never-ceasing wail of the siren.

It sounds paradoxical to speak of prison life as having a veneer of civilization—but it has. No inmate is ever in doubt as to his inferior status, of course, but there is a pretense of civilized behavior generally. With the escape attempt, that disappeared. There were two groups of people: the hunted and the hunters, and we all knew at once to which group we belonged. Every man of us, including the COs, was with the hunted. We did not know who they were, or what they had done or were doing, but profanely and bitterly we prayed the hopeless prayer that they'd make it—that the sons of bitches with guns and clubs would be outwitted.

The prison was not noisy, aside from the siren. The men did not howl or scream, but were unnaturally silent. We walked restlessly back and forth in our cells, and occasionally shouted something unimportant to one another through the doors or windows, and felt our hearts pound heavily in tempo with the siren. All the decent, peaceful, neighborly living outside seemed centuries and leagues away. *This* was the real thing: hunter and hunted! *This* was man's real nature: peril and hatred and terror his bedfellows.

The two-time losers told us amateur lawbreakers what dire things would follow the break. If the men were not found, they said, we would all be kept in our quarters, without meals even, indefinitely. One man had gone through a break where no one had had any meals for 72 hours. (We glanced worriedly at the slim commissary stores in our lockers, and reflected ruefully that they would not last any 72 hours.) Other men told us that the prison would be "much rougher" for months now: guards would tighten up, infractions of minor rules would be punished severely, the little existing fraternization between hacks and inmates would disappear. We only half listened: the wail of the siren kept stirring something primitive and reasonless and terribly frightened in us.

Then, suddenly, the siren stopped. We pressed against our windows, trying to see through the bars toward the front, where the action seemed to be taking place. There was a shot, muffled by the buildings but unmistakably a shot. Some of the men in our block could see the smoke, but no one could tell who was doing the shooting or at what. Then one of the would-be fugitives ran across our limited field of vision and disappeared around a corner of the building, closely pursued by two guards wielding wicked-looking pick handles. We could not understand what he hoped to gain by running, since he was inside the wall, but I suppose a man runs instinctively when men with pick handles come for him. The other two passed immediately after, flanked by more guards. I could recognize only one of them then: a 36-year-old military prisoner, in on a homo rap, who was grinning as he walked by. I know the guy—in fact, he sat directly across from me at breakfast this morning. I would have thought him not especially bright but relatively harmless. He had only a five-year sentence, which is short for military prisoners, and would have come up for parole next spring. Now, of course, he'll get an additional "bit" to do.

When I got back to the office this afternoon I learned who the other two were. One is a chap named Rush, whom I don't know, but who was in for 16 years, military. The other was the young kidnaper, Tom, of whom I wrote in here before. He also sat at breakfast with me this morning. He is 19 years old and is serving a civil sentence of 77 years! A boy still in his teens—he must have been 17 when he was sentenced—for whom society could find no better fate than three-quarters of a century of incarceration!

He is a tough boy—there is no doubt about that. It would require a hopeless sentimentalist to gloss over his crime, but that hardly justifies the retaliation society has wreaked on him. I have never approved of capital punishment, but I should rather be executed than condemned to rot my life away in a cell. And what good does it do? For a boy of 19, life in here under such a sentence must be such torture as would repay the deed he did many times over. He is a frustrated boy, with a warped and perverted mind, but no psychiatrist can change him under such conditions. And for years, I should guess, he will continue to be a threat to the lives of guards as he plots desperately for another "all-or-nothing" attempt. As Mr. Schick said when we came to the office this afternoon, "In his shoes, I'd keep trying any way there was until I was free or dead . . ."

Everyone takes it for granted that the three men have been beaten up, down in solitary. The procedure, I am told, is to send in several of the huskier guards, who proceed methodically to punch the men into insensibility. I cannot either prove or disprove that story for the obvious reason that no inmates will be allowed to see them, but two of the parole officers have all but admitted to me that such is the case.

Guards were more plentiful and sterner looking when we finally were let out of our cells for dinner. I suspect that the "rougher" time ahead will not be wholly imaginary. . . .

It is doubtful if the doggedness with which our system of "justice" goes on doing the wrong thing in a given case was ever more clearly demonstrated than in the sequel to the cases of Martin, Anders, and Rush. Martin, as I have already noted, was a near-moron with a five-year military sentence for sodomy. He had no previous criminal record, according to the parole officer with whom I discussed the escape during the next week, and might well have been paroled next spring. Apart from his homosexual tendencies, which flowered in the Army and were presumably reinforced by the even more unnatural atmosphere of prison, he was a good-natured, relatively harmless guy.

Rush, according to the same parole officer, began his current prison career with a six-month military sentence for some minor offense. He attempted to escape, was caught, and had a couple years more added to his sentence. He tried again, and the same thing happened. BY THE TIME HE REACHED LEWISBURG, HE HAD PILED UP SIXTEEN YEARS IN SENTENCES AS A RESULT OF AN ORIGINAL OFFENSE FOR WHICH EVEN THE ARMY, NOTORIOUS FOR HEAVY PENALTIES, HAD GIVEN HIM ONLY SIX MONTHS! "Rush," said the parole officer, "is one of the guys you see now and then who literally can't endure confinement. He'll keep trying till he makes it or is killed!"—almost the same words with which Mr. Schick had forecast Tom Anders' future.

Anders himself I have already written about. What impulses drove him to the crime he committed I don't know; what I do know is that a sentence of three-quarters of a century is so fantastically cruel as to stun the imagination. On Anders himself, of course, its effect was to produce a state of perpetual desperation and a determination to escape at any price.

A few weeks after the escape attempt the three men were taken in a prison bus to Harrisburg, where they were quickly tried and sentenced to AN ADDITIONAL TWENTY-ONE YEARS each for attempted escape, and ordered transferred to Alcatraz. When I typed up the cards that went with them, I noted that Anders' sentence, with "good time," would expire in the year 2014, and that he would be eligible for parole in 2007!

—Alfred Hassler, *Diary of a Self-Made Convict*

ALCATRAZ: THEY DIDN'T COME TO STAY

Ralph Roe and Ted Cole were from Oklahoma, as their easy drawling speech suggested. Roe, thirty-two, a lanky, friendly sort, serving ninety-nine years for bank robberies, once escaped from McAlester Prison in Oklahoma by riding out on a truck hidden in a crate. Cole, seven years younger, runt-sized but hard and crafty, was a murderer at seventeen, saved from execution by his mother's eloquent appeal. He later killed a cellmate at McAlester, then managed an escape as uncomplicated as Roe's from that prison, in a laundry bag. Picked up on a federal kidnap rap and awaiting trial, he fled the county jail in a garbage can. He was easily recaptured, but continued to saw cell bars and, on trips to court, to wriggle out of leg irons. When he landed on The Rock, to do fifty years, he boasted, "Don't think I'll like it here. Doubt I'll stay long."

On December 16, 1937, a tulle fog, a motionless mist, clung to the bay. Roe and Cole worked in the ground-floor mat shop on the north tip of the island, making rubber mats for the Navy out of used tires. The guard counted in the crew at one o'clock, then went to the adjacent machine shop. Roe and Cole ran to a window where they had already cut two bars, concealing their handiwork with a smear. They now bent the bars, broke two panes (the sound apparently drowned by the noise in the machine shop), sawed a sash and slipped out, taking along a Stillson wrench. They moved through the fog, invisible to the tower guards; smashed a gate lock in the cyclone fence and tossed the wrench aside; groped to the edge of a cliff and jumped twenty feet onto a mound of discarded casings from the mat shop. They plunged on into the bay.

At one-thirty the guard returned to the mat shop for the half-hour count, found Roe and Cole missing, discovered the smashed window, phoned the Armorer. For the first time since Alcatraz became a superbastille, the warden heard the rising wail of the siren. It was a signal to herd the prisoners back to their cells; a summons to off-duty guards to grab a rifle from the armory and get with it; a call to the skipper of the launch to cast off and warily circle the island.

Throughout the afternoon and night the cell house rang with a great clamor as the convicts celebrated. Roe and

Cole had proved that the unbeatable Rock could be beaten.

Did they survive? At the time they struck out, an ebb tide was racing past Alcatraz and out the Golden Gate at seven knots, about eight miles an hour. "Small boats could not have bucked that current," said Lloyd C. Whaley, a San Francisco city engineer. "A strong swimmer starting at Alcatraz would have found himself going out the Gate in the fog before he had expended sufficient energy to reach shore in still water." . . .

. . . Still, some insist, an escaping Alcatraz convict has one big factor in his favor: incentive. . . .

Other escapes were marked by greater artistry and less risk. One prisoner who did clerical work vanished but did not, as Roe and Cole presumably did, go out the Gate on a swift ebb tide. On a day when the commandant was off the island, he simply wrote out an order for his own release, forged the commandant's signature, put on his cap, trotted down to the wharf, presented it to the sentry, boarded the boat, rode over to Fort Mason, walked down the gangplank, presented the order to that sentry, caught a streetcar downtown.

On another occasion, an officer on the commandant's staff died, and the widow ordered a mourning outfit from the city. Not long after it arrived, the widow, weeping behind the heavy black veil, appeared at the wharf. The sentry, reluctant to ask her to produce her pass, considerately helped her onto the boat. The dock sentry at Fort Mason, equally sympathetic, helped her off and on her way. Hours later the commandant's office received an inquiry from the widow—about her mourning outfit.

—J. Campbell Bruce, *Escape from Alcatraz*

LISETTE

It was 1941. I'd been in prison eleven years. I was thirty-five. I'd spent the best years of my life in either a cell or a dungeon. The only freedom I'd had was the seven months with my Indian tribe. The children I had by my two Indian wives must be eight years old. Jesus! How the time had flown! But as I looked back, those hours and minutes became cruelly long, each one seperately imbedded in my stations of the cross.

Thirty-five years! Where were Montmartre, Pigalle, the Place Blanche, the ball at the Petit Jardin, the Boulevard de Clichy? Where was big Nénette with her madonna's face, like a cameo, and her huge black eyes filled with despair as she cried out at the trial, "Don't worry, baby, I'll get you out of there!" Where was Raymond Hubert with his "We'll be acquitted"? And the prosecutor? How were my father and my sisters' families doing under the German occupation?

So many *cavales*. [From *cavaler*, to beat it, or scram, especially from the police.] How many had there been?

The first was when I knocked out the guards and escaped from the hospital.

The second was in Colombia, at Rio Hacha.

That was a beautiful *cavale*. A real success. Why did I leave my tribe? A quiver of physical longing flowed through my body. It was as if I were feeling again the sensations of making love to my wives.

Then there were the third, fourth, fifth and six at Baranquilla. What lousy luck I had had with those *cavales!* The stunt at mass that ended so badly. . . . The dynamite that fizzled, and the next time when Clousiot's damn pants caught . . . and the sleeping potion that wouldn't work. . . .

The seventh was on Royale when that filthy bastard, Bébert Celier, ratted on me. That one would have worked for sure if it hadn't been for him. If he had kept his trap shut, I'd be free with my poor buddy Carbonieri.

And the last one, the eighth, from the asylum. A mistake, a stupid-ass mistake on my part. I should never have let the Italian choose our launching place. Two hundred yards farther down, near the butcher's, would have been a much better place. . . .

Dreyfus' bench, where that innocent man condemned to death had found the courage to go on living, would inspire me. I would not admit defeat. I would try another *cavale*.

Right. This silky, polished stone hanging out over the rocky shore, where the waves pounded and broke without letup, would inspire me. Dreyfus never gave up; he fought for his vindication to the very end. True, he had Emile Zola and his famous *"J'accuse."* But all the same, if he hadn't had a will of iron, the injustices he suffered would surely have sent him hurtling into the abyss from this very bench. He had held on. I could not be a lesser man than he. But I would give up the idea of a "win or die" *cavale*. I'd forget about the "dying" and concentrate exclusively on winning and being free.

During the long hours I spent sitting on Dreyfus' bench, my brain shuttled between dreams of the past and of a rosy future. Often my eyes would become dazzled by the glare and the platinum reflections of the breaking waves. From looking at the sea so long—almost without seeing it really—I came to know every quirk of the wind and waves. Tirelessly the sea attacked the island's exposed rocks. It worked away at them, searched and stripped them as if to say, Diable, go, disappear, you're in my way, you bar my passage to Grande Terre! That is why, every day, relentlessly, I remove a little piece of you.

When there was a storm, the sea gave Diable the full

force of its fury, raging in to snatch its piece of the island, then sweeping it away. It hurled its water into every nook and cranny so as to undermine little by little the giant rocks that seemed to say, You shall not pass.

And that's how I made a very important discovery. Immediately opposite Dreyfus' bench were some enormous craggy rocks that the waves broke against with particular violence. The tons of water had no place to go because the two rocks formed a horseshoe about five or six yards wide and a cliff rose directly above them, leaving the waves no exit except back out into the sea.

What made this important was that if, just as the wave was flinging itself into the chasm, I was to take a sack of coconuts and jump from the rock directly into its center, it would beyond the shadow of a doubt take me with it as it retreated.

I knew where I could find the jute bags for the coconuts; there were plenty of them in the pigsty.

The first thing was to test my theory. During the full moon the tides were higher, hence the waves were bigger. I would wait for the full moon. I hid my carefully sewn bag of dry coconuts in a cave I knew which could only be reached from the water. I had come upon it one day when I was looking for *langoustines*. The shellfish clung to its ceiling, which was completely under water except at low tide. To the bag of coconuts I strapped another bag containing a rock weighing between eighty and ninety pounds. Since I'd be leaving with two bags instead of one, and I weighed a hundred and fifty-five pounds, the proportions were about right.

I was very excited about the experiment. This side of the island was taboo. Nobody would ever suspect that the most windswept and dangerous spot on the island would be used for an escape.

Besides, it was the only place where, if I did manage to

get clear of the coast, I would be carried out into the open sea without the hazard of cracking up on Royale.

This had to be the place.

The bag of coconuts and the rock were heavy and hard to carry. I wouldn't be able to do it alone so I spoke to Chang, who said he'd come and help me. He brought along some fishing tackle and heavy lines; if we were caught, we could say we were setting up traps for sharks.

"Keep pushing, Chang. A little farther and we're there."

The light of the full moon made it as bright as day. The noise of the waves was deafening. Chang said, "Ready, Papillon? Into this next one?" A fifteen-foot wave lunged at the rocks as if possessed and broke just below us, but the shock was so violent that the crest passed over us and drenched us. Still we were able to throw the sacks in at the moment the wave went into reverse. Like a straw, the bag was swept back toward the open sea.

"That's it, Chang! It works."

"Wait and see if it comes back."

Sure enough. My heart sank when, five minutes later, I saw my bag riding back on the crest of a wave over twenty feet high. It smashed against the rocks, scattering the coconuts in every direction and tumbling the rock into the chasm below.

Wet to the bone, battered and almost swept off our feet, Chang and I left that bedeviled place without so much as a backward glance.

"No good, Papillon. No good, *cavale* from Diable. Royale better. Leave from south coast, much better."

"Yes, but an escape from Royale would be discovered in less than two hours. The bag of coconuts moves only with the waves—they'd catch me in no time. Here there's no boat, and I have the whole night before they find out I'm gone, and even then they'll probably think I drowned while fishing. Also there's no telephone on Diable. If I leave in a heavy sea, they'll have no way of communicating with Royale. So here is where I have to leave from. But how?"

The noon sun was leaden—a tropical sun to boil the brain in your skull; a sun that shriveled the plants not yet grown strong enough to resist it; a sun that, in a few hours, dried up all but the deepest saltwater pools, leaving only a white film of salt; a sun that set the air to dancing—it literally moved before my eyes—its reflection on the water burning my pupils. But that did not prevent me from returning to Dreyfus' bench and taking up again my study of the sea. It was then I discovered what an idiot I'd been.

Only one wave out of every seven was as large as the monster that had flung my sack back against the rocks. The others were little more than half its size. From noon to sundown I watched to see if this was always so, if there wasn't an occasional shift or whim that altered the regularity.

There wasn't. The ground swell never came sooner, never came later. There were six waves about twenty feet high, then, forming about three hundred yards from shore, the ground swell. It came in straight as a cannonball, growing in size and height as it approached. There was hardly any spray on its crest compared to the other six, very little, in fact. It had its own special noise, like far-off thunder. When it broke on the two rocks and hurled itself into the passage between them, crushing against the cliff, its great mass caused it to choke and turn on itself. Then, after ten or fifteen seconds, the eddies would work their way out with a wild churning, tearing off huge stones and rolling them back and forth, making a rumble like a hundred wagonloads of stones being dumped.

I put a dozen coconuts in a sack and added a fifty-pound rock. As the ground swell broke, I threw the sack in. I couldn't follow it with my eyes because of the spray, but I saw it for a second as the water was sucked back to the sea. It did not return. The next six waves lacked the strength to throw it back on shore, and by the time the seventh had formed three hundred yards out, the sack must have drifted beyond it, for I didn't see it again.

Bursting with excitement, I went back to camp. I had it! I had found the perfect launching. No question of luck here. Still I would do another trial run, this time under the conditions of the real *cavale*: two sacks of coconuts tied together and, on top, two or three rocks weighing a total of a hundred and fifty-five pounds. I told Chang about it and he listened closely.

"It's good, Papillon. I think you got it. I help you for real thing. Wait for high tide twenty-five feet. Soon equinox."

With Chang's help and that of the twenty-five-foot equinoctial tide, we threw the two sacks and three rocks into the famous wave.

"What was name of little girl you tried save on Saint-Joseph?"

"Lisette."

"We call wave that take you away Lisette. O.K.?"

"O.K."

Lisette arrived with the roar of an express train pulling into a station. Standing straight as a rampart, she grew larger with every second. It was an impressive sight. She broke with such power that Chang and I were swept off the rock and the sacks fell into the chasm. In the flash of a second we realized we couldn't hold onto the rock, so we threw ourselves back—which didn't protect us from a mighty soaking but did prevent our falling into the chasm. This happened at ten in the morning. We weren't taking any risk because the three guards were busy doing inventory at the other end of the island. The sacks were carried off— we could see them clearly far out from shore. Were they beyond the ground swell? We waited. The six waves that followed Lisette were not able to catch them. Lisette came and went a second time, but still no sacks. They were beyond her reach.

We climbed quickly up to Dreyfus' bench to see if we could see them again and, to our joy, we caught sight of them four different times riding the crest of the waves. And these waves were not coming toward Diable but heading west. We had the proof. I would sail toward the great adventure on the back of Lisette.

—Henri Charrière, *Papillon*

"DEATH TAKE MY PLACE IN LIFE" ("The Psychiatric Unit" by Nellie Sloan)

The rooms in the Psychiatric Unit were like what I imagine the maximum part of a mental hospital to be. There were steel doors and bars, and the whole atmosphere seemed gray and depressive. I never knew when the quiet would be interrupted by someone trying to kill herself, or someone else, or maybe just kill the time by screaming all night, loud, obscene screams, screams that often would begin with a whimper of self-pity and end in a violent, crashing tone of twisted sorrow and hate. In the beginning the sudden explosion of some woman's undirected, uncontrolled hate (a hate so complete and without object that it seemed to be directed at the very cosmos itself) terrified me. I began to wonder how long it would be before I, too, would be acting the same way. Yet, as time passed, I got used to those unpredictable cataclysms of agony, which sometimes ended in the woman being dragged to one of the "quiet cells," as they were tactfully called. The quiet cells were six stripped cells which were used to entomb those who became too loud and hard to handle, or for those who could no longer stand the volcanic misery that tore at their insides. These women were thrown into a bare cell, naked, and with nothing except the chilling certainty that now they were really alone with their misery.

The women like myself who were in the Psych Unit on the ninety-day program were mixed in with the women who were there for long periods of treatment. Most of the women not on the new program were in the Psych Unit to stay, perhaps for their full prison term, for they were considered incorrigible and dangerous to the harmony of those living on the main "campus." There were women in the Psych Unit that desperately needed help. Unfortunately, the help that was given did not always succeed. I learned that heartbreaking fact—a fact that even now, over a year later, somehow makes me feel a deep sense of personal failure—on Christmas Eve. We were decorating the tree when it happened, laughing and talking continuously, trying to forget where we were by losing ourselves in the spirit of the occasion. Dee, the young girl with whom I had become very close friends, was not in the room helping us, and I was having such a good time that I hadn't noticed she was missing. Suddenly, we all heard screams and the crashing of furniture. The supervisor rushed in and ordered us to our rooms. The noise had come from Dee's room, and in a panic I tried to run down the hall toward her. I was stopped and locked in my room. I stayed awake all night hoping one of the supervisors would drop by my room and tell me whether Dee was all right, but no one stopped, even though every supervisor that passed my cell for count found me standing at the bars pleading for information. I saw Dee's

room the next day. She had set fire to her mattress and anything else that would burn. She had broken her chair and
the drawers to her night stand. She had torn all of her
clothing to shreds. Finally in a sudden fit of rebellion and
pain she had cut herself with some glass that she found
somewhere (we were not permitted anything made of
glass), and had written on the wall in her own blood,
"Death take my place in life." In a fit of despair like this
one, the one that ended in her death, Dee would not listen
to authority of any kind, but she would have, I knew, listened to me, but there is not much a friend can do through
a concrete wall.

—Robert Minton, ed., *Inside*

Biographical Notes

ALFRED HASSLER. See notes, chapter 4.

HENRI CHARRIÈRE (d. 1973). Born in France, he was convicted in 1931 of a murder he denied having committed.
He was sent to French Guiana in 1933, and during his
twelve years of imprisonment made nine daring escapes,
only to be recaptured. He was finally successful in 1945
when he escaped from Devil's Island to Venezuela. It was
in Venezuela that he discovered the works of Albertine
Sarrazin (see chapter 4) and was inspired to write his
prison memoirs. He died in Spain of cancer.

NELLIE SLOAN. A narcotics addict, Nellie Sloan was
confined at Corrona, a California correctional facility for
women, and later paroled. She is married to Jack Sloan,
also a former addict.

12.

MISFORTUNE'S WORKSHOP

∴ . . I had never been so truly free . . .

—Malcolm X, Autobiography

The poet Rainer Maria Rilke was moved to write: "With certain prisoners known to history things went so that in the days of complete external privation they strove for and won, in the depths of their being, both themselves and the most inexhaustible freedom."

In spite of isolation and dehumanizing conditions, some individuals have found great inner resources while in prison and become writers, scholars, legal experts, revolutionaries: François Villon, the Marquis de Sade, Nehru, Jean Genet, Malcolm X, Martin Sostre—the names go on through the ages, through all centuries. Their writings, ideas, insights, reforms have been gifts to us, on the outside, at what cost! It is sophistry to argue that such works would not have been accomplished outside of prison: we know what men and women have done, are capable of doing, despite their being confined; we are only beginning to understand how much is lost, will continue to be lost, as long as men and women are imprisoned.

ALBERTA

Alberta, a handsome Negro woman who reminds many people of Lena Horne, was left on the doorstep of a Catholic orphanage in New York City at about three months old. This storybook start in life may sound glamorous but in practical terms it was the only glamor in her life. The nuns were no doubt well-meaning and kind but completely medieval in their thinking. Alberta hated the strict regimentation of her life, the inflexible routine, the severe discipline, the hand-me-down clothes that were all she ever wore. She hated the general gray sameness of every day. At sixteen the sisters found her a job cleaning in a hospital, a room nearby and sent her off to make her fortune with the assurance of the community's prayers.

"I'd never worn lipstick, my hair was still in pigtails, and I just barely knew that boys were different than girls.

"It took me a year to adjust to life in the world but I got hep fast. I didn't do anything you understand, I just kept my eyes and ears open and saw a lot of things. How I hated those pretty white nurses in the hospital. They had everything I wanted. Boyfriends and nice apartments and pretty clothes. I still couldn't afford to buy much, and I lived in one room and cooked on a hot plate. Sometimes all I had for supper was a can of soup. I didn't have any friends either, but I guess that was my fault. I was so full of hate and resentment nobody could possibly like me.

"The only person I ever talked to outside of work was a mulatto guy I saw every night in the diner where I stopped for coffee. One day he just up and says to me, 'Baby, you're sitting on a goldmine. . . .'

"It didn't take me long to figure out what he meant and a few days later I brought it up again. That's how I started prossing. Sounds crazy, huh? Brought up in a convent, out a year and I'm staring at ceilings. If you only knew how I hated being poor nigger trash. When the nuns talked about God I used to sit and say nothing but all the time I was thinking, 'I hate you, God. I hate you for making me black and putting me here.' At Mass I'd say, 'I'm glad they stuck nails in you. . . .' "

When Alberta talked about this part of the story she'd drop her eyes and her voice was barely audible. By the time I knew her, she was a woman of deep and sincere religious convictions and these revelations cost her dearly.

"I worked out of a hotel. My old man made all the arrangements. I stayed in the room and he sent up the tricks. Usually six to ten a night. They paid me and I paid him. Once a month I saw a doctor and he told me how to protect myself from pregnancy or disease. I never felt anything emotionally or physically, it was just a job to me. I used to lie there and think, 'you sucker, you're not such a big man now, are you?' If a customer was white, and most of them were, I used to enjoy it a little. I felt I was getting back at them.

"Who turned me on? Nobody. I did it all by myself. Oh sure, my old man thought it was a good idea. Pimps always prefer to have junkies working for them. It gives them a better hold over you. Anyway I started sniffing cocaine at a party and from there to horse is a short step. I was eighteen when I started. One funny thing about me, my habit never got out of control. I shot once a day regular as clockwork and I never went to sleep without knowing where tomorrow's fix was coming from. Don't ask me why one stayed enough—it just did. The only time I broke the rule was when I'd occasionally speedball (mix cocaine and heroin) at a party. But that was rare. I think one reason my habit never got the upper hand was because of money. It was the only thing I cared about, and I figured if I took off too far I wouldn't be sharp enough to make more. The only reason I started selling junk was to make more money. I didn't need to do that to support my habit. I had a regular group of customers pretty fast, and they knew I was reliable and sold good stuff. Sure I cut it, but never much. You know what else? I continued to work at the hospital. I moved up to a practical nurse job and I worked 3 to 11 shift. I was so busy making money I never had time to spend it. I socked it all away in the bank.

"That's how I lived for ten years and I never even smelled a cop once in all that time. Then I moved into a new apartment in an all white section. I didn't know that one of my neighbors was a cop or that he got suspicious of all the white guys that came to my apartment. I still worked the hotel a few nights a week. The guys that came to my place were dope fiends I sold to. You can cop a fix (buy drugs) a lot faster than you can turn a trick so the fuzz got wise in a while. I never knew anything about it till I went to Connecticut to drop a load. There's good money in that and that's why I did it. The second time I went I got busted with the junk on me. That's five to ten, baby, and it could have been ten to twenty if I didn't have a damn good lawyer.

"You know that one phone call they allow you? I called a priest. I'd known him for a few years. I met him in Central Park, believe it or not. I used to go and talk with him once in a while, and he'd just listen. I didn't believe in anything then, but I kept seeing him anyway. He never pushed me or condemned me, but I guess he must have prayed. When I called him from Hartford he drove up right away. The cops were trying to get me to tell where I bought my junk and I wouldn't do it. He advised me to stick to my guns. 'Alberta,' he said, 'your life won't be worth a plug nickel if you fink.' He was right and I knew it. He's the one that got me the lawyer. I had to sign my bankbook over to that bastard before he'd take my case but he kept me out of a federal pen and it's thanks to him I got five to ten. The day after I was sentenced, Father heard my confession. It was the first time in almost thirteen years and from then on it was up all the way. By that time I'd kicked cold turkey. They were marvelous to me at Niantic. Prison is prison and it's no joke for anyone but I owe that state farm my life."

Indeed she does. Alberta had a rare combination going for her inside. She earned the respect of the girls because she could handle herself, and of the authorities because she

responded phenomenally well to rehabilitative therapy.
However, there are no simple explanations for the apparent success of Alberta's prison term. She received psychotherapy, established close rapport with the chaplain and the correction officers, and did a lot of serious thinking. So do many others, but few profit by it as startlingly as Alberta. Perhaps the seeds of her victory were planted in that orphanage in spite of its inadequacies.

Alberta was paroled to Lataste House [a halfway house] (the chaplain's recommendation) after three years. She spent three months with us during which she did housework by the day. This was the job of her choosing. She didn't want to be in a hospital where she'd be around drugs. The solid common sense way she attacked her problems and the maturity and depth of her piety astounded everyone who came into contact with her. Her parole officer said to me repeatedly, "If I wasn't seeing this with my own eyes I don't think I'd believe it and I've been in this business for fifteen years."

Today Alberta lives with a white family for whom she is the housekeeper and is negotiating to go as a lay worker to some mission, preferably one that works with American Indians. Her record will make it difficult for her to be accepted for such a post, but she faces this as realistically as everything else.

It's still too soon to pronounce Alberta completely free of the jungle. A year of making it relatively on her own must be balanced against thirteen years of vice and crime. On the other hand, can any of us say with certainty what we will do or are capable of doing tomorrow? Alberta, too, is simply you or I with a slight change of detail and circumstance.

—Beverly Byrne, *The Love Seekers*

MALCOLM X

I became increasingly frustrated at not being able to express what I wanted to convey in letters that I wrote, especially those to Mr. Elijah Muhammad. In the street, I had been the most articulate hustler out there—I had commanded attention when I said something. But now, trying to write simple English, I not only wasn't articulate, I wasn't even functional. How would I sound writing in slang, the way I would *say* it, something such as "Look, daddy, let me pull your coat about a cat, Elijah Muhammad—"

Many who today hear me somewhere in person, or on television, or those who read something I've said, will think I went to school far beyond the eighth grade. This impression is due entirely to my prison studies.

It had really begun back in the Charlestown Prison, when Bimbi first made me feel envy of his stock of knowledge. Bimbi had always taken charge of any conversations he was in, and I had tried to emulate him. But every book I picked up had few sentences which didn't contain anywhere from one to nearly all of the words that might as well have been in Chinese. When I just skipped those words, of course, I really ended up with little idea of what the book said. So I had come to the Norfolk Prison Colony still going through only book-reading motions. Pretty soon, I would have quit even these motions, unless I had received the motivation that I did.

I saw that the best thing I could do was get hold of a dictionary—to study, to learn some words. I was lucky enough to reason also that I should try to improve my penmanship. It was sad. I couldn't even write in a straight line. It was both ideas together that moved me to request a dictionary along with some tablets and pencils from the Norfolk Prison Colony school.

I spent two days just riffling uncertainly through the dictionary's pages. I'd never realized so many words existed! I didn't know *which* words I needed to learn. Finally, just to start some kind of action, I began copying.

In my slow, painstaking, ragged handwriting, I copied into my tablet everything printed on that first page, down to the punctuation marks.

I believe it took me a day. Then, aloud, I read back, to myself, everything I'd written on the tablet. Over and over, aloud, to myself, I read my own handwriting.

I woke up the next morning, thinking about those words —immensely proud to realize that not only had I written so much at one time, but I'd written words that I never knew were in the world. Moreover, with a little effort, I also could remember what many of these words meant. I reviewed the words whose meanings I didn't remember. Funny thing, from the dictionary first page right now, that "aardvark" springs to my mind. The dictionary had a picture of it, a long-tailed, long-eared, burrowing African mammal, which lives off termites caught by sticking out its tongue as an anteater does for ants.

I was so fascinated that I went on—I copied the dictionary's next page. And the same experience came when I studied that. With every succeeding page, I also learned of people and places and events from history. Actually the dictionary is like a miniature encyclopedia. Finally the dictionary's A section had filled a whole tablet—and I went on into the B's. That was the way I started copying what eventually became the entire dictionary. It went a lot faster after so much practice helped me to pick up handwriting speed. Between what I wrote in my tablet, and writing letters, during the rest of my time in prison I would guess I wrote a million words.

I suppose it was inevitable that as my word-base broadened, I could for the first time pick up a book and read and now begin to understand what the book was saying. Anyone who has read a great deal can imagine the new world that opened. Let me tell you something: from then until I left that prison, in every free moment I had, if I was not reading in the library, I was reading on my bunk. You couldn't have gotten me out of books with a wedge. Between Mr. Muhammad's teachings, my correspondence, my visitors—usually Ella and Reginald—and my reading of books, months passed without my even thinking about being imprisoned. In fact, up to then, I never had been so truly free in my life.

—Malcolm X, *Autobiography*

ETHERIDGE KNIGHT

Some convicts begin their artistic endeavors as a hobby; some begin out of relief from the sheer, screaming boredom of prison. But the point is that artists, writers, and musicians—the primary prison art colony—abound, and out of the many are those outstanding figures who instantly strike the spark of true artistic creativeness from the moment they take up the instrument of their craft. In prison you never have to walk far or look long to find this man. Etheridge Knight, a black poet, perhaps serves best my purpose of drawing a composite of the true prison-born artist.

Knight was a contemporary of mine on the prison newspaper for almost a year. When I got to know him, he was well along with his writing career, having already published in *Negro Digest* and *Goulliard's Poetry Magazine.* He had also published a volume of his collected poems and was halfway through a definitive work on Denmark Vesey, a Negro who led a slave uprising in Pre-Civil War South Carolina.

Etheridge found his way to Indiana State Prison by virtue of a ten-to-twenty-five-year robbery sentence. A confirmed drug addict, he grabbed an old woman's purse, nearly crippling her in the process, to get some money for his habit. He was unfortunate to have been caught at a time when public sentiment in Indianapolis (the place of the "happening," as he for years referred to his crime) was running high against such crimes. Two elderly women had been similarly robbed and beaten shortly before, and the police were running around in circles scratching their collective ass trying to seize a suspect upon whom the outraged community could justly vent its frustrations.

When Knight fell into the police net he fitted the bill nicely. He lay in jail for more than a year angling for a short sentence, but the police, the judge, the newspapers, and the public were insistent that only by meting out the full measure of "justice"—a ten-to-twenty-five-year term —could the best interests of society be served, although Knight complained to me many times that "they sure as hell never convinced me that they were acting in my best interests with a sentence like that."

All things considered, Knight did have some justification for his attitude. Many times he told me that day after day while he lay in jail waiting trial, he saw men return from court with light sentences for crimes worse than his. "I was a junkie, a petty thief, and a drifter," he used to say, "and when the detective told me, 'Nigger, you're goin' to prison!' I believed him."

He didn't have much going for him in confinement. His work record was spotty; he had a limited education; and his outlook on life was blackened by his sense of injustice. He was assigned to menial jobs and was in and out of the hole for refusing to work. His friends called him a "low rider," a real sonofabitch. And so Knight, like countless thousands of convicts before him, wallowed in a haze of red anger and self-pity.

It wasn't long before officials transferred him from State Reformatory to the prison as an incorrigible, which amounted to stamping his packet with the recommendation that he "serve his maximum sentence." Consequently, his first look at Indiana State Prison scared the hell out of him.

We talked often, Etheridge and I, of our first impressions of prison and the effect it had upon our thinking. He told me time and time again that he had almost no recollection of his first few months in the reformatory, he was so angry. Not until months later would he be suddenly overwhelmed with the utter hopelessness and futility of his situation.

Of that time he said, "I knew goddam well that there had to be something better for me in life than a ten-to-twenty-five-year sentence stretched endlessly before me."

From that day, Knight devoted every ounce of his energies toward getting out of prison. He read books like they were going out of style and applied himself in many areas —philosophy, art, science, and religion. In five years he covered a wide field, and he found a bit of Etheridge Knight in all of them. He found a sense of worth, a yardstick of measurement for himself. In his discovery he became an articulate spokesman for the prison Negro population. He gained a reputation, which, in an unguarded moment, he let slip that he valued highly. He became the Negro voice for "telling it like it is."

From the beginning of his artistic awakening, Knight's medium for "telling it like it is" was poetry, sweet, flowing, rhythmical, but at times harsh and bitter, at times ironic and snickering, at times plaintive and sad—but always truthful and exact, his soul expression, as he called it.

I watched him furtively, many times, a gaunt hulk of a man with hamhock hands and stubby fingers, hunched over his typewriter digging at the keys in utter consternation, and I thought, "If that bastard is creating something, I'll eat my hat." He never voluntarily offered any of his finished material for my inspection; I had to dig it out of him. And every time I did, there it was, a thing of perfection. I knew it. And I knew, too, from the first day I experienced this knowledge, that goddam convict or not, anyone with such a keenly attuned sense of esthetic expression had to be more than just the sum total of a long prison sentence.

"I died in Korea from a shrapnel wound," Knight told me once in conversation summing up his life, "and narcotics resurrected me. I died in 1960 from a prison sentence, and poetry brought me back to life."

I know that at heart Knight was always a poet, gentle and easygoing, his brutish crime notwithstanding. It only remained for the proper circumstances to awaken his dormant, untapped poetic talent. He told me often that he disliked writing about prison and prisoners, but paradoxically those stories he wrote of his fellow convicts were consistently his best literary efforts—the ones he marketed. He had much to say about prison, about social injustice to his race, and about himself. A constant theme, predominant and unashamed, ran throughout all his writings: he emphasized the lengths to which men are driven in seeking their identity.

Knight found through writing what he had been searching for through narcotics, a way to express, a way to be himself without violating the social restraints of his fellow men. When he writes, then, he is functioning, and he likes the feeling.

—Art Powers, *An Eye for an Eye*

ROBERT STROUD

Living in a small barred room with a tame sparrow and a score of warbling canaries, Stroud was forging obligations and responsibilities that kept him busy day and night. He fed his birds, talked to them, built cages for them and studied their habits. He made a schedule and within the bounds of his tiny empire, he rose, washed, ate, worked, exercised, rested, studied, read and slept like a citizen of the world outside. Since he was excluded from people, his people were his birds. Birds were his family, wife, children and afternoon matinee.

Hours sped away on the wings of birds. He had the shortest distance from avian theory to avian life of any bird breeder in the world. He need only look up from his book and snap his fingers, in order to place his hands upon a living bird.

Examining his birds with sensitive fingers, he verified, detail by detail, their external parts. Where others took for granted the amazing thing known as a feather, Stroud studied the intricate structure of feathers—the million-pointed hooklets of the barbicels and their assembly into barbules; nature's ingenuity in constructing an effective airfoil. When his birds molted in August, he watched the process as though it were a drama.

He asked permission to get a hand glass, and was

thrilled by new horizons looming before his tired eyes. He put his new glass on Runt's game leg and compared it with the good one of that surprised sparrow.

Stroud began to apply his two outstanding characteristics, often associated with genius: an accurate memory, amounting to almost total visual recall; and limitless patience.

The more he discovered about birds, the more absorbed he became. With the prisoner's fascination for something which can fly away, he investigated these hot-blooded wonders of the skies until he could call their parts and feathers in his sleep.

Around him, other lifers were sinking slowly into vacant-eyed stupor. But Stroud became deeply engrossed in the cycle of mating, birth, childhood, courtship, parenthood, sickness and death in the short, quick life spans of his canaries. He was witness to some tiny drama each day.

Beginning as a prisoner seeking a way to improve himself and help support his mother, Stroud was gradually being transformed into another man—a man with an overwhelming passion to know, and to know why.

Each day brought new problems, unanswered questions. Why did sunlight eliminate the ungainliness of his baby birds? What had killed Manuel's pet sparrow? Why and how did birds molt their feathers? What was the structure of birds that enabled them to fly—and thereby capture the fancy of every prisoner since the beginning of rooms with bars?

When one of his nervous warblers somehow broke both a wing and a leg, Stroud was forced to release the sufferer from its misery. This was an opportunity to learn how to dissect a bird. Carefully, he made incisions into the tiny body with his razor blade. One by one, he freed the organs from their fascia and laid them neatly on white drawing paper. His best instruments were his only ones—long, sen-

sitive fingers with sharp, uncut fingernails. Stroud verified
the internal organs from anatomy drawings in his books,
and wrote his observations. He could not have known how
these drawings would prove help later. . . .

. . . Stroud, the lifer, had found his life's work. He was
thirty-eight years old. He had spent nineteen years in
prison and twelve years in solitary.

Stroud now worked eighteen hours a day. He would
douse himself with cold water while the prison slept, and
perform the morning chores of a farm hand in an area of
seventy-two square feet. After feeding and watering 300
birds, he would clean their cages, examine each canary
with meticulous care for mites, fever, swellings, feather
problems, egg trouble and diet deficiency. He would carefully dissect birds which died, and draw what he saw.
He made detailed notes.

Using the morning bucket of hot water from the cell-
tender, he would bathe some birds by hand, lathering
them with a shaving brush and swathing them in hand-
kerchiefs.

At exercise time on sunny days, he would transfer
every cage of his twittering songsters to the bull pen,
where he would arrange them along the wall for the noon-
day sun. Then he would cultivate greens growing in flat
boxes.

In the afternoon he would hand-print laborious answers
to his growing correspondence with bird breeders. His
correspondence privileges were increased and he received
new bird journals. Absorbing bird lore, physical sciences,
pathology and dietetics, he behaved like a celled monk
pursuing some hidden alchemy. Without any social obligations, required to do a minimum of dressing and un-
dressing, eating alone from a tray and shaving once a
week, he became the only man in the world who spent

twenty-four hours a day with his birds. Pleased officials allowed him to have extension cords and brighter lights. Throughout the evenings and on into the night, guards going off shift grew accustomed to the tiny square of yellow light which shone in the north end of the Isolation Building.

"We don't know when he sleeps," exclaimed a watchtower guard, going off shift. While other prisoners sank into a sea of stupor, the lean Stroud could not find enough time for his activities. He was approaching his prime of life, making a future of a futureless existence.

—Thomas E. Gaddis, *Birdman of Alcatraz*

How much the rice must suffer under the pestle!
But, after the pounding, it comes out white like cotton.
The same thing often happens to men in this world:
Misfortune's workshop turns them to polished jade.

—Ho Chi Minh, *Prison Diary*

Biographical Notes

BEVERLY BYRNE. See biographical notes, chapter 3.

MALCOLM X (1925–1965). Black leader, Muslim, and former pimp and dope peddler, Malcolm was arrested just before he turned twenty-one, and sent to Charlestown State Prison in Massachusetts. In prison he was converted to the Black Muslim religion and discovered the world of books.

Released from the Norfolk Prison Colony in 1952, he began a close association with Elijah Muhammad, becoming heir apparent to Elijah. He became a symbol of black revolt in the United States. Before his murder (reputedly committed by Black Muslims from whom he had broken), Malcolm had all but abandoned his separatist approach in favor of a more conciliatory one.

ART POWERS. See notes, chapter 7.

ROBERT STROUD (d. 1963). A convicted murderer, known as the "Birdman of Alcatraz," Stroud served fifty-four years in prison, forty-two of them in solitary confinement. At eighteen, he surrendered to a United States marshal after having killed a bartender, and was sent to Federal prison in the state of Washington. After stabbing a fellow convict he was confined at Leavenworth where he killed a guard in a fit of anger. In 1920 he was condemned to life in solitary confinement. During this time, Stroud studied pharmacology, medicine, bacteriology, and became one of the world's leading authorities on bird diseases. In 1942, *Stroud's Digest of the Diseases of Birds* was published; it is regarded as a classic in its field. That same year Stroud was removed from Leavenworth to Alcatraz. His last application for parole was denied just seven months before his death at age seventy-three.

HO CHI MINH (1892–1969). President of the Democratic Republic of Vietnam. In 1942, Ho was arrested by Chiang Kai-shek, who was not enthusiastic about the prospect of a Communist government to the south of him. During his fourteen months of imprisonment, Ho was confined in thirty prefecture and district prisons. Released because of American intervention (Ho was strongly anti-Japanese, and thus an invaluable ally to the United States), he returned to Vietnam in 1943.

13.
THE ETERNAL SOURCE

Doctrine vs. doctrine; church vs. state. Religious beliefs as punishable crimes is a concept that has been with us for centuries. The cries Heretic, Anticleric, Nonconformist have caused the excommunication, imprisonment, or execution of countless persons of differing beliefs. Out of the vast number of religious martyrs, many are now seen as luminaries, great reformers, saints, and writers without peer. John Huss, Jeanne d'Arc, Savonarola, St. John of the Cross, Rabbi Akiba, John Bunyan are notable examples. Today conscientious objectors and other war resisters have become our "religious martyrs"; we do not execute them, but imprison them or consign them to demeaning work.

Prisoners convicted for other crimes are frequently not untouched by religion during imprisonment. For some it is consolation; for a few, the only hope of deliverance; it becomes, in the words of St. John of the Cross, "the eternal source, the light by which we see"; for others, like Malcolm X, it brings a change in values. But for many, it has caused bitterness and a hatred of clerical hypocrisy creating irrevocable loss of faith: for these, the way in which religion is travestied in prison is the greatest sacrilege.

Paul and Silas bound in jail all night long
Who shall deliver poor me?

Paul and Silas moaned all night long
Who shall deliver poor me?

Believe in the Lord and you shall be saved
all night long

Who shall deliver poor me?

—Negro Spiritual

"...BUT THE LORD NEVER CAME..."

I began to lose confidence in God. Three times I was sentenced to die for something I never did. What was the Lord doing about it? Nothing. I saw it so I almost wished I was dead. I felt I should kill myself just to get out of misery. I had such thoughts. I didn't want for the state to get the credit of killing me. I was already treated bad enough without having death in that place.

Many religious groups got in touch with me. But they were for the state of Alabama. They were working for them; did me no good. Religious people came there. They talked to the other guys. I began to turn away from them. I would say, "I got a Bible. I read it. I don't care to say anything now." I read into the Bible long after I began to lose confidence in it. I saw many things there, they contradicted themselves. I wondered about that. Even so I read it for what was good in it. I had religious pictures on my walls. I would view them: but the Lord never came there. Nothing but his pictures on the walls. I heard so much praying in the death row. It was very moving. So serious that it would move me, make me feel that I should pray too. I saw guys pray and cry all hours of the night. What they prayed for they never got.

I studied how these guys came by their religion. The average guy there, he got religion. He professed great feelings about God. They only pretended, the way it looked to me. They wanted any help they could get, to make it lighter for them. When you are drowning in the death row the Bible is the straw you grab.

White and black churches both tell my people to tell the white man the truth. A majority of colored children on the farm, they will hear their ma and pa say, "If you tell Old Master a lie, I flog you. Tell old white man the truth every time." That's what makes stool pigeons out of Negroes today. That's what makes many Negroes bad leaders for their people when they get high up. They were taught to respect white folks more than black. Few colored parents I ever knew to tell their young ones to stand up like men and fight. Just bang their backsides with a rod in one hand and flog their brains with the Bible in the other, and say, "Now just you mind that white man and do like he say. You get along with him then."

A man with religion in jail, he was a dangerous man. He'd come into court against you—guilty or innocent. He'd go up against himself and his own people. I saw too many guys done up in the Lord all of a sudden rat on somebody in the next cell.

Most of all I saw the white man wanted a black man to get down on his knees and be a pray-man. They just loved that. Then you were their "nigger." That alone taught me it couldn't be such a good thing for black folks to be so fetched up in all that Bible stuff.

—Haywood Patterson and Earl Conrad, *Scottsboro Boy*

CHRIST BEHIND BARS

Thank you for accepting this note. I wish to review events of the last few days, and offer a few suggestions.

One grows resigned to a certain degree of cruelty in prison; still, each new instance comes with a new shock. I am told that the guards, guns, and chains used to transfer a priest and ten other nonviolent men were fit for a gang of killers.

Again, would it have seriously interfered with your "plans" if I had been allowed to say goodbye to my brother?

Mr. Norton, I have been a guest in your hostel for just one year. A certain experience of your style entitles me perhaps to offer a suggestion to you and the other Catholics on your staff, especially to Mr. Noon and Mr. McDonald.

It is by now clear that the duplicity, cruelty, and moral inertia which are your usual methods against prisoners, must now be turned against priests as well. All to the good. I now speak to you as a priest. And I urge you—stop calling yourselves Catholics. Stop practicing religion in a way which is an abomination in the eyes of God—devotion on Sunday, breaking human lives all week. Concentrate rather on your "jobs." In such a way, you will at least be acting consistently. But do not deceive yourself any longer by thinking you can worship God and destroy men.

The work you do is simply without human meaning. It serves nothing, except your own interests. But as far as the inmates are concerned, you are only keepers of the keys in a human zoo.

How then could your religion not be in violation of the

command of Jesus—"Love your enemies, love your brothers."?

But if you were to cast off this vile "religious" pretense, perhaps your children would one day thank you for refusing to live a lie. They might say of you, at least he did not mock God, worshipping Christ yet crucifying Him in his brothers.

There is no one of you who does not know I am speaking the truth. You know that you are neither rehabilitating men, nor treating them with dignity, nor helping them to change their lives. You know that you are pawns in a system that amputates men from family and community, embitters and saddens them, weakens their hope, exploits them with slave labor—and so embitters them that a majority of them return to lives of crime. In this crime, you bear large responsibility. I tell you so before God.

Of course, another alternative is open to you. You might simply quit your jobs because you wish to be men. In such a case, your religious problem would be solved.

I have a true story to close with. A friend, a distinguished rabbi, told me that in his native city in Poland, the Germans had built an extermination camp for Jews. Each Sunday the townsfolk could see the buses arriving to take the Catholic personnel to Mass. Then they would return to the camp for their week's "work." The rabbi added that it was not until he met my brother and me that he realized Catholics could be different: different, i.e., than destroyers.

You might wish to ponder this story.

In any case I am your prisoner, and proud of it. I wish you could be as proud of your lives, before God. If I were in your shoes, I would fear His wrath.

—Daniel Berrigan, *Absurd Convictions, Modest Hopes*

GOD IS DEAD IN RAHWAY

Most men arriving at Rahway Prison are hurt physically and spiritually although most would conceal their spiritual hurt and need. Forsaken by family and friends, and deliberately rejected by the society they so wronged, we wander like lost sheep until finally, for lack of adequate religious guidance we become mired in lust and perversion, originally the principal cause of our incarceration.

This is not to say that the thirteen hundred men here at Rahway are without religious representation. To the contrary, Catholic and Protestant services are scheduled for every Sunday; Bible Classes and religious tracts are available in abundance; religious medals and rosaries are yours for the asking. Salvation of the SPIRIT is the theme —but little, if anything is said of our PHYSICAL needs.

Of what practical value is a bible to me (except to roll cigarettes when I run out of cigarette paper) when I need someone from my hometown to keep me informed about my ailing children? Or how can the Sermon on the Mount help a youngster who is on the verge of suicide and cannot find anyone to speak to who is in a position to help him?

It seems almost unnatural that our clergymen, evangelists and Christian teachers should segregate themselves from their flocks. It is here, in prison, that most men are vulnerable to religious indoctrination.

Most members of the clergy seem to feel that quoting Scripture from memory and spouting off a lot of silly numbers ends their obligation to their fellow man. Seldom do I hear anyone refer to Spiritual guidance as an integral part of a man's rehabilitation. Little, if any emphasis is placed on religious guidance for men released from prison. Few, if any, Christians are willing to come forward and embrace an exconvict in true Christian fellowship—without the "Jesus Saves" overtone.

During my many years of incarceration I have spent what would amount to at least four years in solitary confinement. At such times my only companion was a bible which I have read and re-read. I must admit that it served its purpose—it occupied my time even if it didn't do a damned thing for spirit or empty stomach. It didn't convert me, I didn't see the *light* and if anything, it has only served to further shaken my belief in God.

I say, keep your bibles, tracts, medals and organ music. Instead, give us of yourselves, your time and help just as He gave of himself to the sick and poor and the needy. Come out from behind your cloaks of hypocritical self-righteousness and wallow a while with us thieves, pimps, drug addicts and murderers.

If religious training is in fact an integral part of rehabilitation and our Christian brothers continue keeping themselves aloof from the men in prison, then let me be the first to proclaim that GOD IS DEAD!

—A. Puchalski, *Fortune News*, October 1970

CHRISTMAS CHEER

Folsom
December 24, 1970

Dearest Mom & Dad:
Well its Christmas Eve—"and all through my cell, not a creature is stirring, except maybe a mouse, or two, or three—smile."

I am spending this Christmas in a room called the "hole"—this condition is the result of what the authorities claimed was a minor rule infraction. I will also be spending the New Year in this room—it's all a part of the prison's idea of Christmas spirit. It is quiet here, and pretty dark—but I am imprisoned only in body—my mind remains free and it will supply me with reasons to retain the Christmas spirit. A belief in the future sure helps in this regard.

I was just interrupted by a jailer and his flashlight. He was making his rounds, counting his prisoners. I wished him a Merry Christmas—but he just slammed the heavy steel door and trampled off down the corridor rattling his keys. I am sure that he thought that my remark was just a method of mocking him and his job—but it was sincerely meant: For who but a person like he needs a greeting of good cheer? It's impossible to hate a person like him—he requires pity for with him its a matter of having a free body—but a imprisoned mind and spirit— For how else could a person accept a job wherein he is paid his silver at the expense of so many others misery?

Your check arrived tonight—too late for Christmas, but I will be able to buy some food items next week—and that will help because people put in the hole are put on reduced food rations—the inmates in the hole call the stuff they feed us in here, a dog bisket. It's made by pressing left over foods into a block and then drying it out. I don't eat the stuff—not solely because of pride, but because of the smell. But I am saving up some of the crumbs for a little cockroach that I am trying to tame. He is a smart little fellow and a good holiday companion. It's too bad that he can't appreciate the little Christmas tree that I drew on the wall. When I am allowed to buy some food items I will buy him a piece of cheese as a Christmas gift.

Things might work out next February—but I am not holding out much hope—I have so often in the past—only to be disappointed. Tomorrow I will try not to think of homes filled full of bright lights and happy people, that will only make me sad. I will also try to hide my worry and concern for my children at the back of my mind, instead I will think of you and Dad, and be happy with such good thoughts. So my Christmas Cheer will be the result of such wonderful parents and the equally wonderful memory of them.

I will also spend my Christmas thinking of a man born on this day so long ago. I will think of all that he taught and wonder why so many people talk about what he taught but live out their lives by the rules of his tempter.

I have spent a great deal of time researching the history of Christ. Jim the Chaplain here has supplied me with over 100 books on this subject. More than anything else I have come to see the great difference in what he taught and the way the people who claim to follow him live. Because of this I respect him, but I will never recognize the religions who have betrayed his word. I cannot respect people who talk love, peace, forgiveness, and practice hate, greed, and selfishness. All in all I will have a happy Christmas, Thanks To Both Of You,

Love, Wayne

P.S. My pet cockroach sends his best wishes.

—Eve Pell, ed., *Maximum Security, Letters from Prison*

RULES AND REGULATIONS

FEDERAL CORRECTIONAL INSTITUTION
LOMPOC, CALIFORNIA

Dear Robert Minton,
    You have been selected by .... (Name)
.... (Number) as the person from whom
he wishes to receive his Christmas package.

    Each inmate is permitted to receive one package at
Christmas time, the weight of which shall not exceed five
pounds, plus the weight of one book.

THE PACKAGE MAY CONTAIN ONLY THE FOLLOWING ITEMS:
Glazed Fruit   A Ballpoint Pen   A Pipe   One Pair of
Tennis Shoes
Candy and/or Cookies—These items must be in a commer-
    cially wrapped box or container. Homemade candy or
    cookies cannot be accepted.
Nuts—Any type, without shells.
Book—Subject matter may include standard non-fiction,
    western, science-fiction, historical novels, humor, auto-
    biographies, travel, and adventure stories. Contents
    must be of an acceptable nature and the institution re-
    tains the right of disposing of indecent and salacious
    matter.

    Packages must be sent through the mail and none will
be accepted by the Visiting Room Officer. Packages should
be mailed so as to arrive here no later than December 21.
Your package should be securely wrapped and addressed
as follows:

INMATE'S NAME AND NUMBER

P. O. BOX W

LOMPOC, CALIFORNIA 93436

Secure wrapping and proper addressing are of extreme importance, as packages that are damaged or which cannot be delivered because of illegible name or number may cause some individual to be without his Christmas package.

J. B. Bogan
Warden

—Robert J. Minton, Jr., ed., *Inside*

THE DIFFERENCE
December 17, 1943

From the Christian point of view there is no special problem about Christmas in a prison cell. For many people in this building it will probably be a more sincere and genuine occasion than in places where nothing but the name is kept. That misery, suffering, poverty, loneliness, helplessness, and guilt mean something quite different in the eyes of God from what they mean in the judgment of man, that God will approach where men turn away, that Christ was born in a stable because there was no room for him in the inn—these are things that a prisoner can understand better than other people; for him they really are glad tidings, and that faith gives him a part in the communion of saints, a Christian fellowship breaking the bounds of time and space and reducing the months of confinement here to insignificance.

On Christmas Eve I shall be thinking of you all very much, and I want you to believe that I too shall have a few really happy hours, and that I am certainly not allowing my troubles to get the better of me. . . .

—Dietrich Bonhoeffer, *Letters and Papers from Prison*

Biographical Notes

HAYWOOD PATTERSON (d. 1952). Arrested when he was sixteen, Haywood Patterson was one of the nine Scottsboro Boys—protagonists in one of America's most famous trials. In 1931, in Alabama, nine black boys, all under twenty, were accused of raping two white women, who were known prostitutes. Eight were sentenced to die; one, sentenced to life imprisonment. But in 1932, the decision was reversed on the grounds that the defendants had not had adequate representation by counsel; the Supreme Court pronouncement that defendants in capital cases must be represented by counsel was considered a landmark decision. The case attracted worldwide attention and was seen for what it was: a grave miscarriage of justice. Patterson escaped from prison in 1948, to Detroit; in 1950, he was convicted of manslaughter and sentenced to the Michigan State Prison for fifteen to twenty years. He died in prison of cancer. The last of the Scottsboro Boys, Andy Wright, was paroled in 1950.

DANIEL BERRIGAN. See biographical notes, chapter 7.

A. PUCHALSKI. Puchalski has been released from the New Jersey State Prison.

DIETRICH BONHOEFFER (1906–1945). Famous German theologian and minister, he was educated in Berlin and New York. Safe in America in 1939, he returned to Germany to be with his own people during the war. He was arrested for resistance activities in 1943, and executed on a Nazi gallows two years later.

14.

SURVIVING: The Last Freedom

People in Auschwitz. Prisoners on Death Row. Against all odds, there is always the will to survive.

How do prisoners survive in a world that at worst denies them that right? Battles are waged for a cigarette, and power is asserted; memories and dreams become anodynes against the reality of despair; out of odds and ends art is created; uniforms are altered, giving a touch of individuality by whatever means. Little material to work with requires ingenuity, and all small things become efforts toward survival.

The will to survive is as strange as it is eternal; among prisoners it is the quality most suspect by authority. If rehabilitation were an actuality and not a gesture, the very ability of the prisoner to survive would be recognized as a strength to be utilized—not feared—in building a different life.

THE MANUSCRIPT

To the island of Trinidad, washed up on the tail end of a Caribbean hurricane, had come a slender water-logged indian canoe. In it, the *Trinidad Guardian* said, were six starved and almost drowned Frenchmen—fugitives who had, after seventeen days on the tossing sea, successfully escaped from Devil's Island and the penal colony of French Guiana.

Out of curiosity several British colonists and I went

down to the military barracks to see the fugitives. They were not under arrest; there is something of the sportsman in every real Englishman no matter how far away he is from home, and the Officer-of-the-Port voiced the thoughts of everyone (but the French Consul) when he said: "I am not going to turn these poor men over to the French Consul. Let him tear his hair all he wants! French Guiana is a plague on the face of civilization. We will feed the fugitives, give them a place to rest, give them a better boat and give them a chance to continue their escape!"

In a large comfortable room six men greeted us with an eagerness to smile that was pathetic. Five of them were big, tremendously powerful men—they might have been prize fighters, Canadian lumber-jacks, soldiers of the Foreign Legion. They were men of brute strength, brute living, and brute mentality. The sixth man, in contrast, was astoundingly little, less than five feet, very thin, and weighing under ninety pounds. But he had fire in his eyes, fire fanned, as I was to learn, by fifteen years of living death, by four previous attempts to escape, and now by an almost fanatical decision to either make good his fifth attempt or die.

He had with him only one possession, an oil cloth covered package which contained over thirty pounds of closely written manuscript—the detailed record of fifteen years of prison colony life; the most amazing document of biography, of crime and of punishment which I had ever seen. . . .

"But that manuscript of your life in French Guiana and the documents," I said as he was tightly sealing the oil cloth covering, "why don't you let me send it safely to the United States for you and find a publisher. It's impossible for you actually to gain permanent freedom. You'll be lost at sea or, landing in some unfriendly port, you'll be arrested and sent back to Cayenne."

"I'll make it this time," Belbenoit said. "I am going to reach the United States and I am going to take the manuscript with me."

Twelve months later I was in the jungles of Panama. I saw a little man with a big butterfly net in the forest trail ahead of me. He stood still for a moment and looked at me as though he couldn't make up his mind whether to run or not. I recognized him.

"René Belbenoit!" I said. "Congratulations!"

"Not yet!" he answered. "Panama's only half way to the United States. It's taken me a year to get here!"

"Where are your companions, the others who were with you in Trinidad?" I asked.

"I am the only one who is still free," he said. I could not help but turn over in my mind as I looked at his thin, worn body and face the fact that in the year since I had seen him—the year which for me and most people in the world had been quiet routine—his life must have been a continuous nightmare. A whole year it had taken him to get from Trinidad to Panama! We sat in front of his little thatched butterfly hunting shelter, many miles from civilization—ten miles, he said—from the *Chakoi* village in which he lived with primitive Indians. Again I asked him to let me take his manuscript safely to the United States.

"You can't continue lugging thirty pounds of paper through Central America," I said. "You've still to pass through Panama, Costa Rica, Nicaragua, Honduras, Salvador, Guatemala and Mexico, countries that now guard their frontiers with the vigilance of hawks. You've no passports. You're a fugitive. What you are trying to do is impossible. Let me take the manuscript to the United States and get it published. It is an amazing document, and an extraordinary story. The publishers may be able to help you win permanent sanctuary and freedom."

"Thank you, again," he said politely, "But I think I can make it. I want to take it to the United States myself. The United States is the land of the free, isn't it? The Land of Liberty. I have been fifteen years in hell. If I can reach the United States I may be able to put an end to the sufferings not alone of myself but of thousands of other human beings. If I am caught somewhere, if it looks as though I will be sent back to French Guiana, I will send the manuscript to you—before I kill myself!"

I thought I would never see him again, that the story of man's inhumanity to man which he had transcribed painfully during fifteen years of torture would be lost to all other readers, lost in the jungle or in the sea which would be his grave also. But I was mistaken. René Belbenoit, after twenty-two months of superhuman trying and many amazing adventures, finally reached the United States. He crossed the frontiers in rags, but his manuscript was always safely wrapped in oiled paper.

His book, *Dry Guillotine,* begins with his exile from society and civilization. It is the story of Devil's Island, of Iles Royale and Saint Joseph, of Cayenne, the capital of a colony of sin, of *liberés* living like jackals, of men going crazy in solitary dark cells, of life more terrible than death and deaths more gruesome than fiction. . . . He says that he hopes the publication of his book will accomplish just one thing. He hopes, with all his heart; it will cause France finally to do away with French Guiana and send no more human beings there to suffer—on the *Dry Guillotine.*

—René Belbenoit, *Dry Guillotine,* from Introduction by William La Varre

𝔄𝔡𝔳𝔢𝔯𝔱𝔦𝔰𝔢𝔪𝔢𝔫𝔱𝔰

WANTED—A home-like home.   Present one, not what it is cracked up to be.   Address Clinton 4,320.

WANTED—A good night's rest.   Gallery shouters and instrumentalists take note.   Nemo, Star Office.

WANTED—An eraser, (must be mighty sharp) to blot out the past.   A stock of experience, (fringed and threadbare) given in exchange.   For particulars, Auburn 20,101.

WANTED—That *rara avis*, the con who does *not* think he is better able to manage the STAR than the present Editor.   Applications solicited by Sing Sing 51,094.

WANTED—A few blank pages in the Book of Life, wherein we desire to make some new entries—on the Cr. side.   Address *Summa Summarum*, New York State Prisons.

WANTED—Immediately—an Opportunity.   Price no object if goods are fair and in good working order. Anxious, Clinton 4,298.

WANTED—Anno Domini 1902.   Will give in exchange one and a quarter yards of warranted genuine, home-made Spring po'ms—just *too* lovely for every day wear. Samantha, Auburn 595 (W. P.).

LOST—Five days' 'short time.'   Finder can have same by arranging with the Powers That Be.   Address Nostalgic, Auburn 20,210.

—*Star of Hope*, May 19, 1900 (a Sing Sing publication)

BLACK TUESDAY, BLACK HUMOR (by Joshua Hill)

5 *May 70*

Black Tuesday. The store man didn't bring any candy and peanuts to sell this morning and a lot of dudes are beginning to panic, since they cannot subsist on the slop doled out at meal times. Many people depend on candy and peanuts for their very sustenance. Poor devils. Some of them are talking suicide. I can see the newspaper now:

46 INMATES COMMIT SUICIDE IN THE COUNTY JAIL

Forty-six inmates at the Los Angeles County Jail committed suicide today because there was no candy or peanuts available for them to buy. Names are being withheld pending notification of relatives.

Jail officials stated the majority of the victims either cut their wrists or hung themselves. However, two men were drowned attempting to flush themselves down their toilets. Also, one man died as a result of having his genitals bitten off after attacking a group of sixteen deputies, and one other inmate died of a fatal overdose of corn-beef at dinner.

Mayor Samuel Yorty ("Mayor Sam") has termed the Jail a disaster area, and for reasons known only to himself, declared Martial Law.

Sheriff Peter J. Pitchess ("Sheriff Pete"), in

an effort to put an end to the serious outbreak of suicides ("It ain't natural and it's bad for morale"), has ordered his men to roam the jail shooting any inmate caught trying to take his own life.

—Stephen Levine, ed., *Death Row*

MAKING DO
(Flowering Beauty)

That spring the prisoners acquired an unusual interest in aesthetics. Flower gardening suddenly became a hobby of the entire outside work detail. Petition was made to beautify the paved courtyard with a large circle of flowers around the center flagpole. From this hub ran bordered walks, spoke-like, to every gate and building.

This meant that large areas of cobblestone and brick pavement were broken up, and in place of a colorless expanse of gray courtyard there were circles, triangles, squares, ellipses and octagons of color. Flower beds had never been so beautiful or so well watered.

Spring had never been so phony. . . .

My men were rapturous about this opulent landscaping.

"Imagine!" chuckled Scott. "All this in a penal institution, a house of correction!"

"It couldn't happen in Italy," said Punch with a straight face.

"It's a wonderful country, democracy is safe," sighed Gibbs.

"Jeez—ain't it *amazin'* what goes on under that flag?" said Connie piously.

I remembered this doubletalk vividly when during the summer, concurrent with all this flowering beauty, a visiting narcotics agent with one of our bachelor buttons in his lapel made his tour of the cell block—and smelled marijuana. Opening one particular cell he found a groggy novice trying to light uncured marijuana leaves.

The agent stalked out into the courtyard and discovered that growing between the hollyhocks and sunflowers were marijuana plants.

The captain's face was rosy with something besides Irish humor when he ordered demolition squads to tear up the beds. It was just as well, he rationalized, it was getting so there was no place to walk.

Following this vigorous housecleaning job the men's interest in aesthetics sunk to such an abysmal pitch that most of the legitimate blooms pined for water, and in a matter of days the place reverted to the original beds which were tended by the few real gardeners among the prisoners.

—Donald Powell Wilson, *My Six Convicts*

CONSCIENTIOUS OBJECTOR IN DANBURY

Lowell Naeve, an artist in segregation here, has been experimenting with a new material that he has made out of cooked oatmeal, newspaper, and water. From this he has made drawing boards, picture frames, a two-foot globe (painted and in relief) and a perfectly shaped guitar. The only tools he uses are old razor blades and sandpaper.

—From *The Grapevine*, No. 3, July 1945 (a prison newspaper)

KILLING THE BLUES

I missed the drinks even more than the women and a number of guys agreed with me. When you get the blues on the outside you can always kill them with a couple of drinks. But in jail you just have to wait until the blues wears off and that may take a long while.

As a substitute, some of the men took nutmeg or ginger which was sneaked out of the kitchen. Mixed with water, either one will set you up. I tried nutmeg in Danbury for the first time. Because it does not dissolve, the drink is like sawdust but within a couple of hours you feel lighter than air. It is strange to have a nutmeg jag in prison and to laugh at the ridiculous screws with their keys and whistles. One little Negro who had a stiff bit ahead of him after Danbury, managed to keep high most of the time. He was always laughing.

So much nutmeg and ginger disappeared from the kitchen that the authorities put these spices under lock and key. That made them become highly valued connections. The kitchen is the main center of the connections trade. Men working there smuggle out eggs, meat, pies, apples and other food at the risk of being put in the hole. Some give the connections to their friends. Others sell them, and these prisoners are called merchants. . . .

Nutmeg and ginger are not wholly satisfactory substitutes for alcohol. Occasionally a resourceful prisoner would build a crude still, but no inmate was able to produce liquor in helpful quantities before the operation was discovered by the screws. At Christmas it was usually possible to get a drink or two, the rumor being that one lieutenant and a couple of screws would sell whiskey at $25 a bottle.

—Jim Peck, *We Who Would Not Kill*

MEDIUM OF EXCHANGE

"Three for two me two boxes until I draw," is a commonly heard phrase in the nation's prisons. It simply means a man is attempting to borrow two cartons of cigarettes until he is able to make his monthly canteen purchase and is willing to pay the "three-for-two" loan "shark" a carton "interest." All of which is to say that while the Dollar, Yen, Lira, Peso and Rupee are easily recognizable as currency in various parts of the world, strange as it seems, the legal tender for approximately 230,000 men and women is none of these nor anything remotely familiar.

Far more negotiable to the denizens of the nation's 680 camps, reformatories and prisons is an everyday item absently used by millions of Americans and inhabitants of countries throughout the world—cigarettes!

Cigarettes! The controversial tobacco leaf product which constantly being either praised or panned by growers, retailers, doctors, advertisers and research clinics is THE medium of exchange in most prisons.

. . . Since nothing has caused as much friction in prison as gambling, (with sex a close second,) where cigarettes are naturally constantly changing hands, all too often debts incurred result in assaults and killings. In an attempt to curtail problems in this area, authorities forbid gambling in many States and often limit the amount of cigarettes a prisoner may have in his cell or in his possession. This, of course, does little to curtail the trafficking in Funny Money.

... What will Funny Money buy? Practically anything except the companionship of a woman. Some typical prices:

*Enough "home-brew" alcohol for a good drunk: 5 packs

*Three grilled cheese sandwiches: 1 pack

*A starched and pressed ("bonarooed" is the word used to describe custom pressed clothing) pair of pants and shirt: 2 packs

*Sex with a homosexual: 2 packs and up

*The death of someone: 2 cartons and up. (The death of individuals has been "contracted" (arranged for), on occasion, for less than 2 cartons as unbelievable as this may seem).

—*Western Confectioner and Tobacconist*, November 1971

FATEFUL TRANSFORMATION

Guilty or innocent, the prisoner changes form and colour, and assumes the mould that most easily enables him to secure a maximum of those minimal advantages possible within the framework of the prison system. In the world outside, now faded to a dream, the struggle is waged for position, prestige, power, women. For the prisoner those are the heroic battles of Olympian demi-gods. Here inside the prison walls the struggle is waged for a cigarette, for permission to exercise in the courtyard, for the possession of a pencil. It is a struggle for minimal and unworthy objects, but a struggle for existence like any other. With this difference, that the prisoner has only one weapon left to him: cunning and hypocrisy developed to the point of reflex action. Of all other means he has been deprived. The hearing and sense of touch of a man who has been blinded are intensified; there is only one direction in which the prisoner can evolve—that of increasing artfulness. In the hot-house atmosphere of his social environment he cannot escape this fateful transformation of his character. He feels his claws growing, a furtive and dejected, an impudent and servile look creeps into his eyes. His lips become thin, sharp, Jesuitical, his nose pinched and sharp, his nostrils dilated and bloodless; his knees sag, his arms grow long, and dangle gorilla-like. Those who uphold the Theory of Race and deny the influence of environment on the development of the human being should spend a year in prison and observe themselves daily in a mirror.

—Arthur Koestler, *Dialogue with Death*

"I WAS THERE . . ."

. . . I worked on splitting myself in two and developed a foolproof method: in order to roam among the stars, to summon up various stages in my life or build my amazingly realistic castles in Spain, I first had to tire myself out. I would walk for hours without sitting down, never stopping, thinking about nothing in particular. Once I was truly exhausted, I stretched out on my bunk and wrapped the blanket around my head. This way, the little air there was in my cell was further cut off. My lungs became asphyxiated and my head started to burn. Suffocating with the heat and lack of air, I suddenly found myself in flight. Ah! What indescribable sensations! I spent nights of love that were more intense than real ones. I could sit down with my mother, dead these seventeen years. I could play with her dress while she stroked my curls, which she had left long to make me look like a girl. I caressed her slender fingers, her soft silky skin. She laughed over my foolish desire to dive into the river as I had seen the big boys do one day on a walk. I even saw the way she wore her hair, the love that flowed from her bright eyes, her gentle words: "My little Riri, you must be good, you must be very good so that your mummy can love you a lot. Later on, when you're a little bigger, you can dive into the river too. You're too small now, my treasure. The day will come soon, too soon, when you'll be a big boy."

Hand in hand, we followed the river home. I was actually there, in the house of my childhood. I held my hands over my mother's eyes so that she had to play the piano without looking at the music. I was there; it wasn't my imagination. I was with her, standing on a chair behind the piano stool, and I pressed my small hands against her large eyes so she couldn't see. Her nimble fingers continued to skim over the piano until she had played "The Merry Widow" to the end.

Neither you, inhuman prosecutor, nor you, dishonest policemen, nor you, miserable Polein, who bought your liberty for the price of a lie, nor the twelve jurymen who were such cheeseheads they believed the lot of you, nor the guards here in the Réclusion—worthy associates of *la mangeuse d'hommes* [one who feeds on men]—no one, absolutely no one, not even these thick walls, nor the remoteness of this island lost in the Atlantic, nothing,

nothing physical or mental, can stop my delicious wanderings, bathed in the rosy hue of bliss.

—Henri Charrière, *Papillon*

A TRIP THROUGH THE MIND JAIL FOR ELDRIDGE (by raulsalinas)

la loma

Neighborhood of my youth
    demolished, erased forever from
    the universe.
    You live on, captive, in the lonely
    cellblocks of my mind.
Neighborhood of endless hills
    muddied streets—all chuckhole lined—
    that never drank of asphalt.
    Kids barefoot/snotty-nosed
    playing marbles, munching on bean tacos
    (the kind you'll never find in a café)
    2 peaceful generations removed from
    their *abuelos'* revolution.
Neighborhood of Sunday night *jamaicas*
    at Guadalupe Church.
    Fiestas for any occasion
    holidays holy days happy days
    'round and 'round the promenada
    eating snow-cones . . . raspas . . . & tamales
    the games—bingo   cake walk   spin the wheel

making eyes at girls from cleaner neighborhoods
the unobtainables
who responded all giggles and excitement. . . .
Neighborhood of Spanish Town Cafe
first grown-up (13) hangout
Andres,
tolerant manager, proprietor, cook
victim of bungling baby burglars
your loss: Fritos n' Pepsi-Colas . . . was our gain
you put up with us and still survived!
You too, are granted immortality.
Neighborhood of groups and clusters
sniffing gas, drinking muscatel
solidarity   cement hardening
the clan   the family   the neighborhood   the gang
    Nomás!
Restless innocents tattoo'd crosses on their hands
"just doing things different"
"From now on, all troublemaking mex kids will
be sent to Gatesville for 9 months."
Henry home from *la corre*
khakis worn too low . . . below the waist
the stomps, the *greña* with duck-tail
    —Pachuco Yo—
Neighborhood of could-be artists
who plied their talents on the pool's
bath-house walls/intricately adorned
with esoteric symbols of their cult: . . .
the art form of our slums
more meaningful & significant
than Egypt's finest hieroglyphics.
Neighborhood where purple clouds of *Yesca*
smoke one day descended & embraced us all.
Skulls uncapped—Rhythm n' Blues
    Chalie's 7th. St. Club

loud funky music—wine spodee—odees—barbecue—
grass
our very own connection man: big black Johnny B. . . .
Neighborhood of Reyes' Bar
where Lalo shotgunned
Pete Evans to death because of
an unintentional stare,
and because he was *escuadra,*
only to end his life neatly sliced
by a prison barber's razor.
Durán's grocery & gas station
Guero drunkenly stabbed Julio
arguing over who'd drive home
and got 55 years for his crime.
Ratón: 20 years for a matchbox of weed. Is that cold?
No lawyer no jury no trial i'm guilty.
Aren't we all guilty?
Indian mothers, too, so unaware
of courtroom tragi-comedies
folded arms across their bosoms
saying, *"Sea por Dios."*
Neighborhood of my childhood
neighborhood that no longer exists
some died young—fortunate—some rot in prisons
the rest drifted away to be conjured up
in minds of others like them.
For me: only the NOW of THIS journey is REAL!
Neighborhood of my adolescence
neighborhood that is no more
YOU ARE TORN PIECES OF MY FLESH!!!
Therefore, you ARE.
LA LOMA . . . AUSTIN . . . MI BARRIO . . .
i bear you no grudge
i needed you then . . . identity . . . a sense of belonging.

i need you now.
So essential to adult days of imprisonment,
you keep me away from INSANITY'S hungry jaws;
    Smiling/Laughing/Crying.

    i respect your having been:
    My Loma of Austin
    my Rose Hill of Los Angeles
    my West Side of San Anto
    my Quinto of Houston
    my Jackson of San Jo
    my Segundo of El Paso
    my Barelas of Alburque
    my Westside of Denver

Flats, Los Marcos, Maravilla, Calle Guadalupe, Magnolia,
Buena Vista, Mateo, La Seis, Chiquis, El Sur and all
    Chicano neighborhoods that now exist and once
    existed; somewhere. . . . . , someone remembers. . . . .

—Antonia Castaneda Schular, Tomas Ybarra-Fausto, and
Joseph Sommers, eds., *La literatur chicano*

DIFFERENT

I finally get up and put on my *bonaroo* clothes, special
starched jobs that cost me four packs a week. To most
people they probably look like nothing more than blue
denims, neat as denims can be. But here they mean you're
"clean." If you're sharp on the outside, you've gotta be
sharp on the inside, too, and just because everyone has to
wear the same clothes, you can still set yourself off as
different by being a good enough hustler to be able to

afford having your clothes specially done. The con with the concession in the laundry separates my clothes when they come in, does them special, and sends them back through normal channels.

—Anthony J. Manocchio and Jimmy Dunn, *The Time Game*

THE BIRTHRIGHT

The uniformity and conformity of the clothing is a significant element in the blandness and drabness of prison life. As bad as clothing fads on the outside may be, they are to be preferred to prison fashion. In our culture, men and women distinguish themselves, in part, by the clothes they choose to wear. There is an attempt on the part of prisoners to do likewise; however, the limited variety of apparel available makes the attempt sometimes look ludicrous. Thus the Black Muslims can be distinguished from other prisoners by the fact that they invariably button the top buttons of their shirts. Other prisoners may elect to wear a distinguishing cap and at times, wear it inside the dormitory. Still others use India ink to paint words and pictures on their sweat shirts. There are innumerable variations on these themes, and while they often seem trivial they should not be casually dismissed: they represent aborted attempts at asserting one's individuality. As prison officials insist upon homogeneity, the men being so treated insist on being recognized as individuals. Each one knows that he, though a prisoner like every other prisoner, is still a man, a bit different and distinct from every other man. Subverting one's prison uniform is at once a significant and pathetic attempt to retain this birthright.

—Howard Levy and David Miller, *Going to Jail*

A GLIMPSE OF FREEDOM

We had for some time in the prison an eagle, one of the small eagles of the steppes. Someone brought him into the prison wounded and exhausted. All the prisoners crowded round him; he could not fly; his right wing hung down on the ground, one leg was dislocated. I remember how fiercely he glared at us, looking about him at the inquisitive crowd, and opened his crooked beak, prepared to sell his life dearly. When they had looked at him long enough and were beginning to disperse, he hopped limping on one leg and fluttering his uninjured wing to the farthest end of the prison yard, where he took refuge in a corner right under the fence. He remained with us for three months, and all that time would not come out of his corner. At first the convicts often went to look at him and used to set the dog at him. Sharik would fly at him furiously, but was evidently afraid to get too near. This greatly diverted the convicts. "Savage creature! He'll never give in!" they used to say. Later Sharik began cruelly ill-treating him. He got over his fear, and when they set him on the eagle he learnt to catch him by his injured wing. The eagle vigorously defended himself with his beak and, huddled in his corner, he looked fiercely and proudly like a wounded king at the inquisitive crowd who came to stare at him.

At last everyone was tired of him; everyone forgot him, abandoned him, yet every day there were pieces of fresh meat and a broken pot of water near him. So someone was looking after him. At first he would not eat, and ate nothing for several days; at last he began taking food, but he would never take it from anyone's hand or in the presence of people. It happened that I watched him more than once. Seeing no one and thinking that he was alone, he sometimes ventured to come a little way out of his corner and limped a distance of twelve paces along the fence, then he went back and then went out again, as though he were taking exercise. Seeing me he hastened back to his corner, limping and hopping, and throwing back his head, opening his beak, with his feathers ruffled, at once prepared for battle. None of my caresses could soften him; he pecked and struggled, would not take meat from me, and all the time I was near him he used to stare intently in my face with his savage, piercing eyes. Fierce and solitary he awaited death, mistrustful and hostile to all. At last the convicts seemed to remember him, and though no one had mentioned him, or done anything for him for two months, everyone seemed suddenly to feel sympathy for him. They said that they must take the eagle out. "Let him die if he must, but not in prison," they said.

"To be sure, he is a free, fierce bird; you can't get him used to prison," others agreed.

"It's not like us, it seems," added someone.

"That's a silly thing to say. He's a bird and we are men, aren't we?"

"The eagle is the king of the forests, brothers," began Skuratov, but this time they did not listen to him.

One day, after dinner, when the drum had just sounded for us to go to work, they took the eagle, holding his beak, for he began fighting savagely, and carried him out of the prison. We got to the rampart. The twelve men of the party were eagerly curious to see where the eagle would go.

Strange to say, they all seemed pleased, as though they too had won a share of freedom.

"See, the cur, one does something for his good, and he keeps biting one," said the convict who was carrying him, looking at the fierce bird almost with affection.

"Let him go, Mikitka!"

"It's no use rigging up a jack-in-the-box for him, it seems. Give him freedom, freedom full and free!"

He threw the eagle from the rampart into the plain. It was a cold, gloomy day in late autumn, the wind was whistling over the bare plain and rustling in the yellow, withered, tussocky grass of the steppes. The eagle went off in a straight line, fluttering his injured wing, as though in haste to get away from us anywhere. With curiosity the convicts watched his head flitting through the grass.

"Look at him!" said one dreamily. "He doesn't look round!" added another. "He hasn't looked round once, lads, he just runs off!"

"Did you expect him to come back and say thank you?" observed a third.

"Ah, to be sure it's freedom, It's freedom he sniffs."

"You can't see him now, mates. . . ."

"What are you standing for? March!" shouted the guards, and we all trudged on to work in silence.

—Dostoevsky, *The House of the Dead*

THE LAST FREEDOM

. . . Once, a group of naked prisoners about to enter the gas chamber stood lined up in front of it. In some way the commanding SS officer learned that one of the women prisoners had been a dancer. So he ordered her to dance for him. She did, and as she danced, she approached him, seized his gun, and shot him down. She too was immediately shot to death.

But isn't it probable that despite the grotesque setting in which she danced, dancing made her once again a person? Dancing, she was singled out as an individual, asked to perform in what had once been her chosen vocation. No longer was she a number, a nameless, depersonalized prisoner, but the dancer she used to be. Transformed, however momentarily, she responded like her old self, destroying the enemy bent on her destruction, even if she had to die in the process.

Despite the hundreds of thousands of living dead men who moved quietly to their graves, this one example, and there were several like her, shows that in an instant the old personality can be regained, its destruction undone, once we decide on our own that we wish to cease being units in a system. Exercising the last freedom that not even the concentration camp could take away—to decide how one wishes to think and feel about the conditions of one's life—this dancer threw off her real prison. This she could do because she was willing to risk her life to achieve autonomy once more. If we do that, then if we cannot live, at least we die as men. . . .

Those prisoners who blocked out neither heart nor reason, neither feelings nor perception, but kept informed of their inner attitudes even when they could hardly ever afford to act on them, those prisoners survived and came to understand the conditions they lived under. They also came to realize what they had not perceived before; that they still retained the last, if not the greatest, of the human freedoms: to choose their own attitude in any given circumstance. Prisoners who understood this fully, came to know that this, and only this, formed the crucial difference between retaining one's humanity (and often life itself) and accepting death as a human being (or perhaps physical death): whether one retained the freedom to choose autonomously one's attitude to extreme conditions even when they seemed totally beyond one's ability to influence them.

—Bruno Bettelheim, *The Informed Heart*

Biographical Notes

RENÉ BELBENOIT. See biographical notes, chapter 9.

JOSHUA HILL. See biographical notes, chapter 10.

DONALD POWELL WILSON. See biographical notes, chapter 1.

LOWELL NAEVE. Imprisoned as a conscientious objector during World War II, Naeve now lives in Canada, where he and his wife operate a summer camp for children.

JIM PECK. See biographical notes, chapter 5.

ARTHUR KOESTLER (b. 1905). Distinguished novelist and essayist, Koestler was born in Hungary. He worked as a foreign correspondent in France and Germany, and was imprisoned by Franco during the Spanish Civil War as a Communist; three months later he was released on May 12, 1937.

HENRI CHARRIÈRE. See biographical notes, chapter 11.

raulsalinas. A chicano poet, raulsalinas is imprisoned at Leavenworth.

ANTHONY J. MANOCCHIO. See biographical notes, chapter 4.

JIMMY DUNN. See biographical notes, chapter 4.

HOWARD LEVY and DAVID MILLER. See biographical notes, chapter 5.

FYODOR DOSTOEVSKY (1821–1881). One of the world's great novelists, he was born in Moscow and went later to St. Petersburg to study engineering. He resigned his commission to devote himself to literature. In 1849, he was arrested as a Socialist; charged with "having attempted with others to circulate anti-Government writings with the aid of a private press," he was sentenced to eight years penal servitude; the sentence was commuted to four years. From 1850 to 1854, with nothing to read but the Bible, Dostoevsky served out his sentence in Omsk prison. The account of these years, *The House of the Dead,* was his most popular work during his lifetime.

BRUNO BETTELHEIM (b. 1903). Head of the University of Chicago's Sonia Shankman Orthogenic School, he was born in Vienna, and first began to practice psychoanalysis in that city. After a year in the concentration camps of Dachau and Buchenwald, he same to the United States in 1939. Out of these experiences he wrote his famous study *Individual and Mass Behavior in Extreme Situations.*

15.

IN HELL TOGETHER

It occurred to me that if one day we should all be in hell together it would be very much like this place.

—Dostoevsky,
The House of the Dead

Despite heroic efforts of prisoners to hold onto their identities, some have lost this capacity, and merely survive without a sense of self. For Ezra Pound, charged with propagandizing for the enemy and imprisoned by American troops in Italy in 1945, it was "fatigue deep as the grave." For draft resisters confined during the Vietnam War in a California prison, it is described by Dr. Lewis Merklin as a state of nonbeing: ". . . if I notice nothing, then nothing is happening . . . if nothing is happening, then nothing is happening to me." The feeling that one's life is superfluous and meaningless, no more important than the number assigned it, is a feeling some prisoners experience only intermittently; for others it is a gradual downhill process, and irreversible. When selfhood is stripped, one moves from "hell" into "the house of the dead."

PRISON STUPOR

At the age of sixteen I was working as office boy for a commission merchant who owned a warehouse in the freightyards near the State Prison. Occasionally I was sent on errands which took me past the main gate of the prison, through the steel-barred gate of which I could usually see one or more trusties raking the lawn or working in the garden. One day I stopped, leaned against the steel pickets of the fence which enclosed the prison courtyard, and looked in. A trusty in a suit of striped overalls was standing with his arms folded lazily against the handle of the rake, his head resting dejectedly on his arms, his whole attitude that of a man who had worked all day and was very tired, although it was only about nine o'clock of a cool spring morning. He seemed almost in a coma. There was an expression of utter indifference on his face, and his eyes were glazed with absent-mindedness. He was, although I did not know it then, a living example of the total, final, devastating effect of imprisonment upon the human being.

Six years later I was serving my first term of imprisonment in this very prison. As I stood in the line at "bucket parade" one morning, another column of convicts marched past us. In it was a young man of about my own age (twenty-two) who was surreptitiously laughing and joking wih a companion. He was apparently a recent arrival and certainly a first-termer; his face, his movements, his whole attitude expressed youth and health and unconcerned gaiety. An old-timer who was standing beside me said, out of the corner of his mouth, "This place will take a lot of that steam out of him in pretty short order!" There was a kind of admiration tinged with sadness in his eyes as he said it. "I was like him a few years ago," he added. Without knowing why, I somehow knew that the old-timer was right; that imprisonment would eventually rob the young prisoner of his gaiety, his spirit and something I call the gaiety of his tissues. I thought of the somnolent trusty I had seen years before. All about me I could see men with the same expressionless faces, the same sluggish, lifeless movements. The deadening result of imprisonment.

What was this horrible thing, I wondered, which could make weak dawdlers of men who had been full of health and strength a few years ago? As the years rolled past, I began to learn. The remarkable thing about it, I thought, was that the convicts were aware of its wide prevalence and yet seemed powerless to keep out of its constricting clutches. It struck me that there must be something very devious and dangerous about an affliction which could attack men who were conscious not only of its unconcealed presence, but also of its cruel power. There was, and there is! To this day, I have never lost my fear of it. I dread it as I dread the thought of being gripped by some powerful and unbreakable habit like drug addiction. For I will go so far as to say that I consider its effects as enervating and demoralizing as the effects of a habit-forming drug. That a man may come out of prison penniless, lacking friends, without a home or a job, is, to my mind, not nearly so awful as that he may come out a victim of prison stupor (as some of us term this malady).

—Victor F. Nelson, *Prison Days and Nights*

I didn't sing a note the whole time I was in Alderson. I didn't feel like singing. So I didn't. A lot of the girls in there were nice kids. They used to beg me to perform and they'd get sore at me when I refused. It didn't matter. I couldn't have sung if I'd wanted to. If they'd understood my kind of singing they'd have known I couldn't sing in a place like that. The whole basis of my singing is feeling. Unless I feel something, I can't sing. In the whole time I was there I didn't feel a thing.

—Billie Holiday, *Lady Sings the Blues*

BEING SUPERFLUOUS
(Nazi Germany)

Once . . . a prisoner was to have gotten a flogging but was discharged before it happened. A newcomer was given his prison number and a few days later the punishment was administered to him, since the whole transaction was recorded under a number.

The punisher had no interest in knowing why the punishment was inflicted, or on whom. The unit beaten was just "a prisoner." Certainly punishment as such had purposes: to increase output, to debase prisoners, to increase the Gestapo's sense of power, to intimidate the prisoners and the population at large. But for such purposes any prisoner would do as well as any other. So even his supreme suffering now had nothing to do with the individual as such. He died because Jews had become superfluous, because there were too many Poles, or because civilians outside the camps had to be taught a lesson.

—Bruno Bettelheim, *The Informed Heart*

DEHUMANIZATION
(Prisons in New York, 1900)

AUBURN (WOMEN)

ANNIE M. WELSHE, ... Matron.

CLINTON

DAVID F. DOBIE, ... Warden.
ELIJAH VOGAN, ... Principal Keeper.
REV. JOHN E. METCALFE, ... Chaplain.
JULIUS B. RANSOM, M.D., ... Physician.

EDITORIAL STAFF

No. 1,500, Sing Sing . . . . . Editor-in-Chief.
No. 1,501, Sing Sing . . . . . Assistant Editor.
No. 25,818, Auburn . . . . . . Local Editor.
No. 3,965, Clinton . . . . . . Local Editor.
No. 196, Auburn, Women's Prison . . Local Editor.
No. 336, Auburn, Women's Prison . Asst. Local Editor.

—Masthead of *Star of Hope*, Sing Sing, May 5, 1900

THE EDGE

Soledad
Jan 5, 1971

[*From Mass of Desperate Papers*]
As a human being I have grown dependent on belonging to others and as a creature I am dependent upon freedom

and exposure to nature—as a prisoner I am removed from both of these things.

I am so afraid that my mind cannot accept reality of being trapped here. On approaching realization—big hysterical claustrophobia—suffocation comes. I realize that I live in delusion of hope of possible release or resumption of life. Life is ended. I can no longer live in imagination of hope. My mind is broken—but I cannot admit that this is true. Many here go insane too . . . They scream in terror as articulated patterns of mind terminate abandoning them to the reality they can no longer avoid. One screamed "Hot and cold, hot and cold," Another "Help me, please let me out of here." I know this fear now and often. To realize that I am subject to people who regard me in such a way as to treat me thus is fear but real terror is the phenomena itself—the moments passing. This is attack on mind—to torture. It makes no sense to express reasons why I should not be tortured this way because there is no sane reason to do this to me. These words are the only thing my mind hangs on as I write I am unable to re-read. Please do what you can to get me out of here as soon as possible. Yes, I am weak. Yes, I am insane. Reality is claustrophobia for me now. Hysteria.

It is Sunday morning, about 3 a.m. Rolling and smoking cigarettes blot out fear—divert. That everyone has abandoned me to this leaves no identity—no love—no together with any-one. To be alone, on an island, would be different. This is like a mine cave in where nobody digs to free you.

Smoke smoke. Nobody responds to what I say. But this is song for life and is good-right song and laws song-to assassinate is bad-wrong song. So I say I cannot communicate with anybody. I write many letters mail none for a long time. Then hysteria allayed by writing letter and tem-

porarily put down by sending but only gone by release.
Then not gone until law made right, follow outside too.
I am afraid of law, I do not respect it. This is what has
bothered my whole life—I do not trust law for good reason.
I am afraid of people for good reason. Truth and right and
equality no good against guns, or money, or force.

Bryce

—Eve Pell, ed., *Maximum Security, Letters from Prison*

HARD ROCK
RETURNS TO PRISON
FROM THE HOSPITAL FOR
THE CRIMINAL INSANE

Hard Rock was "known not to take no shit
From nobody," and he had the scars to prove it:
Split purple lips, lumped ears, welts above
His yellow eyes, and one long scar that cut
Across his temple and plowed through a thick
Canopy of kinky hair.

The WORD was that Hard Rock wasn't a mean nigger
Anymore, that the doctors had bored a hole in his head,
Cut out part of his brain, and shot electricity
Through the rest. When they brought Hard Rock back,
Handcuffed and chained, he was turned loose,
Like a freshly gelded stallion, to try his new status.
And we all waited and watched, like indians at a corral,
To see if the WORD was true.

As we waited we wrapped ourselves in the cloak
Of his exploits: "Man, the last time, it took eight
Screws to put him in the Hole." "Yeah, remember when he
Smacked the captain with his dinner tray?" "He set
The record for time in the Hole—67 straight days!"
"Ol Hard Rock! man, that's one crazy nigger."
And then the jewel of a myth that Hard Rock had once bit
A screw on the thumb and poisoned him with syphilitic spit.

The testing came, to see if Hard Rock was really tame.
A hillbilly called him a black son of a bitch
And didn't lose his teeth, a screw who knew Hard Rock
From before shook him down and barked in his face.
And Hard Rock did *nothing*. Just grinned and looked silly,
His eyes empty like knot holes in a fence.

And even after we discovered that it took Hard Rock
Exactly 3 minutes to tell you his first name,
We told ourselves that he had just wised up,
Was being cool; but we could not fool ourselves for long,
And we turned away, our eyes on the ground. Crushed.
He had been our Destroyer, the doer of things
We dreamed of doing but could not bring ourselves to do,
The fears of years, like a biting whip,
Had cut grooves too deeply across our backs.

—Etheridge Knight, *Black Voices from Prison*

Biographical Notes

VICTOR NELSON (1898–?). Born in Sweden, he came to the
United States with his family while still a boy. Between
the ages of fourteen to thirty-four he spent most of his life

in prisons for drunkenness and theft. He aroused the interest of Dr. Abraham Myerson, Psychiatric Examiner of Prisoners for the Commonwealth of Massachusetts, and was paroled in his care in 1932.

BILLIE HOLIDAY (1915–1959). One of the great jazz musicians of all time, Billie was born in Baltimore, but came to New York City at an early age. She was for a time a prostitute and maid, but her vocal talent was discovered before she was twenty. She was arrested in Philadelphia in 1947, and charged with illegal use and transportation of drugs. Sentenced to the Federal Reformatory for Women at Alderson, West Virginia, Billie took the cure and was released in ten months. Throughout the years she was persecuted by the government, and because of her record denied the right of a cabaret license, thus depriving her of an important source of income. She died at the age of forty-four, with seventy cents in the bank and $750 in fifty-dollar bills taped to her leg.

BRUNO BETTELHEIM. See biographical notes, chapter 14.

BRYCE. A prisoner at Soledad, California.

ETHERIDGE KNIGHT. See biographical notes, chapter 7.

16.

THE MILITARY DISSIDENT

In 1971, inmates of Attica Prison in New York state rebelled against conditions in the prison. The State Police were called in and at the end of the riot, thirty-nine people —thirty prisoners and nine hostages—were dead. This massacre alerted the world to the horror of American prisons. In 1968, the brutality that passes for army discipline was revealed through the Presidio incident. A group of military prisoners in the San Francisco stockade attempting nonviolently to present a list of grievances against inhuman conditions in the prison were forcibly disbanded without being granted a hearing and then court-martialed for the capital offense of "mutiny." By the very desperation of their act, the men of Presidio caused us to wonder if the army should be, in the words of the Supreme Court, "a specialized community governed by a separate discipline from that of the civilian."

Since the army is totalitarian, and, indeed, must be, say its supporters, dissent within its ranks is punished as a criminal act. The court-martial and subsequent imprisonment of Privates Dennis Mora, David Samas, and James Johnson, the "Fort Hood Three," is but another incident in many, proving that conscience is not always an inalienable right—at least, not if one is wearing the uniform of the United States Army.

In the most technical sense, the Fort Hood Three and the thousands of other war resisters were political prisoners. They questioned, then defied a policy of their government which, as loyal citizens, they were expected to carry out. Imprisoned for refusing to kill, condemned to suffer the same problems in prison as those who are there because they have killed, *the Fort Hood Three and men like David Miller were victims of the times—of a flawed national morality.*

BALLAD OF THE FORT HOOD THREE

Come all you brave Americans
    and listen to me.
If you can spare five minutes
    in this twentieth century,
I'll sing to you a story true
    as you will plainly see.
It's about three soldiers,
    they call "the Fort Hood Three."

"We've been told in training that in
    Vietnam we must fight,
"And we may have to kill women and
    children, and that is quite all right.
"We say this war's illegal, immoral,
    and unjust.
"We're taking legal action, just the
    three of us.

"We'll report for duty, but we won't
    go overseas.
"We're prepared to face court martial,
    but we won't fight for Ky.
"We three have talked it over, our
    decision now is clear.

"We will not go to Vietnam, we'll
fight for freedom here."

—Pete Seeger

Private David Samas: "I was opposed to the war in Vietnam before I was drafted, but I entered the service with an attitude that I fear I shared with thousands of other men: that is, that my convictions would never be put to a test, because I probably would not be sent to Vietnam. Everyone to some extent has the attitude that 'it' always happens to the other guy. On June 10, I received my orders for Vietnam. It had happened to me, and I had to make a decision to either follow my orders and go to Vietnam or to hold fast to my beliefs and refuse to go. . . .

My grandparents came to this country because it offered them a chance to work, to live as a free people and raise their families as they believed best, and to speak and worship as they pleased. They came and worked in the coal fields of Pennsylvania and the stockyards of Chicago. Our country welcomed them because it had the freedoms they sought. It had fought for and won its independence. The Vietnamese now are struggling as once we did. They are fighting for their liberty against the most powerful country that ever existed. Ironically, they fight against us.

They have a right to their freedom, just as we did. I will not deny them their rights. . . . *I will not go to Vietnam.*"

PFC James Johnson: "In my case the fact that I am Negro makes the fact of U.S. involvement even more acute. . . . The Negro in Vietnam is being called upon to defend a freedom which in many parts of this country does not exist for him. . . . Just as Negroes are fighting for absolute freedom and self determination in the United States, so it is with the Vietnamese in their struggle against the Americans. . . .

On December 6, 1965 I took an oath to obey my authorized superiors. Nevertheless I must obey my conscience and convictions first. I can do this by not going to Vietnam. I emphatically refuse to serve in Vietnam."

Joint Statement read at press conference by Dennis Mora: "We have decided to take a stand against this war, which we consider immoral, illegal and unjust. We are initiating today, through our attorneys, . . . an action in the courts to enjoin the Secretary of Defense and the Secretary of the Army from sending us to Vietnam. We intend to report as ordered to the Oakland Army Terminal, but under no circumstances will we board ship for Vietnam. We are prepared to face Court Martial if necessary.

We represent in our backgrounds a cross section of the Army and of America. James Johnson is a Negro, David Samas is of Lithuanian and Italian parents, I am a Puerto Rican. We speak as American soldiers."

—*Liberation*, July 1966

THE INHERITANCE

The existing system of military justice is un-American, having come to us by inheritance and rather witless adoption out of a system of government which we regard as fundamentally intolerable; it is archaic, belonging as it does to an age when armies were but bodies of armed retainers and bands of mercenaries; it is a system arising out of and regulated by the mere power of Military Command rather than Law; it has ever resulted, as it must ever result, in such injustice as to crush the spirit of the individual subjected to it, shock the public conscience and alienate public esteem and affection from the Army that insists upon maintaining it. . . . The system may well be said to be a lawless system. It is not a code of law; it is not buttressed in law, nor are correct legal conclusions its objective. The agencies applying it are not courts, their proceedings are not regulated by law. The system sets up and recognizes no legal standard, and has no place for lawyers and judges. Whatever is done with the final approval of the convening commander is done finally beyond all earthly power of correction.

—Lt. Colonel S. A. Ansell, U.S. Army, *Cornell Law Review*, 1919

PRESIDIO!

There were tears and shouts of joy outside the barren one-room courthouse on the afternoon of June 7. Fourteen GI's charged with mutiny for conducting a peaceful sit-down demonstration last October at the San Francisco Presidio stockade had just been given light—by Army standards—sentences. Two of the 14 had been found guilty of lesser crimes than mutiny and sentenced to three and six months additional confinement. Of the 12 convicted of mutiny, Private Richard L. Gentile, a Vietnam veteran, was rewarded for his year of battle duty with a sentence of only six months at hard labor; others, whom the Army tagged as leaders of the mutinous cabal, were let off with just 15 more months in the brig. To add to the euphoric feelings, Lt. Col. Richard Potter, president of the five-man court-martial panel, assured the prisoners, "You fellows pull yourselves together and you'll be home for Christmas."

Mounting public pressure was responsible for the shorter sentences imposed upon the latest batch of "mutineers" to be court-martialed. (The first three demonstrators to be tried received sentences of 14, 15 and 16 years confinement, subsequently reduced by the Judge Advocate General's office in Washington to two years each.) And perhaps some of them would be home for Christmas, if they could withstand the strain of more dismal months inside an Army stockade. But the reason these young men were on trial in the first place was that they could not play the cover-your-ass games demanded of them by the Army. Each of them, sooner or later in their military experiences, had cracked, gone AWOL, and been thrown in the Presidio stockade.

—Peter Barnes, *The New Republic*, July 5, 1969

THE COMFORTABLE LIFE

At the time of the sit-down there were 140 prisoners at the Presidio, of whom 120 were imprisoned in space meant to hold 88. There was one toilet for about every thirty-five prisoners because not all of the toilets had seats and some were stopped up and unusable. Much of the time there was no toilet paper. The clogged toilets backed up into the shower rooms, the floors of which were sometimes two or three inches under water. Human feces floated in the water, so it was sometimes best to wear one's boots while taking a shower. Prisoners had to buy their own soap, and if a prisoner ran out in the middle of the week, he couldn't have another bar until the next week. If he lost his toothbrush, he couldn't get another until the following month. Prisoners in segregated cells were sometimes not permitted to bathe or brush their teeth for a week. The barracks were crowded and prisoners lying on the top tier of the bunk beds were suffocatingly close to the ceiling. Once there was a fire in a segregation cell and prisoners on the top floors of the stockade found themselves locked in. On the day of the sit-down, as on other days, the stockade was short of food. There were only fifty-four drinking cups for the whole prison population. Recreation consisted of one movie a week, chosen by the chaplain. The prison library, which closed at 4 P.M., before the men came back from work, was in the basement and accessible only by making one's way around garbage cans; the books were ancient ones, on such subjects as mysticism and military history. Families could visit prisoners, but it was against the rules, for example, for an inmate father to hold his baby. Everywhere were filth and the smell of human waste. And, of course, there were rats.

But the men who sat down in the prison yard that fine October morning in 1968 had deeper worries than arise from poor living conditions. There was an atmosphere of brutality about the Presidio stockade that made them panicky.

An official Presidio press release claimed that "prisoners live a more comfortable life than the regular soldier who performs his duties properly." Then why the fifty-two suicide attempts in 1968? Colonel Harry J. Lee, provost marshal for the Sixth Army, had a reply: "There have been no suicides nor has there been a bonafide suicide attempt at the stockade in the memory of personnel now serving at the facility since at least June, 1966." The Army does not call them suicide attempts; it calls them "gestures." Private Roy Pulley, one of the protesters, told how one gesture struck him: "I was lying on my side on the bunk reading one night, and this guy across the room was sitting on his bunk. He tied something around his arm to make the veins swell up so he could cut them better. And when he cut them, the blood flew about twenty feet—hit me right in the back of the neck."

A total of six gestures was made by Ricky Lee Dodd. On one occasion he cut his wrists when he was imprisoned in solitary. He was taken to the hospital, where the wrists were sewn up and bandaged, and he was returned to the stockade. This time he removed the gauze from his wrists and hanged himself. When he arrived back at the hospital he was pronounced dead, but he was revived. He had previously attempted suicide by slashing and hanging. After one of those earlier attempts, a guard had handed him a razor blade with the cheerful encouragement, "If you want to try again, here we go." After another, a guard had squirted him with urine from a water pistol.

—Robert Sherrill, *Military Justice Is to Justice as Military Music Is to Music*

"FUCK IT, IT AIN'T WORTH LIVING."

The spark that ignited the October 14 demonstration was the killing by a guard of 19-year-old Private Richard Bunch, a frail, boyish-faced brooder whom everyone inside the stockade knew was insane.

Bunch got through the first year of his Army duty with no apparent problems. Then he was transferred to Fort Lewis and something went wrong. He went AWOL, wandered through Haight-Ashbury on drugs, then turned up at his mother's home in Dayton, Ohio. Mrs. Bunch scarcely recognized her own son. He babbled that he had died twice and been reincarnated as a warlock. She tried to have him hospitalized for psychiatric treatment but no institution would accept an AWOL GI. In desperation she called the Army and received a written promise that her son would receive psychiatric care. Instead, he was thrown into the stockade, first at Fort Meade, Md., then at the Presidio.

It didn't take long for Bunch's fellow-inmates to realize he was mentally deranged. Bunch would sit on his bunk in a lotus position and mumble about his reincarnations. He would announce that he could walk through walls, and then he would walk into them. At night the whole stockade would be awakened by Bunch's frantic screams.

One day in October, Bunch asked a prisoner to recommend a fool-proof method of committing suicide. The prisoner suggested running away from a shotgun detail. On Friday, October 11, while on a shotgun detail, Bunch asked a guard, "If I run will you shoot me?" The guard replied, "You'll have to run to find out." Bunch requested the guard to shoot at his head, then skipped away directly in front of him. He had gone barely 30 feet when the guard killed him with a 12-gauge shotgun blast straight at his back. No one had heard the guard yell "Halt."

When word of the shooting reached the stockade, the prisoners could barely contain their fury. Someone walked over to Bunch's bunk and found a hand-written note that said, "Fuck it, it ain't worth living." Stockade officials quickly declared the shooting a "justifiable homicide." To the prisoners it was the last straw in a long train of cruelties that threatened their sanity and now, they thought, their lives. In their agitated state, some inmates talked of killing a guard or burning down the stockade. By Sunday night, passions had cooled enough for the prisoners to agree upon a nonviolent, orderly demonstration the following morning. The idea was to sit down until someone listened to their grievances.

A list was drawn up on a DD-510 form with seven main demands: elimination of shotgun details, complete psychological evaluations of all prisoners and guards, elimination of racist guards, rotation of guards to prevent the build-up of antagonisms (guards worked 12-hour shifts with nine days on and three days off), better sanitary facilities, decent food in sufficient quantities, and a chance to tell the press the prisoners' version of Bunch's slaying. Surely, they believed, if only those in authority could know what was *really* going on in the Presidio stockade, help would be quickly forthcoming. Human beings couldn't be treated this way; *Americans* couldn't be treated this way. If only people *knew*. . . .

Monday morning at 7:30, 27 prisoners broke from the roll-call formation, sat down in the grassy area of the stockade and asked to see Capt. Lamont, the stockade commander. Lamont arrived, accompanied by a fire truck and an Army photographer who circled the demonstrators, taking pictures from all angles. Private Walter Pawlowski, one of the three "mutineers" who has since escaped to Canada, stood up and started to read the list of grievances. Lamont was not interested in grievances. He had been tipped in advance about the impending demonstration and was interested only in mutiny. He walked over to a loudspeaker in an MP patrol car and proceeded to recite Article 94 of the Uniform Code of Military Justice, the mutiny article. ("Any person subject to this code who, with intent to usurp or override lawful military authority, refuses, in concert with any other person, to obey orders or otherwise do his duty or creates any violence or disturbance, is guilty of mutiny.") Then he ordered the demonstrators back to Building 1213.

The prisoners didn't budge. They remained in a circle, chanting for the press, for freedom, and for Terence Hallinan, a young San Francisco attorney with several clients in the stockade. They sang "America the Beautiful," "This Land is My Land," and "We Shall Overcome." They flashed the V sign.

After about 40 minutes, Lamont turned to the chief of the fire truck—a civilian—and requested him to hose down the demonstrators. The fireman refused. Lamont then ordered 25 MP's to escort the demonstrators back to their cellblocks. According to an Army fact sheet, "no force was required other than physically carrying some of the prisoners off." The Army photographer had to admit it was a "very moving demonstration."

Dr. Price M. Cobbs, co-author of *Black Rage*, subsequently examined several of the prisoners. "They reacted like black people," he said. "They sat down and sang 'We Shall Overcome.' That was probably the first time in their lives they had ever sung that song. They reacted in a non-violent fashion, like Martin Luther King."

Nonviolent or not, the deed at the Presidio had been done and the wheels of Army "justice" quickly began to spin. Under the UCMJ—the US military code adopted in George Washington's day from the British Articles of War and revised only minimally since then—the commanding officer of a soldier's unit brings the charges against him, appoints military counsel, selects the court-martial panel (jury), and even approves or disapproves of the verdict and sentences levied. In the case of the San Francisco Presidio, headquarters for the US Sixth Army, the commanding officer is Lt. Gen. Stanley R. Larsen, a three-star general whose rapid ascent in the ranks was much the envy of his fellow-officers. (They're not so envious any more: Larsen's mishandling of the Presidio demonstration may well have cost him his fourth star.)

Larsen could have brought charges less serious than mutiny, a capital offense. Or he could have handled the whole problem administratively. But Larsen was evidently determined to show that youthful dissent would never be tolerated in the Sixth Army as long as he was in command. He decided to back up Lamont and call it a mutiny.

Not all of the brass at the Presidio felt this was wise. After a pretrial hearing required by Article 32 of the UCMJ (the military's equivalent of grand jury proceedings), hearing officer Capt. Richard J. Millard recommended that the demonstrators be tried by special court-martial with a maximum sentencing power of six months, or instead be simply separated from the Army with less than honorable discharges. "The charge of mutiny under Article 94 does not apply to the facts of 14 October 1968," Millard stated in his official report. "There are three elements to the offense of mutiny, one of which is the intent to override lawful military authority. The element is absent in the present case." Millard noted that conditions in the stockade were "not up to the standards we should expect," and that the prescribed grievance procedures for prisoners, as implemented at the Presidio, were "shoddy and inefficient." "To charge [the accused] with mutiny, an offense which has its roots in the harsh admiralty laws of previous centuries, for demonstrating against conditions which existed in the stockade, is, in my opinion, an overreaction by the Army." But Larsen, egged on by Col. James Garrett, Judge Advocate of the Sixth Army, ignored Millard's report and plunged ahead with the mutiny charges.

The court-martial trials of 22 of the demonstrators at various West Coast bases are now part of history. (The last two demonstrators are currently being tried in San Francisco.) At Fort Ord, where 14 were tried, Terence Hallinan conducted a brilliant defense that included extensive testimony about stockade conditions and statements from 15 prominent psychiatrists concerning the effects of such conditions upon the defendants. The trial record contained over 1½ million words and is believed to be the longest court-martial in US history. . . .

. . . If the Presidio mutiny trials have dramatized one thing above all else, it is that the feudalistic nature of American military justice must now be critically reexamined. At a time when civilian courts have taken enormous strides forward in protecting the civil rights and civil liberties of citizens, the UCMJ and the military courts seem scarcely to have discovered the 178-year-old Bill of Rights.

Grievance procedures in any large bureaucracy are likely to be "shoddy and inefficient," to quote Capt. Millard; but only in the military are citizens *punished* for peacefully attempting to express legitimate grievances. Only in the military can one man—the commanding officer—come so close to serving, or having his representatives serve, as prosecutor, jury and judge. Only in the military can an officer "order" citizens to cease exercising their constitutional rights; any civilian law officer who prevented a citizen from exercising his constitutional rights would be guilty of a federal offense.

Now that an enormous standing Army has become a seemingly permanent fixture in American society, some clearly defined civil rights for GI's—and more humane standards for treating soldiers who shouldn't be soldiers—are an urgent necessity. If the Presidio "mutiny" stirs Congress, or the Army, into action on these fronts, then perhaps Richard Bunch did not die in vain.

—Peter Barnes, *The New Republic*, July 5, 1969

Biographical Notes

DAVID SAMAS, JAMES JOHNSON, DENNIS MORA. For refusing to obey an order to go to Vietnam, Privates Mora, Samas, and Johnson were court-martialed in 1966. All three were found guilty, received dishonorable discharges with forfeiture of pay, and sentenced from three to five years at Leavenworth. They were released in 1968.

LT. COLONEL S. A. ANSELL (1875–1954). Former Acting Judge Advocate General U.S. Army, during World War I.

17.

THE NEW PRISONER: A Change in Consciousness

. . . if any of you gentlemen own dogs, you're treating them better than we're treated here.

—Inmate to team of observers, Attica State Prison, September 1971

In Virginia in 1942, Odell Waller, a black sharecropper, was executed for having killed his landlord during a quarrel over fifty sacks of wheat owed him: he had been convicted—in the name of justice—by a white jury. During the same period, in the same place, and with the same presiding judge, a white man charged with killing a black was—also in the name of justice—acquitted.

Since the death of Waller, the growing influence of the Black Muslim religion, the civil rights movement of the fifties and sixties, and the writings of Malcolm X, Eldridge Cleaver, and George Jackson have created a new mood of protest inside prison and without. Questions are being asked that have never been asked before: are there prisoners of society? is there a convicted class? what is a politicized prisoner? Trials, judgments, and inequities in sentencing are being studied in the light of a new political consciousness.

Inmates, no longer content to play the scapegoat role traditionally assigned them, now feel themselves objects of an exploitative social order, members of an oppressed class without choice, doomed to suffer—whether in or out of prison—conditions essentially the same. The 1970 prison strike at Folsom (the longest strike in California prison history) and the Attica massacre in 1971 have won new support for the prison movement; liberal-minded citizens now welcome prison militants into the vanguard of social change.

While correctional officers and politicians are debating prison reform in their most civilized manner and fringe groups such as the Symbionese Liberation Army of 1974 engage in self-defeating struggles that are concerned more with revenge against society than with basic problems of injustice and inequality—the New Prisoners are coming into the arena; and with the blacks, the Chicanos, the Puerto Ricans, the Indians, and the armies of Women's and Gay Liberation they are not asking for, but are demanding their rights.

What will be the answer?

YESTERDAY

We owe to the officers and the prison management the duty of living not only within the letter but also within the spirit of the prison rules, that their task, which is not a pleasant one by any manner of means, may be made lighter and our imprisonment made thereby shorter.

We should in our work give the State the best that is in us, for only in giving our best do we show, not only that we are truly repentant, but are making atonement for the wrongs we committed.

—*Sing Sing Bulletin,* convict's statement, December 1920

–AND TODAY

We the convicts and our people imprisoned or at large throughout the state of California are being subjected to a continuous cycle of poverty, prison, parole and more poverty; the same cycle that prisoners the world over have endured since the first man was enslaved. It is more than a game of Crime and Punishment; it is a social condition of inequality and degradation that denies us the opportunity to rise up and pursue a dignified way of life as guaranteed by the UNITED STATES CONSTITUTION. Once convicted, forever doomed has been the practice of society. We are the first to be accused and the last to be recognized. We are branded the lowest of all people: we the CONVICTED CLASS.

The right to organize for protection and survival is an inalienable right which is guaranteed to all people regardless of their social, racial, religious, economic, or political condition. Therefore, we the CONVICTED CLASS have banded together to form a cooperative Union to be hereafter called the UNITED PRISONERS UNION. We believe the creation of this Union will enable us to put an end to injustice, protect the lives and interests of our people, gain our constitutional rights and free us of our bondage.

—Preamble to the Constitution of the United Prisoners Union, 1971

Whereas formerly prisoners tended to regard themselves as unfortunates whose accident of birth at the bottom of the heap was largely responsible for their plight, today many are questioning the validity of the heap. . . .

Increasing numbers of prisoners are beginning to look upon the whole criminal justice system, with the penitentiary at the end of it, as an instrument of class and race oppression.

—Jessica Mitford, "Kind and Usual Punishment in California"

THE MYTH

THE ICED PIG

Number 1

Attica Newsletter

Power brothers! Poder hermanos! This is t first issue of what will be a continuing project. A project that will help to bring each other to an understanding of our place & role in neo-fascist Amerika & t American Auschwitz known at Attica.

Of primary importance is t coming awareness of ourselves as *political prisoners*. No matter how heinous t "crime" u have been convicted of, no matter how many people u offed, drugs u pushed, whores u ran, places u robbed, u are a political prisoner just as much as Angela. *Every act has a cause & effect.* T *cause* of your "crime" is that u found yourself in a society that offered no prospects for a life of fulfillment & sharing with your brothers & sisters. A society where u were taught to compete & beat t guy next to u because if u didn't, he'd beat u. A society whose every facet & angle is thoroughly controlled by t Pigdogs of t corporation giants of Amerika. T apparent *effect* of your "crime" is that now u find yourself locked behind tons of steel & concrete, completely brutalized, cut off from any warmth & affection. But t *real effect* is that u have become waste material to Amerika's ruling class. By your "crime" u have shown Amerika's bosses that u can't cooperate in t "free enterprise" system. That is to say, u won't accept $100 a week for breaking your balls while some fat-assed capitalist drives around in t Mercedes u paid for. By your "crime" u were only doing in a crude way what t Rockefellers & Fords have been doing since they stole this country from t Indians 200 years ago.

Yes brothers, in every sense of t word we are political prisoners. And now we owe it to ourselves & t great masses of struggling humanity, to teach ourselves t truth of Amerika's myth. To forge ourselves into dedicated cadres committed to t construction of a society that will serve t needs of t people & make us into whole human beings at last.

—Samuel Melville, *Letters from Attica*

ATTICA: THE END OF THE LINE

Forty-three citizens of New York State died at Attica Correctional Facility between September 9 and 13, 1971. Thirty-nine of that number were killed and more than 80 others were wounded by gunfire during the 15 minutes it took the State Police to retake the prison on September 13. With the exception of Indian massacres in the late 19th century, the State Police assault which ended the four-day prison uprising was the bloodiest one-day encounter between Americans since the Civil War.

Prison is the end of the criminal justice line—for inmates, for supervisory personnel, and for members of the public who have conveniently forgotten the institutions to which they abandon their most difficult fellow citizens. But official indifference and public forgetfulness is unacceptable. When society places a person behind walls, it cannot put aside its obligation to try to change and help that individual. Chief Justice Warren E. Burger made the point in an address:

When a sheriff or a marshal takes a man from a courthouse in a prison van and transports him to confinement for two or three or ten years, *this is our act. We* have tolled the bell for him. And whether we like it or not, we have made him our collective responsibility. We are free to do something about him; he is not.

Attica, one of those forgotten institutions, housed more than 2,200 inmates on September 9, 1971. There, as at other institutions, the emphasis was on confinement and security. Despite brave talk about rehabilitation as a prime objective of detention, the shortage of trained personnel and the inadequacy of facilities made rehabilitation an impossible dream. In fact, it is not even clear that it was then, or is now, a real objective of the American prison system.

At Attica there was no meaningful program of education for those who wished to learn and no rehabilitation program for those who were willing to rejoin society as constructive citizens. Idleness was the principal occupation. Most correction officers were not equipped by training to communicate with their inmate charges, and did not consider it their duty to understand or to resolve inmate problems. It is scarcely surprising that the original uprising developed almost spontaneously out of small misunderstandings only indirectly related to the major grievances that smoldered below the surface.

—*Attica, The Official Report of the New York State Special Commission on Attica*

THE DISINHERITED

. . . Only twelve days before the uprising, State Correction Commissioner Russell G. Oswald sent a taped message to the 2,000 inmates outlining the steps he was working on to make conditions more nearly bearable. "What I'm asking for is time," he told the prisoners, but time ran out on him. About half the prisoners rose in what amounted to an insurrection which, prudent foresight suggests, is a harbinger of worse to come. They had no firearms. The assault force, also numbering about 1,000, was heavily armed. When they had done their work, thirty-nine men were dead—nine hostages out of the thirty-eight that the convicts had seized, and thirty convicts.

Could this bloody outcome have been avoided? One can only conjecture, but the consensus among enlightened observers is that it could. Mayor Kenneth A. Gibson of Newark termed the suppression "one of the most callous and blatantly repressive acts ever carried out by a supposedly civilized society on its own people." Now Governor Rockefeller is calling for the formation of a five-member panel to investigate what happened. It is to consist of "some top people in the correctional field." In Commissioner Oswald he had a top man, who negotiated with the inmates and seems to have made a good impression on the committee of observers. But the Governor refused to come to Attica, although his mere presence in the town—no one expected him to go inside the prison walls—might have cooled things off sufficiently to enable an agreement to be reached. And, knowing nothing of the circumstances, President Nixon expressed his support of the Rockefeller hard line.

There was undoubtedly a lunatic fringe among the inmates—those who demanded their release to a "nonimperialist power"—but the great majority of those who took part in the insurrection were rational men. Some were rational in the sense that all they wanted was better living conditions and the respect due them as human beings. Others were rational in a revolutionary sense: they were ready to die rather than continue to submit to society's treatment of them. They died, and they won. America's image is further tarnished before the world and, as Senator Muskie said, "the Attica tragedy is more stark proof that something is terribly wrong in America." That view contrasts with Rockefeller's statement that the uprising was brought on by "the revolutionary tactics of militants," and that the investigation would include the role that "outside forces would appear to have played." Whatever outside forces were involved could not have moved a thousand men to such desperation.

The Attica massacre, in one aspect, was a victory of the "tough" school of penologists and the reactionary elements in American society over the modernists. Oswald never had the support of the Attica staff, nor of the townspeople, most of whom make their living from the prison. They favored the former commissioner, who had come up through the ranks and was noted for his toughness. It was the reactionary elements that circulated a report that the nine hostages had had their throats cut by the convicts, and that one had been castrated. This lie was nailed by Dr. John F. Edland, the county medical examiner, who made an impressive appearance on TV. He examined eight of the bodies and found that all had died from gunshot wounds. Another medical examiner came to the same conclusion with regard to the ninth victim. The insurrectionists appear to have been responsible for only one death—that of a guard who was thrown out of a window and who died before the battle in the prison began.

Canards of this virulent type usually mark unjustified action by the guardians of law and order. At Kent State sniper fire was alleged to have impelled the Guardsmen to fire on the students. The commanding general fell back on this excuse and clung to it long after it had been disproved.

Several hundred thousand Americans are inmates of American prisons. At Attica, 85 per cent were Negroes or Puerto Ricans, in the custody of guards who, as one shouted on TV, hated "niggers." Society locks them up to get rid of them—the "correctional" label is a farce. Even separated as they are by incarceration in numerous state and federal penitentiaries, they constitute, morally and even physically, a formidable force. To return to Senator Muskie's evaluation: the rebellion shows that "we have reached the point where men would rather die than live another day in America." The only solution, he said, was "a genuine commitment of our vast resources to the human needs of all the people."

Failure to heed such words would be not only inhumane but stupid. The observers invited into the prison by the insurrectionary inmates . . . were impressed by the tactical skill, the poise and the single-mindedness of the defiant men. These prisoners were politicalized, using the term here not primarily with respect to whatever ideological convictions they may have held, but in the sense that they were aware of themselves as a considerable group sharing common experiences and goals. The uprising at Attica very little resembles prison riots of the past, when goaded men suddenly began beating on their cell bars, hurling their food to the mess hall floor and screaming obscenities at their jailers. This was group action, not mass hysteria. It is the latest, but not in all probability the last, manifestation within a penitentiary of what for lack of a better term is called today black nationalism. But Attica was not a racist movement; blacks and Puerto Ricans were predominant in the resistance, as they predominate in the prison, but many whites stood with them. It was a class action—the class of the disinherited.

When men who have nothing discover that they have one another, they combine into units that are incalculably formidable. That is why the words of sane and compassionate men must be heeded. American prisons have never been institutions; they have always been receptacles. But prisoners are not garbage. It is bad enough—indeed, it is probably wicked—that we deprive them of their freedom, but from now on if we also take from them all hope of a future, we may expect Attica to become the name for a new kind of war. Commissioner Oswald knew that before the first hostage was seized; Rockefeller and Nixon will no doubt fade into the recesses of history with their eyes unopened.

—*The Nation*, editorial, September 27, 1971

AN ANNIVERSARY FOR ATTICA

Elliot Barkley died a year ago today. He died in the yard of D block at Attica. Barkley was 21 years old and black. He was in Attica for violation of parole. He had violated parole by being unemployed, and he was unemployed because he was fired when his boss discovered he was an ex-con.

A year ago today, Walter Dunbar, the Deputy Commissioner of Corrections, stood outside the gray, 30-foot wall of Attica and informed the media that inmates had murdered nine hostages by slitting their throats, and that one hostage was castrated, his testicles stuffed in his mouth. Dunbar said the storming of the prison was "an efficient, affirmative police action."

A year ago today Nelson Rockefeller released a statement from his home on Fifth Avenue that began: "Our hearts go out to the families of the hostages who died at Attica." He pointedly offered no sympathy for Elliot Barkley's mother, living in Buffalo's black ghetto, or for the children and widows of the 29 inmates who died by his decision.

It is now a year later, the picture has slowly emerged, and I think it is clear who should be punished.

* * *

Every hostage who died on Sept. 13, 1971, was killed by state police guns. The official version of slit throats and castration was disproved by the autopsies. We now know thanks to the McKay Commission hearings that between fourteen and seventeen corrections officers, without permission, fired into the yard of D block with their own hunting guns, and that they killed two inmates. We now know that the state police were firing dumdum bullets, which are outlawed under international law and the Geneva Convention. We now know that 450 rounds of ammunition were fired into the yard in that "efficient" action, hitting one out of every ten inmates. We now know the inmates had no guns and fired no bullets. We now know, after a public screening of the official film of the police assault, that the first warning to the inmates to surrender came after four minutes and twenty seconds of heavy shooting. We now know that it wasn't only the inmates, and the hostages, and observers' committee who pleaded with the Governor to come to Attica, but that Corrections Commissioner Russell Oswald, on three separate occasions, implored the Governor to come.

There is also now sufficient evidence to suggest another factor in the Attica massacre not mentioned by Governor Rockefeller or Commissioner Dunbar. That factor is racism.

On Sept. 13, 1971, 70 per cent of the 2,254 men in Attica were blacks and Puerto Ricans; whites somehow end up in nice prisons like Walkill. But not one of the guards at Attica was black or Puerto Rican. And not one of the 2,800 residents of the town of Attica was nonwhite. The guards in Attica called their batons "nigger sticks."

Of the 600 state police who stormed Attica, not one was black. When they surged into the yard, they were chanting, "White power, white power."

The racism even extended beyond death. In the Attica morgue, the dead guards were tagged with their names. The dead inmates were tagged, "P-1," "P-2," and so on.

Conditions inside Attica today are worse than before the riot. Most of the 28 inmate demands that Commissioner Oswald quickly agreed to, and admitted were "long overdue," have still not been implemented. There is still no narcotics program for inmates, the food is still served with glass, bugs and hair in it, there are still frequent complaints of brutality and race-baiting by guards.

More than eighty Attica inmates, presumed "militants," have been locked in solitary confinement for the last 365 days. Most have been dispersed among other upstate prisons, but twenty are still held in Attica's isolation unit. The men are in 6 by 8 cages that have no chair, no mirror, no desk. The windows in their cells have been painted over so they have not seen the sun in a year. The cells are arranged so the men cannot see each other. They are permitted to exercise ten minutes a day, and granted one three-minute shower a week. Some have lost as much as 50 pounds. And they have not been formally charged with anything or given a hearing.

One of the most deeply felt of the 28 demands was the

removal of the two prison doctors, Sternberg and Williams. They are still there. One inmate in isolation went to Dr. Williams with severe chest pains. He was refused medication and told: "You should have died in the yard, nigger." Another inmate has a chronic bone infection in his leg. For months he was denied antibiotics, and given twenty aspirin a day. He will soon have his leg amputated.

Attica was not unique in our recent history. Several times we have watched the state kill, and the killers receive the special amnesty of the powerful. At the Algiers Motel, at Orangeburg, at Kent State, at Jackson State, the law acted as an outlaw and escaped accountability.

On this first anniversary of Attica, I meditate on the short life of Elliot Barkley, and know that Nelson Rockefeller will never be held to account.

—Jack Newfield, *The New York Times*, September 13, 1972

GUILTY!

The criminal courts are political institutions. They reflect in kind many of the inequities and hypocricies of our society as a whole. The courts enforce laws that are politically made, and they maintain the status quo against forces seeking change. The courts mirror and perpetuate racism in that the vast majority of judges are white even though the defendants in any urban area are overwhelmingly black or of Spanish descent; the courts discriminate against the poor who are not able to post even low bail, or afford a lawyer, and who face alien middle-class standards in sentencing. The alcoholic, the drug addict, the psychologically troubled, the rebellious, the political activist, and those on the fringes of society are dealt with the only way the court knows how: repressively. . . . The ineluctable fact remains, however, that the criminal law works best for those already advantaged or privileged.

—National Lawyers Guild, 1970

"WE ARE POLITICAL PRISONERS."

A frequently heard cry from behind the walls of our prisons and jails is: "We are political prisoners."

Most of America turns away in disbelief as they hear this assertion. "Surely," they reassure each other, "the mugger, the robber, the addict, etc., can't think of him- or herself as a political prisoner." For these doubters, the political prisoner is a communist, a spy, a draft evader, etc.

Many of the people in our cages know that their crimes were not of a political nature. But what many have come to learn is that *the politics of our country placed them in circumstances in which crime flourishes*—but even more important—*that the politics of our criminal justice system brought about their imprisonment.* For many Black, Puerto Rican, Chicano, and poor White prisoners know that if they were in different financial and sociological groupings that their arrest, their detention, their bail, their trial, their sentence, and their parole consideration would be vastly different.

George Jackson, at the age of 18, robbed a gas station of $70. 10 years later, before his assassination, he had still not made parole. But Clifford Irving's swindle of $750,000 brought him a 2 year federal prison sentence, and he should be paroled in a year.

Was George Jackson not a political prisoner?

Whether you, sitting in your living room think so or not, George Jackson in his cell knew he was. And all of the George Jacksons in all of the cells are giving more than lip service to this idea today.

Someone had better listen to the sound of thunder.

One of the cries from Attica was: "We are not beasts and we do not intend to be beaten or driven as such . . . What has happened here is but the sound before the fury of those who are oppressed."

—*Fortune News,* August 1972

IDEOLOGY BEYOND PRISON

. . . such a group [Symbionese Liberation Army], originating in the harsh conditions of prison life, can have a potent appeal for those confined offenders who see themselves as the scapegoats of an "oppressive, racist society."

The S.L.A. apparently evolved from a black "cultural association" in California's Vacaville Prison. It has momentarily [1974] caught public attention with its acts of political terrorism. The S.L.A., however, is only one extreme expression of a profound change taking place in prisons in the United States: the politicization of the inmate population and the formation in prison of activist groups organized around the theme of ethnic militancy. . . . Prisons used to be damned as schools of crime by those who knew the futility of life behind the walls and the frequency of recidivism. Now there are many prison officials who are ready to damn the prison as a school for radical ideologies. . . .

American society has long remained indifferent to its prisons and prisoners, but the uprising at Attica in 1971 forced the society to think about the questions. The report of the Attica special citizens commission, directed by Dean Robert McKay of New York University's law school, made clear how the lack of meaningful work, the limited recreational facilities, the authoritarian regime of the guards, and the inadequate medical services all set the stage for a riot. In addition, the McKay report described two other features of the Attica prison which are present in many American prisons and which are changing the nature of the custodial institution.

First, the average age of inmates in many prisons today is lower than in the past. This is true partly because of a change in the age structure of the United States and partly because serious crimes are being committed by younger persons. Prison populations are no longer made up of old, dispirited prisoners easy to control; rather, many prisons have a large number of young offenders, alienated and full of energy.

And second, an increasing proportion of the population in many prisons is black—a "new breed," as they are described by the McKay report, a group of blacks—or Chicanos—who see themselves as the victims of an oppressive society. . . . Large segments of prison populations have coalesced into unified groups, such as the S.L.A., and they and their ideology are clearly capable of enduring beyond prison.

—Gresham Sykes, *The New York Times*, editorial, April 21, 1974

HUEY NEWTON

The prison cannot gain a victory over the political prisoner because he has nothing to be rehabilitated from or to. He refuses to accept the legitimacy of the system and refuses to participate. To participate is to admit that the society is legitimate because of its exploitation of the oppressed. This is the idea which the political prisoner does not accept, this is the idea for which he has been imprisoned, and this is the reason why he cannot cooperate with the system. The political prisoner will, in fact, serve his time . . . Yet the idea which motivated and sustained the political prisoner rests in the people. All the prison has is a body.

—Huey Newton, *To Die for the People*

GEORGE JACKSON

. . . Believe me, when I say that I begin to weary of the sun. I am by nature a gentle man, I love the simple things of life, good food, good wine, an expressive book, music, pretty black women. I used to find enjoyment in a walk in the rain, summer evenings in a place like Harrisburg. Remember how I used to love Harrisburg. All of this is gone from me, all the gentle, shy characteristics of the black man have been wrung unceremoniously from my soul. The buffets and blows of this have and have-not society have engendered in me a flame that will live, will live to grow, until it either destroys my tormentor or myself. You don't understand this but I must say it. Maybe when you remember this ten or twenty years from now you'll comprehend. I don't think of life in the same sense that you or most black men of your generation think of it, it is not important to me how long I live. I think only of how I live, how well, how nobly. We think if we are to be men again we must stop working for nothing, competing against each other for the little they allow us to possess, stop selling our women or allowing them to be used and handled against their will, stop letting our children be educated by the barbarian, using their language, dress, and customs, and most assuredly stop turning our cheeks.

—George Jackson, *Soledad Brother*

A CHANGE IN CONSCIOUSNESS

It is too obvious that the legislative and judiciary systems of the United States were established in order to protect a capitalist minority and, if forced, the whole of the white population; but these infernal systems are still raised against the black man. We have known for a long time now that the black man is, from the start, natively, the guilty man. We can be sure that if the blacks, by the use of their violence, their intelligence, their poetry, all that they have accumulated for centuries while observing their former masters in silence and in secrecy—if the blacks do not undertake their own liberation, the whites will not make a move.

But already Huey Newton, Bobby Seale, the members of the Black Panther party, George Jackson, and others have stopped lamenting their fate. The time for blues is over, for them. They are creating, each according to his means, a revolutionary consciousness. And their eyes are clear. Not blue.

—Jean Genet, in Introduction to *Soledad Brother*

Biographical Notes

SAM MELVILLE. See biographical notes, chapter 7.

HUEY NEWTON (b. 1942). Cofounder with Bobby Seale of the Black Panthers in 1966 in Oakland, California, Newton was arrested when hostility between the Panthers and the Oakland police erupted into violence in October 1967 in a midnight ghetto confrontation in which a policeman was killed in an exchange of gunfire. Newton was tried for first-degree murder, and in a compromise verdict, was convicted of voluntary manslaughter and sentenced to a two-to-fifteen-year term in Los Padres Men's colony in San Luis Obispo, California. After a four-year court battle during which the California State Supreme Court reversed his conviction, and two retrials (each ending in a deadlocked jury) the DA dismissed charges. Newton had already served three years.

GEORGE JACKSON (1941–1971). At eighteen, Jackson was sentenced from one year to life: he had stolen $70 from a gas station. During the next eleven years in prison, eight and a half of them were spent in solitary confinement. When he was twenty-eight he was indicted for murdering a prison guard at Soledad Prison. Two days before his trial he was shot and killed by a tower guard at San Quentin; prison authorities say that he was attempting to escape. In the short span of his life he became a symbol of resistance for the inmate population—his writings, when they are able to be secured, are rented for a pack of cigarettes a night; inmates feel themselves lucky to pay so small a price.

JEAN GENET. See biographical notes, chapter 5.

18.

I'M COMING OUT!

While they were getting you ready for a lifetime of jailing, they forgot to tell you about out here.

—Fortune News, July 1972

Prison is a secret society. Only those who have lived through the prison experience can understand the complexities of its rituals. From getting busted (handcuffs, fingerprinting, confiscation of personal possessions, delousing) to doing time (sleeping, getting up, eating, in the yard, eating, sleeping), every hour is regulated, every moment planned.

Once released, the ex-con enters what is now a foreign world. He finds the demands of freedom more terrifying than demands of the world inside. Decisions must be made: how and where to spend the twenty-five dollars given him, if released from a Federal prison or the dollar if released from the city jail. But how does one make a decision when ability to do this has been systematically destroyed by life inside? The challenges of getting out proving too great, the ex-con begins to think of "home"—a "sound enough reason to abolish the institution of prison itself" as William Styron wrote of James Blake. Being alienated together seems preferable to being alienated alone; a job is pulled; the ex-con becomes a prisoner again.

If the prisoner's capacity to live independent of the criminal fraternity is ultimately broken, the cause lies within the very society that condoned his extreme penal regimentation. The vital problem of adjustment is largely ignored by parole authorities. It is also overlooked by the society that is reluctant to give a prisoner another chance, trust, employment, and a new direction.

Now one of these mornin's
And the time ain't long,
That man's gonna call me,
And I'll be gone.
I'll be done all my grievin',
Whoopin', holl'in', cryin',
I'll be done all my worryin'
'Bout my great long time.

—American Folk Song

"I'VE GOT THE STREETS . . ."

I know what I am. I'm a convict and nothing the state can do can make me change, because I know I got the better go. I've got something that most guys, especially the Joe Squares, don't have. I've got hope! I've got the streets, and I'm going out there again. I've got something to look forward to. Joe Square has the rut, the routine, and there's no hope for him. When I get out there again I can make up for everything that's happening to me now. I'll be free, free to live the way I want and to do what I want. I know Joe Square can't make that statement. I can shoot dope, steal, rob, pimp whores. I can live as fast and as good as I want. And when they nail me again, I can come back "home" for a vacation and wait it out until the next time.

—Anthony J. Manocchio and Jimmy Dunn, *The Time Game*

THERESA DERRY
(Out of the Same Bag)

"When I got out of there—after nearly four years away from civilization—I felt like I was walking around with a big tag on me: *Look at me. I just came out of prison,*" Terry Derry said, six years after she left Muncy.

"They take a city girl and put her in prison and she picks tomatoes for four years—it's oblivion—and then they send her back to the city as 'socially adjusted.' I was so 'adjusted' that even the bus ride back to Philadelphia scared the shit out of me—the noise and the people talking and moving around. I just shut my eyes and prayed to survive the trip.

"After I didn't see my family for so long, everything seemed so strange to me . . . and it was so hard to adjust. I really wanted to be a totally different person from when I had gone in. I had studied so hard. I had decided I wanted to be a registered nurse and a good mother. I could tell you every bone in the body by name, and exactly how the circulatory system works. I came out with all these dreams . . . and then started getting doors slammed in my face.

"But I was fortified because I had a husband who was my inner strength . . . who loved me . . . and I had a daughter who loved me and needed me. And I was determined to do right by her."

Presently Terry is working in Philadelphia as a court-prison administrator for a release on recognizance program funded by the Pennsylvania Program for Women and Girl Offenders. She goes into the prisons to interview women awaiting trial who can't raise bail. She tries to work out problems with them and arrange for their release on recognizance. She uses her own house as a center for women who have nowhere else to go.

"If you have a sick or stray animal you can call the SPCA, but try to find a place for a woman just out of prison . . . and you learn there ain't no such creature. I don't know—this work is like my blood to me—I can relate to these women 'cause we've all come out of the same bag. I can tell them honestly they haven't done half the things I've done. I've done it all, and baby, I've come through it alone. I didn't have no mother to hold my hand.

"For a while I tried to deny my past, I wanted to be totally new and all that. But then I told myself, 'Look, girl, you've done all these things, they're part of your past.' I'm not wearing it all as a badge of honor, but then who should go to jail? Me at 13? Huh-uh, baby; not me or nobody else."

—Kathryn Watterson Burkhart, *Ramparts*, June 1971

PAROLE: POSTPONED

Michael Gardner is twenty-two and looks sixteen. Frail, narrow-shouldered, quavery-voiced, pale, he seems out of place here. He ought to be at the high school dance, standing uncomfortably against a wall. He grew up in a small textile mill town in the poorest part of the state. Kicked out of school at sixteen, he retaliated by ransacking the building. At seventeen it was larceny, at eighteen, breaking into a car. A reformatory sentence. An escape. Thirteen more months in the reformatory. Then a string of robberies, finally a sentence of two to eight years. He looks frightened, anxious. He brings out the grandfather in Gates.

"This is your first time in prison," Gates begins in a soft voice. "Now you've had some time to think. What's the story? What causes you to do this, do you think?"

Gardner looks at the floor. "I think it was my own stupidity. I didn't stop to think."

"Well, a young fella your age, it's a waste of time if you don't come up with some ideas about where all this is coming from and where you're going. . . ."

Gardner answers slowly, the words measured: "I know where it's coming from and I know where I'm going. I've done something to better myself in here. I've become an apprentice carpenter. And I've taken the time to think. . . ."

Gardner is ringing bells with the board. He's done something to *better himself*. He may be *rehabilitated*. And maybe he is. He wasn't a carpenter when he came in. He was a thief, and not much of one. "If they've got the tiniest bit of smarts they know what this board wants to hear," an ex-inmate has told me. "If you show some inclination to self-help, don't just do your time the old-con way. They want to see you run a little."

Gates seems particularly impressed. He believes in work, and here's a man with a trade. "We live to work, we don't work to live," Gates likes to say. "We've been growing away from that in this country."

Gates is gentle with him, avuncular. "Well, you know you got a long sentence this time, but it's nothing to what you'll get next time."

"Yessir." Gardner almost swallows his reply.

Sacks has taken his coat off. He has a sudden thought: "Do you think prison is a good thing for rehabilitation or not? Do you think we ought to close the prisons?" It's time for a commercial.

Gardner sees the opening. "No," he says, "I wouldn't say close the prisons. I may have a different outlook than some of the people in here, but I mean to me it's helped me see myself. I made my apprenticeship."

Rawlins is looking thoughtful, puffing on his pipe. Sacks is toying with his glasses. Gates looks like a statue—erect in his chair, not a wrinkle. His eyes have the cool, subdued glow of a distant star. "When was the last time you saw your father?" Sacks asks. They have seen the probation officers' presentence report; Gardner's father has been stepping on him for years.

"About four weeks ago."

"How do you get along with him?"

"I get along with him good now." The answer comes too quickly.

"I mean, we have our arguments like every family does, but . . ."

His last parole officer had reported: "His father and him beat the hell out of each other whenever they saw each other. I couldn't even talk to the old man if I wanted to get anywhere with Mike."

Rawlins senses something: "Did you say you wanted to live with your family?"

"Yes. I figure I owe them something. I mean they done a lot for me."

A week earlier, the father had told me: "The kid's asked me to speak to the parole board for him, but the way I look at it he's on his own now. Why should I lose a day's pay and go down there? He can live here if he wants to, but he's got to behave." The mother was no softer: "The doctor told us when he was ten that he wasn't getting enough affection at home. He got the same as the rest. He got clothes, food, all a kid could want."

Gardner looks close to tears now. He gets up and leaves the room. The board did not ask his feelings about parole, but the day before Gardner had described it as "a bunch of crap. You got to go out and live like a human being, not with someone watching you all the time. Out there you can't listen to anyone, you gotta look out for yourself."

"I'm going to vote to parole," Gates says. "He's just a youngster, younger than his age. I think this might be the time, prison might have awakened him. This is a kid. He's different from the others with long records and set in their ways."

"I vote for parole," says Sacks. "One thing that impressed me was his answer on what prison does. It made sense."

Rawlins still wonders. "My concern is that he may have problems at home. I see a fragile guy. . . . He may be hurting more deeply than he showed here." ("One of the weaknesses of our operation," Sacks will say later, "is that usually nobody checks out the family, what he's going out to. We should know what it's like.")

All three agree to parole. Of the seventeen men who come before the board on this day, six will be granted parole, nine denied and the decisions in two cases will be postponed; usually, between 50 and 60 per cent win parole.

Gardner is expressionless when he gets the word. "I'll probably still get in trouble if I stay in that little town," he had said. "Everybody knows me there. I gotta get some money and then take off." The old parole officer had said he felt Gardner had a chance "if he can latch onto something for his ego, a good job, a girl, so he can say, 'Look, Dad'. . . ." Now, the board members are saying they want to get Gardner in a work-release program, but they are not sure they can. It means a month's delay in his release. Gardner doesn't understand, and Gates doesn't feel he can explain it. "We think you can stand at least another month because you're learning something," he says instead. "Okay? Now take care of yourself."

Gardner looks uncertain as he walks out.

"Gee," Sacks says quietly, "he looked so downhearted."
"He's a kid," Gates says.

(Note: Gates, Rawlins, and Sacks are members of the Parole Board.)

—Donald Jackson, "Parole Board," *Life* magazine, July 10, 1970

IN THE DARK

In California, sentencing and paroling of male convicts is entrusted to a nine-member Adult Authority, according to its published literature "composed of persons who have demonstrated skills, abilities and leadership in many fields."

Its members are appointed by the governor for four-year terms. The composition of the present board is not easily squared with its self-appraisal. It is, with the lone exception of a retired dentist, drawn from the ranks of law enforcement and Corrections: former policemen, prosecutors, FBI and prison personnel. This board wields total, arbitrary, despotic power over the destinies and liberties of California's state prison population, not only while they are in custody but also after they have been released on parole. . . .

The crucial moment in the prisoner's life is his hearing before the Adult Authority, which will determine whether or not to set his sentence, whether or not to grant a parole date. If he is serving five years to life, he is legally eligible for parole after twenty months, one third of the minimum term. His first hearing will be eighteen months after he enters prison, and he will come before the board annually thereafter until it is ready to fix an "individualized" maximum term short of life and set a date for his release on parole.

The Adult Authority is under no legal obligation to set the sentence, and in practice it does not do so until it is ready to grant parole. By keeping the prisoner in perpetual suspense, never knowing from year to year what portion of his one-to-twenty or five-to-life sentence he will serve, the Adult Authority maintains maximum control over him for the entire period of his incarceration.

Assisted by a number of full-time case-hearing representatives, the Adult Authority makes the circuit of the prisons, splitting up into teams of two, to conduct the prisoner interviews. A prison staff member is present to brief the panel on the inmate's record, to make notes on his "attitude" during the hearing and comments made about him by the panel members after he has left, and to record the panel's decision.

Presumably to ensure a decision uninfluenced by the possible bias of prison authorities, the staff worker is not permitted to make recommendations to the panel. But since he is charged with reporting the institution's evaluation of the prisoner, the outcome is generally predetermined by his presentation.

There are no written guidelines for the conduct of the hearing, and if parole is denied, the prisoner is not entitled to know the reason. No transcript is made of the hearing. The prisoner's family, his counsel, and the press are excluded.

Compared with the prison disciplinary committee, the Adult Authority claims it is lavish in the time it accords to the convicts who come before it: according to its literature, the average is a little less than seventeen minutes per prisoner. At that, the panel does not give him its undivided attention. While one panel member conducts the interview, the other is reading the file on the next case.

From one who has been through it several times, I learned something about the interview from where the prisoner sits. Nasty, short, and sometimes brutish, he found it. "Seventeen minutes may be the mathematical average," he said. "In my experience, five to seven minutes is more like it."

The panel bases its decision largely on the contents of the prisoner's central file folder, a formidable pile of paper work containing everything the authorities know, or think they know, about him: probation officer's report, comments of trial judge and district attorney, psychiatric evaluation, reports by guards of disciplinary infractions. While guards are encouraged to familiarize themselves with the contents of the folder, neither the prisoner nor his lawyer is permitted to see it. The rationale: it contains "confidential psychiatric material"—a curious distortion of the privileged doctor-patient relationship, which is supposedly for the patient's benefit and subject to waiver by him. In prison, the privilege is waived not for the "patient" or his counsel, but for policing agencies and the FBI, who are permitted full access to everything concerning him.

Adult Authority policy is to rotate the panels, so that the man whose parole is denied year after year will confront a different duo each time. Nostrums for his rehabilitation vary, depending on the idiosyncracies of the individual panel members. "Panel Member A may be hipped on religion, and tell the prisoner to go to church every week," said my informant. "But fifty-two Sundays later, he comes before Panel Member Y, whose bag is Alcoholics Anonymous, and even if the prisoner doesn't happen to have a drinking problem, he'll be told, 'Attend the AA for a year and then we'll see about a parole date.' This can go on indefinitely, as long as they haven't set his sentence. If he shows his true feelings and says, 'You're arbitrary and unjust,' they will say he's not ready for parole. If he says

he has benefited enormously from the rehabilitation programs, they may put him down as a smoothie and deny
parole anyway. The prisoner is totally in the dark; he has
no way of knowing on what they base their decision. Is it
any wonder that when he eventually comes out he's bitter
and full of revenge?"

—Jessica Mitford, *Atlantic Monthly*, March 1971

The National Commission on Reform of Federal Criminal
Laws has recommended that, in addition to the explicit
condition of refraining from committing further crimes, the
United States Board of Parole have the power to require
a parolee to:

> (a) work faithfully at a suitable employment or
> faithfully pursue a course of study or of voca-
> tional training that will equip him for suitable
> employment. . . .

—Ronald L. Goldfarb and Linda R. Singer, *After Conviction*

LICENSES
AND PROSCRIPTIONS

The licensing and bonding requirements applicable to
many jobs present still further obstacles to the employment
of ex-offenders. Licensing regulations, which apply to occu-
pations ranging from law and medicine to collecting gar-

bage and cutting hair, frequently contain broad enough standards of competency and honesty which result in flat proscriptions against all offenders. Often there is no rational connection between the restrictions placed on a former offender's occupation and the crime he committed. For example, although one of the most popular vocational training courses in the New York City Reformatory is the barber school, New York State often delays or denies applications for apprentice barber's licenses when the applicant has a prison record. Motor-vehicle departments frequently deny or delay driver's licenses to former prisoners.

Ex-offenders also have difficulty in meeting employers' requirements of bonding against theft, a common practice in many retail and service businesses. In addition, prospective employers sometimes insist on bonds from people with criminal records that they would not require from other employees. Many bonding companies flatly refuse to underwrite bonds for ex-prisoners.

—Ronald L. Goldfarb and Linda R. Singer, *After Conviction*

> (h) remain within the geographical limits fixed
> by the Board, unless granted written permission
> to leave by the Board or the parole officer;

—National Commission on Reform of Federal Criminal Laws

PRISON WITHOUT BARS

Charles Noyes . . . was paroled in May of 1967 to the owner of a Little Rock bowling alley who promised him a forty-hour week at a fair salary. Within a month, Noyes telephoned. "I'm uptight about the job," he said. "Can I come down and talk to you?"

I said, "Sure, come on down."

When he walked in I scarcely recognized him. He had lost at least twenty pounds and his face was haggard, his eyes bloodshot. He had been working sixteen hours a day, seven days a week, and getting considerably less money than had been promised, even though he had got married on the strength of his having a job. The long hours were also wreaking havoc with his domestic life.

Noyes was also forced to do heavy work, although a condition of his employment specified that he be given only light work because of an earlier back injury.

When he told his employer he couldn't keep on working under such conditions, he was told that if he complained or tried to get another job, the employer would call his parole officer and Noyes would be sent back to prison.

Noyes asked me if he could come to work at the prison. I cleared his employment with the parole director and became Noyes's parole sponsor as well as supervisor. He worked out extremely well, and a few months later we hired his wife, too, to work as a secretary.

Noyes's story was typical. This was the psychological situation of the convicted prisoner, from which there was no escape but the grave, because he could not legally leave Arkansas while on parole. And if a parolee managed to make it through his parole period, he still lived on the razor's edge between the freeworld and the prison, because the system, once set in motion, continued to work against him.

Local authorities were well aware that he was a former prisoner. If he was ever picked up again on any charge it was most likely he would be sent back to prison. In Arkansas, as in most other states, a convict's word is worthless in court. Any kind of sentence in Arkansas for any offense, resulting in imprisonment in the Boys' School or the prison farms, is tantamout to a lifelong sentence of apprehension, anxiety, and harassment.

—Tom Murton, *Accomplices to the Crime*

NO HARD FEELINGS

By the Associated Press.
Montgomery, Ala., June 9, 1950

—Andy Wright, last of the "Scottsboro boys" still in prison, left on parole today with "no hard feelings" toward anyone.

His parole "pay" amounts to $13.45. . . .

Wright and eight other Negroes were arrested in 1931, on charges of raping Mrs. Victoria Price and Ruby Bates aboard a freight train. Three of them went free after a court action that lasted six years. Wright was sentenced to ninety-nine years.

Thirteen dollars and forty-five cents and nineteen years, two months, and fifteen days. Now with such a paltry sum in his black hand he was being returned from living death to life in a white world.

—Allan K. Chalmers, *They Shall Be Free*

Gratuities given prisoners on release are minimal in most states and not enough to support most releasees. In some states the assistance is scarcely enough to get the prisoner home, let alone sufficient to see him through his transition period and to the point where he is earning a living.

—Ronald L. Goldfarb and Linda R. Singer, *After Conviction*

CLOUDED VISION

. . . They had kept her locked up for five years. But now she had done her time. She would go out.

Presently I, too, would go out. And we both would be tagged. We both would be listed as having criminal records. And so she must not communicate with me, for I would still be under the supervision of the Parole Board for two more years and contact between us could be held against me as a parole violation.

So, willy-nilly, the State had set us here together, and willy-nilly it would move us on. We had walked and laughed together, given each other a helping hand. When the inward pressure of worry had become too much for her, she had turned to me with a rush of confidence that bared the struggle in her own soul, and showed her passionate desire to rescue her children from the environment that had caused her own tragedy. We were two human beings caught in the strange whirlpool of life. Storm-swept to the same spot together, like two soldiers drafted in the same regiment, our friendly interest had nothing to do with crime, but was based on human companionship.

But the State said: "No! The black ink of your finger-prints has blotted out your human rights as individuals. You are 'cases' in a Criminal Court. You are 'numbers' in a prison. You are 'women with a record'!"

There are many associations made in prison that are pernicious, but on the other hand there is many a friendship that can do more to encourage and strengthen the individuals involved toward right living than all the laws and parole officers combined. For helpful understanding grows with mutual suffering. But authority, blind in its arrogance, peers with clouded vision at the individual and declaims: "You have broken the law! From now on you are a discredited person. You can have no motive that is altruistic. Move on!"

So Melly and I moved on, she in one direction, I in another. I hope she has achieved her goal—work, security and a future for her children.

—Edna V. O'Brien, *So I Went to Prison*

The board of parole in releasing a prisoner on parole shall specify in writing the conditions of his parole, and a copy of such conditions shall be given to the parolee. A violation of such conditions may render the prisoner liable to arrest and re-imprisonment. . . . Such rules, both general and special may include, among other things, a requirement . . . *that he shall abandon evil associates and ways.*

—McKinney's Consolidated Laws of New York annotated, Book 10B, Correction Law

STIGMATA

The widespread availability of law-enforcement records has created a pariah class of millions of persons made up of ex-convicts and people arrested but not convicted. That pariah class is the crime problem, or at least a large part of it. Crime is centered in those cities and those parts of cities where people go when they are trying to escape their past records. The time-honored way of escaping was to lie when asked, "Have you ever been arrested?" As law-enforcement agencies and private companies improve the efficiency of their dissemination of records, lying no longer works. The truth about the past record catches up, no matter where a person moves.

Shocking as the notion might be, those lies served an important social purpose. When a man with an arrest record could lie his way into a job, all of us had a little less to fear. Today, when we expose the lie, we simply insure that one more person won't be able to escape his arrest record and integrate himself into society.

Judicial and legislative action to control the use and distribution of arrest records will not have much impact for a long time to come. The records of people arrested in the past have often been so widely circulated as to make it very difficult, if not impossible, to prevent them from continuing to haunt people for years to come. But action has to start sometime, and the best time is now. There is even a small sign that the F.B.I. is concerned. At the hearing last Feb. 28 to decide whether he should be confirmed as F.B.I. director, L. Patrick Gray testified that he had "purged inactive arrest records of individuals age 80 and older from the fingerprint files." All the octogenarians I know who are out looking for jobs are very grateful.

—Aryeh Neier, ACLU, *The New York Times Magazine,* April 15, 1973

THE SELF-FULFILLING PROPHECY

. . . Most provisional roles conferred by society—those of the student or conscripted soldier, for example—include some kind of terminal ceremony to mark the individual's movement back out of the role once its temporary advantages have been exhausted. But the roles alloted the deviant seldom make allowance for this type of passage. He is ushered into the deviant position by a decisive and often dramatic ceremony, yet is retired from it with scarcely a word of public notice. And as a result, the deviant often returns home with no proper license to resume a normal life in the community. Nothing has happened to cancel out the stigmas imposed upon him by earlier commitment ceremonies; nothing has happened to revoke the verdict or diagnosis pronounced upon him at that time. It should not be surprising, then, that the people of the community are apt to greet the returning deviant with a considerable degree of apprehension and distrust, for in a very real sense they are not at all sure who he is.

A circularity is thus set into motion which has all the earmarks of a "self-fulfilling prophecy," . . . On the one hand, it seems quite obvious that the community's apprehensions help reduce whatever chances the deviant might otherwise have had for a successful return home. Yet at the same time, everyday experience seems to show that these suspicions are wholly reasonable, for it is a well-known and highly publicized fact that many if not most ex-convicts return to crime after leaving prison and that large numbers of mental patients require further treatment after an initial hospitalization. The common feeling that deviant persons never really change, then, may derive from a faulty premise; but the feeling is expressed so frequently and with such conviction that it eventually creates the facts which later "prove" it to be correct. If the returning deviant encounters this circularity often enough, it is quite understandable that he, too, may begin to wonder whether he has fully graduated from the deviant role, and he may respond to the uncertainty by resuming some kind of deviant activity. In many respects, this may be the only way for the individual and his community to agree what kind of person he is.

Moreover this prophecy is found in the official policies of even the most responsible agencies of control. Police departments could not operate with any real effectiveness if they did not regard ex-convicts as a ready pool of suspects to be tapped in the event of trouble, and psychiatric clinics could not do a successful job in the community if they were not always alert to the possibility of former patients suffering relapses. Thus the prophecy gains currency at many levels within the social order, not only in the poorly informed attitudes of the community at large, but in the best informed theories of most control agencies as well.

—Kai Erikson, *The Wayward Puritans*

THE LURE
(1963)

What shakes me in all this is that so many nights I walk the grounds here, feeling the inexplicable pull of the joint, trying to fathom the Why of this incredible homesickness, trying to name for myself the kinship of the doomed I felt for the other cons when I was in. How is it possible, when I hated so many of them, found them dull and brutal and often more square than the squares outside?

This is a fight that still goes on, even at a time when it looks as if I could have something going for me, if only I just stay with it and work at it. But I find myself wondering what the cons back there are doing, how they're making it. And I think of it with nostalgia, so go figure it. The longer I stay out the weaker this demented attraction will become, I hope, and so I struggle all the time.

1965

TERM METED IN
ATTEMPTED DRUG THEFT

Jacksonville, Fla., March 11, 1965—
James William Blake, 44, was sentenced yesterday to five years in the state prison in connection with a burglary to obtain barbiturate drugs.

Blake, who pleaded guilty, was sentenced by Criminal Court Judge William T. Harvey.

Asst. State Atty. William M. Tomlinson said Blake was

arrested outside a medical office building at 225 W. Ashley St. last Dec. 18 after an attempted burglary there.

Blake pleaded guilty to attempted breaking and entering with intent to commit a misdemeanor and received a 2½-year term on that count. He also pleaded guilty to unlawfully possessing a barbiturate drug without a prescription and received an additional 2½ years.

I think it was then I realized I wanted to go back to the tribe, to my people, in the joint. And said to myself, home is where, when you go there, they can't turn you away.

—James Blake, *The Joint*

FUTURE SHOCK

Talk to the men who have been out on the street. Talk with each other about the reality of the streets—and leave the fantasies aside. Make your dreams realistic, so you don't become part of the revolving-door cycle. Prisoners can work together to prepare each other for the street. Each man who is prepared and stays out is one man less who will go back. Every time you surrender out here, you are giving a hack insurance on his pension plans.

*No matter how long you've been away, you haven't handled money. Can you plan a budget for yourself so you don't get into a financial corner? No one in the joint—nor your parole officer—will ever talk to you about this.

*You've been fed your meals every day of your institutional life. Can you walk into a restaurant and order a meal? Can you make basic decisions of survival after the keepers of the cage have been making all basic decisions for you?

*Getting around is important to the city person. Will the subway crowds confuse you? Do you know that you must have the exact change (35¢) to get on a bus in New York City and that the bus driver will look at you with hate and give you no information about new procedures?

*Have you been away so long that you will not be familiar with electric doors that open as you step in front of them? Will you be assured that you won't fall flat on your face in front of a crowd, as you become confused from these doors?

*Will you recognize the sound of a baby's cry? Or be able to dial a telephone and ask for information operator? Will the sound of cars in traffic be alien to you? Will you misinterpret a stranger's friendly smile?

*You've been told when to wake up and when to go to bed every day of your prison life. Will you know when to retire or be able to get up in time for an appointment or to go to work? Will you be able to sleep in a quiet room without a flashlight in your face during the night?

*In prison, you have been taught that kindness is weakness. Will you continue to manipulate out here, because in the joint you had to if you wanted pressed clothes, or enough food to eat, or help with a writ?

*In prison, you contained too many emotions. Correctional officers who ridiculed you or belittled you met your silence. When you get out, you will recognize that you have bottled up years of emotions, angers and frustrations. Will you be prepared for the flood of feelings which will rise to the surface when you come out?

*If your wife or girl has waited for you, will you understand that she has lived many years without your strength and has a kind of independence of her own? Are you ready for a changed relationship with the woman you love?

While they were getting you ready for a lifetime of jailing, they forgot to tell you about out here.

—*Fortune News*, July 1972

Biographical Notes

ANTHONY MANOCCHIO and JIMMY DUNN. See biographical notes, chapter 4.

KATHRYN WATTERSON BURKHART. See biographical notes, chapter 4.

THERESA DERRY. Terry did her six years on parole, and still hopes to be a nurse.

TOM MURTON. See biographical notes, chapter 6.

EDNA V. O'BRIEN (d. 1959). A trader in stocks and bonds, she was arrested on charges of grand larceny and was sentenced to the Bedford State Prison in New York. She did time for fifteen months and was released in 1936.

JAMES BLAKE. In 1962, Blake was released from Raiford State Prison in Florida. Several months later he was hired as an orderly in a mental sanitorium in Westchester, New York. It was there that Blake wrote the letter from which this chapter's excerpt is taken. See also, notes, chapter 5.

19.

THE PRISON EXPERIENCE

*. . . death worth living
and life worth dying . . .*

—e.e. cummings

THE CHANGE

When I came out of prison . . .

. . . I did not perceive that great changes had taken place on the common, such as he observed who went in a youth and emerged a tottering and gray-headed man; and yet a change had to my eyes come over the scene—the town, and State, and country—greater than any that mere time could effect. I saw yet more distinctly the State in which I lived. I saw to what extent the people among whom I lived could be trusted as good neighbors and friends; that their friendship was for summer weather only; that they did not greatly propose to do right; that they were a distinct race from me by their prejudices and superstitions, as the Chinamen and Malays are; that in their sacrifices to humanity they ran no risks, not even to their property; that after all they were not so noble but they treated the thief as he had treated them, and hoped, by a certain outward observance and a few prayers, and by walking in a particular straight though useless path from time to time, to save their souls. This may be to judge my neighbors harshly; for I believe that many of them are not aware that they have such an institution as the jail in their village.

—Thoreau, *Civil Disobedience*

"... WHO WERE THE MAD AND WHO THE SANE?"

... I could only feel darkness and desolation all around me. The bar of gold which the sun left on the ceiling every morning for a short hour taunted me; and late in the afternoon when the cells were dim and the lights in the corridor were not yet lit, a heartbreaking conviction of the ugliness, the futility of life came over me so that I could not weep but only lie there in blank misery.

I lost all feeling of my own identity. I reflected on the desolation of poverty, of destitution, of sickness and sin. That I would be free after thirty days meant nothing to me. I would never be free again, never free when I knew that behind bars all over the world there were women and men, young girls and boys, suffering constraint, punishment, isolation and hardship for crimes of which all of us were guilty. The mother who had murdered her child, the drug addict—who were the mad and who the sane? Why were prostitutes prosecuted in some cases and in others respected and fawned on? People sold themselves for jobs, for the pay check, and if they only received a high enough price, they were honored. If their cheating, their theft, their lie, were of colossal proportions, if it were successful, they met with praise, not blame. Why were some caught, not others? Why were some termed criminals and others good businessmen? What was right and wrong? What was good and evil? I lay there in utter confusion and misery.

When I first wrote of these experiences I wrote even more strongly of my identification with those around me. I was that mother whose child had been raped and slain. I was the mother who had borne the monster who had done it.

I was even that monster, feeling in my own breast every abomination. Is this exaggeration? There are not so many of us who have lain for six days and nights in darkness, cold and hunger, pondering in our heart the world and our part in it. If you live in great cities, if you are in constant contact with sin and suffering, if the daily papers print nothing but Greek tragedies, if you see on all sides people trying to find relief from the drab boredom of their job and family life, in sex and alcohol, then you become inured to the evil of the day, and it is rarely that such a realization of the horror of sin and human hate can come to you.

This workhouse we were in was one of the most modern prisons. It was built on the cottage plan and men and women worked in the fields or sat at machines in the factory and sewed. Yet here were also solitary confinement cells, more bleak and barbarous than I could have imagined such cells to be. There were stories told of prisoners being left in these cells for six months. Six months! The thirty days stretched out before me interminably. I would be utterly crushed by misery before I was released. Never would I recover from this wound, this ugly knowledge I had gained of what men were capable in their treatment of each other. It was one thing to be writing about these things, to have the theoretical knowledge of sweatshops and injustice and hunger, but it was quite another to experience it in one's own flesh.

—Dorothy Day, *The Long Loneliness*

THE LESSON

"For me, prison hasn't been the end of the world. It's been a beginning—a chance to stand aside and look. When I tell you I have grown in the seven months I have been here, I mean it. Not because of any programs—there aren't any. But because of the people I've lived with and the bed I've slept on. And I'm beginning to live with myself and accept myself. I know I am more of a woman, a valuable soul than I ever would have been if I hadn't come here. If six hundred women can each say, 'Hey, I'm a woman,' regardless of being called homosexuals or convicts or being neglected and hurt and made to live under ridiculous rules and ridiculous pressures and mental brutality and heartbreak—*they have something to teach the world*. It was a mind blower to me to see the strength, the tenderness and courage of these women and to find out, hey, I'm a woman, too. I'd just never had the chance."

—Kathryn Watterson Burkhart, *Women in Prison*

GOODBYE TO HELL
(by Wade Eaves in the Pea Pickers Picayune, Cummins Farm Weekly)

How does one say "Goodbye" to Hell?

How do you say goodbye to a nauseous pit of degeneration . . . a *factory* of heart-corroding fear and distrust; a rendering plant that can shred strength and ambition into lifelessness?

How do you say goodbye to the mass of inhabitants of this awesome machine; men who for so long have lived jammed against your very soul. . . .

A friend said, "Don't get Up-Tight, man . . . get the ———— out of here and forget the joint." A formula, of sorts, and one probably used by a thousand men in the past; quick! easy! fade away . . . leave and kill this steel and concrete memory forever.

IS that the way most men go? Leaving not as a human with dignity but fleeing as an animal flees a forest fire. It would be momentarily easy to leap upon a mental white charger and ride off "in all directions at once" but each idyllic path eventually stops at a barrier of reality.

Fleeing can't erase memories of this place. Running only creates distorted and false memories and transforms them to chaotic images of pseudo-status, of power or symbols of some dreamlike toughness or brotherhood of a life that never should have been. "Escaping" is no solution. The scars are here, laced throughout the mind and body, and they must not ever be forgotten.

How do you say good-bye without some regret? You

wonder why you didn't do more to help all the men you *could* have. Like the kid you *knew* was going to escape with the wrong gang . . . he was pathetically simple, easily influenced . . . and he lost his life trying to swim a river. He *could* have been turned away . . . but trying to give good advice isn't the way of the life as accepted here . . . but you should have tried anyway . . . for right is still right.

How many could have been helped . . . dissuaded one time . . . encouraged another . . . so your regret is the shameful knowledge you didn't do all you could to lend a helping hand.

That regret is a gnawing inside, almost a torment, grinding away at you for not being a man when you should.

Paradoxically, this knot of regret comes at a time when your soul is a raging inferno of freedom's fire.

There is also a fleeting flash of fear you might have missed seeing or hearing one hideous act or condition or person you could not possibly forget. You can't afford to forget; you can't flee that which is terrifying, you know you mustn't enjoy the luxury of forgetting. You know you *must* keep this Colossus of Shame in proper perspective or fail.

You've been classified a criminal. You have paid for that accusation. You know where the mistakes of life can, and do, lead . . . you've been there.

You've been to Hell.

—Cynthia Owen Philip, *Imprisoned in America*

"... a new way of life ..."

"When a weekly alcoholic program came in from the outside, I found a beginning. When I got out on parole, that's when people in the program really helped me out. The day I got home, people from the program picked me up. A woman who had spoken at the prison became a friend. I don't think she knew how much she helped me. I was on parole and I was living with a sick aunt. This lady gave me keys to her apartment so I could go there after work or whenever I needed to get away from my aunt. She trusted me. I couldn't believe it. My references were all to jail, then. She said, 'Listen, that's behind you.' And she told me to stop thinking about my past life and start living in my present life. . . .

". . . coming home is so hard. The only thing you've been responsible for is being on the job when you're supposed to work. How can you come out and make a good decision? I was scared to make any at all. I finally had to say, I'll just make the decision and live with it—good, bad or indifferent.

"After I'd been home a while, I wondered if ex-cons were doing anything for ex-cons. I couldn't forget what I'd experienced—the sixteen-year-old kid, the inmate who was put into punishment behind two doors and wound up in a catatonic state because she couldn't stand it . . . she couldn't stand being in a steel cell with only a Bible and a book of rules, a toilet and a bed, with a matron coming by three times a day with a cigarette . . . I couldn't forget the claustrophobia I'd experienced and what it was like to go to the library to look for a book and find that anything pertinent or relevant must have been printed in the 1800s.

"I had come to believe that people destroy themselves by committing crimes and going to jail. It's a way of self-destruction. And I didn't see anything in there to help. Prisons don't serve any purpose but removing women from society. Even though the physical facilities and surroundings where I was at are better than men's prisons, and there is less physical brutality unless a woman fights . . . all the demands made at Attica could fit very well into any women's prison.

"Well, I was struck by the honesty of the people at Fortune. And I found out that I cared, I cared a lot. I became committed then. Both to dealing with myself and to maybe help other people avoid my mistakes and to expose what prisons really are.

"I have a new way of life now. I don't take ordinary things for granted anymore. Ordinary things are gifts to me. I enjoy food. I enjoy going to a good show. I enjoy people. I've had a lot of luck, a lot of good breaks."

—Kathryn Watterson Burkhart, *Women in Prison*

A WAR TO BE WAGED

The existence of the camps is a warning. German society, both because of the strength of its structure and the violence of the crisis that demolished it, underwent a decomposition that is exceptional even in the present state of world affairs. But it would be easy to show that the most characteristic traits of both the SS mentality and the social conditions which gave rise to the Third Reich are to be found in many other sectors of world society—less pronounced, it is true, and not developed on any such scale as in the Reich. But it is only a question of circumstances. It would be blindness—and criminal blindness, at that— to believe that, by reason of any difference of national temperament, it would be impossible for any other country to try a similar experiment. Germany interpreted, with an originality in keeping with her history, the crisis that led her to the concentrationary universe. But the existence and the mechanism of that crisis were inherent in the economic and social foundations of capitalism and imperialism. Under a new guise, similar effects may reappear tomorrow. There remains therefore a very specific war to be waged. The lessons learned from the concentration camps provide a marvelous arsenal for that war.

—David Rousset, *The Other Kingdom*

DIMENSIONS OF EVIL

. . . Instead of seeing the Bogers and Klehrs [Joseph Klehr, S.S. sergeant-major and former male nurse and Wilhelm Boger, guard, were responsible for the murders of hundreds of prisoners at Auschwitz] of Auschwitz as fabulous, myth-sized and inhuman monsters, we come to recognize that people like them are in fact all around us. All they need is the right kind of crisis, and they will blossom out.
. . . Auschwitz worked because these people wanted it to work. Instead of resisting it, rebelling against it, they put the best of their energies into making genocide a success. This was true not only of one or two psychopaths but of an entire bureaucratic officialdom, including not only the secret police and Nazi party members but also managers and employees of the industries which knowingly

made use of the slave labor provided in such abundance by the camp. . . .

It is enough to affirm one basic principle: Anyone belonging to class X or nation Y or race Z is to be regarded as subhuman and worthless, and consequently has no right to exist. All the rest will follow without difficulty.

As long as this principle is easily available, as long as it is taken for granted . . . we have no need of monsters: ordinary policemen and good citizens will take care of everything.

—Thomas Merton on Peace

Biographical Notes

HENRY DAVID THOREAU (1817–1862). Famous essayist, naturalist, and political nonconformist, Thoreau was an active opponent of slavery and a devout pacifist. He was imprisoned for a day as a result of his refusal to pay a poll tax to a government that supported the Mexican War, a war he believed to be a land-grabbing plot of Southern slaveowners. He believed in a moral law superior to constitutions and said, "They are the lovers of law and order who observe the law when the government breaks it."

DOROTHY DAY (b. 1897). Founded, with Peter Maurin in 1943, the Catholic Worker movement which is dedicated to philosophical anarchism, pacifism, and a concern for the poor. The imprisonment described (one of many during Miss Day's long career of social protest) was the result of a group of militant women suffragists' picketing the White House.

MARGUERITE. Represented here by "The Lesson," Marguerite is a prisoner in the California Institute for Women in Frontera.

KATHRYN WATTERSON BURKHART. See biographical notes, chapter 4.

WADE EAVES. "Goodbye to Hell" was contributed by Eaves to the *Pea Pickers Picayune*, Cummins Farm Weekly. The Cummins Farm is a part of the Arkansas State Correctional System.

JEANETTE SPENCER. "A new way of life" exists for Jeanette, now that she has become a bookkeeper and counselor for released female prisoners. Formerly she did time at the old Women's House of Detention in New York City and at Bedford State Prison.

DAVID ROUSSET (b. 1912). French novelist and essayist, he was an early organizer of the resistance movement during World War II. Attempts to win over the German soldiers to the cause of the French underground led to his arrest. He spent sixteen months in concentration camps, one of which was Buchenwald. He was freed by the American 82nd Airborne Division in 1945.

INDEX